ACTS

ACTS

Larry Woiwode

HarperSanFrancisco
A Division of HarperCollins*Publishers*

FIRST EDITION

Library of Congress Cataloging-in-Publication Data

Woiwode, Larry.
    Acts : a writer's reflections on the church, writing, and his own
life / Larry Woiwode. — 1st ed.
    p.   cm.
    Includes bibliographical references.
    ISBN 0–06–069404–1 (alk. paper)
    1. Bible. N.T. Acts—Criticism, interpretation, etc.   I. Title.
BS2625.2.W666   1993
226.6'06—dc20   92–52503
                                                             CIP

93 94 95 96 97 ❖ HAD 10 9 8 7 6 5 4 3 2 1

For G. I. Williamson
in gratitude

For by one Spirit we were all baptized into one body, whether Jews or Greeks, whether slaves or free, and we were all made to drink of one Spirit.

1 Corinthians 12.13

He fell silent for a few moments and stared at his hands. "You know," he said, "these are yuppie words, *happiness* and *unhappiness*. It's not happiness or unhappiness, it's either blessed or unblessed. As the Bible says, 'Blessed is the man who walketh not in the counsel of the ungodly.'"

Bob Dylan, in an article commemorating his fiftieth birthday, *Rolling Stone*

CONTENTS

TO THE READER

W<small>HY</small> A<small>CTS</small>? <small>YOU MIGHT ASK</small>. Because it is the most overtly narrative book of the New Testament, and narrative is the writer's business. It is also, to my eyes and ears, such a shapely narrative I'm not sure its equal exists in either the Hebrew or Greek testaments, and its curious genius is that its teachings are *enacted*. True, there is complex doctrine in many of the sermons that Acts records, but it rises from dramatic speeches within the momentum of the narrative itself. The more attention you pay to the actions and attitudes in Acts, then, besides what is explicitly stated, the more its text begins to open up. It has the power to put pressure on your personal life.

And then the idea of a response to a book of the Bible wasn't my own. By saying this I'm not being mystical; mysticism is, to me, an uncongenial state best reserved to the person experiencing it. Indeed, there were times during the writing of this when I wondered about my wisdom (or temptation toward mysticism) in submitting to the task, although there was never any doubt in my mind about the need, even necessity, for such a book. Which is a way of saying there was never a time when what you hold seemed merely decorative. I have decked it with facts and application, often at the expense of personal exposure, and although you may not always agree with me, I hope there are times when you will have to remove your glasses, or close the blinds, or get out of your chair and pace the room.

The idea that was the genesis for the book came about, like Genesis itself, by fiat. The poet Alfred Corn was asked to edit a companion New Testament volume to a volume of essays, already published, by contemporary writers on the Old Testament, and I was one of several writers he contacted. Yes, I was interested. In which book of the New Testament? Romans or Ephesians, I said, and he mentioned that he had been thinking of The Acts of the Apostles—because of its narrative nature, the novelist in me assumed. But once I looked at Acts again and realized it was one of the two longest books of the New Testament (Luke is the other), I wondered if the choice wasn't partly recompense to a person who wrote such thick novels.

I had recently resigned from a teaching position at a university, and many of the students I had worked with were on my mind or still in touch. A few years earlier, at this university, a group of undergraduates had approached the administration and asked that a course on the Bible be included in the curriculum— either out of a sense of lack in their education, or a desire to know more about scriptures—and at their request a modest religion department was set up.

I knew that most of my students hadn't read the Bible and never would. But a few, I thought, might speed-read an essay with my name attached. I saw the essay as a last chance to reach those few. I wanted to give them a sense of the traditional view of the teachings of the Old and New Covenants and of the Church, and also to acknowledge to them, with their attentiveness to hypocrisy, the ways in which the present church has deviated from the Church that develops in Acts.

When the essay began to grow beyond the space I would be sharing with others, the idea for this book occurred. As I have worked on it, I have tried to hold to my original impulse: to address students who might be hearing about the church and biblical concepts for the first time. But another dimension seemed necessary. When I thought back to the time of my entry into the church, I remembered the trouble I had finding an overarching view of the teachings of scripture—much less one from a writer's perspective, with a writer's gravitation toward contemporary culture, nor the writer so aged he wouldn't need to worry about literary-political correctness or incorrect ecclesiastical politics. So I have tried to address the needs of the student I once was.

As here: "Modern Christians often seem to suppose that piety is somehow opposed to thinking, that hard study should be reserved for secular schools, that the reader of the Bible may afford to be neglectful of the facts. Such an attitude is dishonoring to the divine revelation. Christianity is not wild speculation or bottomless mysticism. It reaches, indeed, to the highest heavens, but its foundation is laid upon sober fact."[1]

I hardly need add that few "facts" that apply to the arts arrive nowadays from the church. It is difficult to find texts that examine the arts, to any depth, from a Christian viewpoint, or that treat literature as other than a mode of exegesis—a term for the method used to explain a text from the Bible. Good groundwork has been done in the visual arts, because of their connections to Christian iconography, but where can you turn, other than to portions of *The Sacred Wood* or C. S. Lewis, to hear a Christian speak from experience about writing? Indeed, among evangelicals there is a tendency to toss a book aside if it offends—toss it aside and turn on the television, which daily presents more violence and machismo and gratuitous sex than any dozen novels.

There always will be a branch of the church, perhaps, that withdraws into a retreat from life. But there will also be, as always, one that searches for a world-and-life view beyond the sanctuary, as here: "It is an easy thing to build a faith when one makes a selection of the facts. But the only faith that is of solid worth is the one that faces every fact. And that is the glory of Shakespeare (as it was the glory of our Lord) that he goes open-eyed through life, and refuses to be blind to anything."[2]

These are reflections, not an attempt to be comprehensive or authoritative, not even about writing—not that I could be. I suggest many possibilities that Acts opens up, hoping that others will pick up from there, and that this might be the beginning of an opening up in general in the church to the arts and other issues of concern. If the church doesn't remain open-eyed, refusing to blind itself to anything, it ends up, as it has in the past, in a false defensive posture, as with the Mapplethorpe exhibition or Scorsese film. Or it tries to convert to fantasy the Bakker and Swaggart scandals. And if the church, which is to be a light on a hill to save lives from shipwreck, isn't working to encourage the arts or discover application for them, the worst shopworn arts will overtake our culture and invade the church. This is indeed what is happening.

So it seemed that before the church took on so much protective coloration it grew indistinguishable from the culture, it was time to respond to that culture from within the church. What follows, then, is my own highly personal (and, as I hope, informative) response, several thousand words arranged in ways that should be viewed, like the sentences of any writer, as a series of premeditated acts.

I

BEGINNINGS

ALL THE WAY BACK to a year or two after the time when I'm first able to remember, at the age of four, I remember waking (or this is the way the sensation arrives) in church and hearing a priest with a German accent declaim in what seemed to me anger, in reference to a passage I now know is from First Corinthians, "Does that mean, wives, that you must submit to him when he asks you to go to *bet* wid him? *Yess!*"

With the fervor of his *yes* I felt my mother next to me stir in the pew, uneasy, then my father shift on my other side, while I experienced at their center my first faint stirrings of sexual intimation—or whatever rough secret it was they shared in their bedroom: scripture had been applied.

I was raised a Roman Catholic. This ancient ark of the church is widely known, for good and ill, as a bastion of tradition, but an effect of my upbringing in the saint-laden, incense-clinging, Tridentine age of the fifties, was that I was brought to revere scripture. In this church, the hub near the center of a village in central North Dakota, I heard sections of the gospels and epistles read in every worship service as I grew up, and one of the teachings of scripture (shorthand for referring to both testaments of the Bible) is that faith comes by hearing. I was aware I was hearing words out of a realm removed even from the priest.

I didn't always know how to respond to what I heard, or how to take it, but the Spirit works independently of us, and for the years that I attended the parochial school of this church, I heard scripture read seven days a week. At that age I was able to enter a story so fully the entry felt literal; I was moving past rocks and trees among people I might embrace. So when the liturgical calendar completed another cycle, I had heard and entered again the substantial ground of the scenes that supported my life: the angels bringing to shepherds the news of Christ's birth, his baptism by John, his appearance in the Temple among the elders; his death on the cross; his resurrection.

The trouble with a ritualistic, cyclical imperative is it can wear patterns and grooves that have your head below the ground before you notice. And then some will call the patterns neurotic, or worse. Of course, there are always those. Labels of the sort only rename a problem or the symptoms of it with pseudoscientific authority, and set you off on a different cycle.[1] They usually offer little remedy. Or the remedy they offer often works for the author of the label only; that person ends up feeling superior.

If, for example, I find it impossible to fathom the depravity of Jeffrey Dahmer, the young man from Milwaukee who was found with a dozen disemboweled and partly cannibalized bodies in and about his house, and so call him "paranoid psychotic," I not only forgo the implications of his act to humanity in general but let myself, a good old normal Joe, *not* a psychotic, off the hook. Nobody is helped by this process any more than Jeffrey Dahmer is.

The Roman Catholic Church did not provide me with an apologetic with which to defend my faith except to say, That's the way it is. This worked well enough to a point, as perhaps it should for a faithful Catholic, but didn't impress my high-school friends or cut any ice with the professional atheists I met in college. They were not about to listen to arguments for the Pope as the successor to St. Peter without evidence. And who, after all, was St. Peter?

In my second year at the university I became an agnostic humanist, a hedonist roarer—the kind you want to stay far from if he's had one too many, which I had more than once too many—so that my life became a blasphemous caroming in every direction that offered change. This could be seen as a coward's caving in, or the sensible route for a maturing young person to take, but I still feel unhappy reverberations from it. A guillotine came down on a way of life I didn't pick up again until my thirties, and I've since wondered if a more effective apologetic might have been, Scripture teaches; or as Christ puts it, It is written. . . .

I suspect it would have, for reasons I'll explain in the proper place, but on the immediate level it would have caused my inquisitors to confront scripture. It was scripture that remained with me through those years and scripture that eventually called me back to the church, by a route other than the sacramental one, and it is scripture that has the power to break apart every deathly, cyclical activity that we have the power to devise, and to make life whole again, because scripture embodies Christ.

Over my years as a reader and a writer I've found it almost impossible to hold anything in memory unless it's framed by a story: certainly down in words, at least. Most any reader can reel off lines of Shakespeare or Frost or Dickinson or Plath, but how many recite Pound's Cantos, or Eliot's Quartets? Narrative poetry is easy to memorize because its unfolding events, often ticked in place by rhyme, are like mileposts along the road to a destination. Even if there isn't a story to encapsulate what we wish to retain—which is, I think, the way memory works—there is always, in anything we're able to remember the rest of our lives, a progression, a narrative thread or pattern, or a set of steps leading from A to C.

It's for this reason, I believe, that the most pungent and memorable portions of the Bible are cast as stories—Adam and Eve, Moses and Pharaoh, David and Bathsheba, Ruth and Naomi, Balaam and his ass—stories that often appear early in the Bible, as you note. This same memorableness adheres to any part of the Law and the Prophets or the Gospels that I'm able to call up at will. Often these are passages that I should have in mind to compare to other, later passages. I suspect that this is why, when Jesus wished to teach a lesson that would stick, both in his auditors' minds and mine, he cast it in the narrative known as *parable*.

However anybody feels about narrative, over and above the purposes we can ascribe to the use of story in scripture, story is the quintessential way in which God has chosen to reveal himself to us.

The Acts of the Apostles is the most narrative book of the New Testament. There are portions of the Gospels that contain passages of narrative power, but the Gospels' progress is largely carried out through a series of vignettes, each with its spiritually pedagogical purpose (though Mark presents some exceptions)—or they are organized, like the Gospel of John, more logically than chronologically, to amplify a central teaching. The Acts of the Apostles is traditionally ascribed to the same Luke who composed the Gospel According to St. Luke, and all the internal evidence points to his authorship. A preface to Theophilus, similar to the one that opens Luke's gospel, is employed, and whenever a curious shift in point of view, from "omniscient" to first person, occurs in Acts (this will be discussed), Luke appears on the scene.

Although Luke is the author of a Gospel, he is not an apostle; that distinction should be made now. He does not possess the credentials for apostleship that he records, through Peter, in the first chapter of Acts. He is a physician and a scholar and, by a curious stroke of providence, the only gentile included in the canon of scripture. In some commentaries you might encounter an academic debate about whether "Luke" is actually Luke and whether this "Luke" then "actually" authored Acts. Or as a recent poem, meant to unmask the worth of deconstructionist criticism, remarks near its end:

> It's a woman posing as Luke.
> It's Luke posing as himself, unsuccessfully.
>
> This isn't Luke.
> It's a lie that reveals the true Luke.[2]

Any debate about the authorship of Acts shouldn't concern the beginning reader. Dedicated scholars may conduct scrupulous research and argue until they're blue in the face about the book's authorship, but unless additional manuscript or historical evidence is uncovered, they won't be any closer to proving their point on the day of their deaths than when their faces started assuming that unusual tinge. Disputing an unprovable point is about as interesting as watching paint dry, and during the last part of this century the American Church has consumed itself on such scholarship.

The European sector is already notably dead from it, via higher criticism (the church's modern version of dancing on the head of a pin, performed in our age by scholars), and similar research that roots not for the truffle but trifle has most American seminaries on a downhill slide. Rather than focusing on the substance of the central message of scripture—or even the subsidiary ones and their application—and teaching young seminarians to properly divide and communicate that word to wasting bodies of the church across the U.S., seminary professors tend to practice and promote a kind of disputatious focus on detail. They do this, I suspect, because they feel, like other professors, that this keeps them au courant. See *The Closing of the American Mind*, *Profscam*, *Illiberal Education*, et al.

I served as a professor long enough (and was tenured, so this shouldn't be construed as sour grapes—Ezekiel 18.2) to know the regimen. My mother was a teacher, my father was; both my brothers are, or have been, as I have. The dedication I saw in my parents is diminishing, along with the professional concern with which committed men and women used to labor to teach actual skills, including the reading of the classics (as some still do) rather than trends in the culture and political advocacy. To get some sense of how far the art of teaching and education has slipped, look at this testimony from John Muir, out of his memoirs of 1912:

> . . . I had committed the whole of the French, Latin, and English grammars to memory, and in connection with reading-lessons we were called on to recite parts of them with the rules over and over again, as if all the regular and irregular incomprehensible verb stuff was poetry. In addition to all this, father made me learn so many Bible verses every day that by the time I was eleven years of age I had about three fourths of the Old Testament and all of the New by heart and by sore flesh. I could recite the New Testament from the beginning of Matthew to the end of Revelation without a single stop.[3]

Our most eminent theologians probably don't have this store of scripture in memory for instant reference, as Muir had when he was eleven. With the training he received, he was actually equipped to make informed decisions, as our present pedagogic philosophy prescribes one should do, in spiritual and cultural matters, at an early age.

My feelings about scholarship in general in secular universities, and Christian scholarship in particular (and there should be a difference, in quality and spiritual discernment and ethics, at the minimum) are summed up by a professor of history and science at the University of Sydney, Australia, who writes, "Much of what goes as the latest wisdom in science and history will yet be shown to be nonsense and those who embrace it enthusiastically will be viewed as dunces by a later age. This is not to say that we need not face the serious problems that are raised by secular scholarship. It is simply to say that a refusal to follow every latest fad of scholarship is not necessarily a sign of obscurantism. Often it shows more wisdom than blind faith."[4]

I will assume Luke to be the author of Acts.

I suspect Acts was attached to Luke's Gospel, until the canon was established, but I do not believe, as some scholars suggest, that it was composed in the second century to refute the Marcion heresy. This idea that emerged from Rome, via Marcion, in A.D. 144 "maintained that Christ was the revealer of an entirely new religion, completely unrelated to anything that had preceded His coming (such as the revelation to Israel in the Old Testament), and that Paul was the only apostle of Christ who faithfully preserved this new religion in its purity (uncontaminated by Old Testament or Jewish influence)."[5]

The British theologian F. F. Bruce, in his commentary on Acts that sets our present-day standard, makes wise use of historical and textual evidence to refute this wrong-headed supposition. Paul himself, under the direction of the Spirit, continually opposes the teachings that will emanate from Marcion, as Acts will illustrate. The Marcion heresy at first appears puzzling, since all of scripture argues so consistently against it, until you realize that strains of it are still present in the modern church. Indeed, it seems that the church replays an ancient heresy every few years, due to its general lack of understanding of scripture and history. This is a further failure of teaching.

When the gospels were gathered together in the first century for their fourfold testimony, Acts was probably given the place in the canon it occupies today, serving as a bridge between the gospels and the epistles—letters directed to specific congregations within the early Christian Church. The followers of Christ who formed the church first came to be known as "Christian" in Antioch, one of the many items of historical information we gather in Acts (11.26). And Acts is, as it were, the Genesis of every epistle. The overall shape and direction the church should take unfolds through the scenes of Acts. Then the epistles, in addressing specific problems within that church, as they always do, continue to narrow the gate by which the church can be entered and still be called a church.

Luke was a scholar, as I have said, and a doctor ("the beloved physician," in the apostle Paul's phrase), so his testimony is particularly apt as the first miracles of the church begin to occur— and will never again occur in such plenitude, in this same way, for reasons to be explained. Acts is Luke's second book of instruction ("so you will understand the subject in which you have been catechized," as a literal rendition of the passage in Luke 1 might read) to an auditor known only as Theophilus, or "lover of God." The name could be symbolic, though as likely it refers to an actual person, since the name was common enough in Luke's time. The point is that one who loves God must *understand the subject in which he or she has been catechized.*

One of the failings of the American branch of the modern protestant branches of the church (on one twig of which I am counted a member) is that it apparently mistrusts catechisms. As this division of the church began to turn broadly evangelical in the 1900s, it seems to have started worrying whether catechizing was, as it were, kosher—as though the method of teaching originated in Rome. Not so, as we learn from Luke. A number of the finest catechisms available were written by protestants, primarily at the time of the Reformation. There is Luther's, a durable artifact that few who fill the pews of the present Lutheran Church know by heart, if they know of it at all.

The Heidelberg Catechism is a secondary standard (scripture being primary) of the Christian Reformed Church, with its predominantly Dutch membership, and the Reformed Church in the

United States, generally called the Eureka-Classis Church (I picture a turn-of-the-century photo of Eureka, South Dakota, with stately Germans wearing the billed headgear of ship captains standing outside a depot). The beauty of the Heidelberg lies in the direction of its questions; they are addressed to *you* or *we*, so that one must answer in a personal way, and as the questions move through a progressive understanding of God and one's relationship to Him, only the iciest heart is able to avoid the application that begins to grow from the humble and lyric answers.

Perhaps the most scrupulous of the catechisms, however, is the Westminster, issued in larger, shorter, and children's versions. It was begun in 1638 by the Assembly of Westminster Divines, who met in Henry VII's Chapel and the Jerusalem Chamber of Westminster Abbey, the source of the catechism's title.[6] These "divines" were British and Scottish theologians and pastors who had received a commission from Parliament to define the doctrine of the newly emerging and (as it was falsely termed by courtiers) "dissenting" Church. The Assembly had intended to rewrite the Thirty-nine Articles of the state Church of England but found these untenable, and composed what became known as the Westminster Confession of Faith. The Catechism is derived from it.

The meeting turned out to be an extended one, according to Dean Arthur Stanley's *Historical Memorials of Westminster Abbey*: "For five years, six months, and twenty-five days, through one thousand one hundred and sixty-three sessions, the Chapel of Henry VII and the Jerusalem Chamber witnessed their weary labours."[7] In 1643 these documents were signed with rejoicing in the Jerusalem Chamber. The Confession and Catechisms were adopted and used, sometimes after revisions, by most of the English-speaking branches of the church, including Baptist and Congregational affiliates, until the twentieth century. But in the last one hundred years, the independency of spirit of

Americanism, it seems, along with a broadening "evangelical" outlook already mentioned, swept most churches clean of catechizing.

Versions of the Westminster Confession of Faith and catechisms are still used in Reformed Baptist churches, and they remain the secondary standards, though often by mere tokenism, in dozens of branches of the American and Scots presbyterian churches. John Muir's family came from one such Scottish branch to America, and the memorization of scripture he underwent was not unusual for the day in his tradition.

The Westminster Catechism is perhaps the fullest and most doctrinally impeccable, after all that labor, as in the Larger Catechism's Question 36: *Who is the mediator of the covenant of grace?*

A. The only Mediator of the covenant of grace is the Lord Jesus Christ, who, being the eternal Son of God, of one substance and equal with the Father, in the fullness of time became man, and so was and continues to be God and man, in two entire and distinct natures, and one person, forever.

Or the simpler and more direct Shorter Catechism on that knotty question, *What is Justification?*

A. Justification is an act of God's free grace, wherein he pardons all our sins, and accepts us as righteous in his sight, only for the righteousness of Christ imputed to us, and received by faith alone.

In the Larger Catechism each phrase bears a footnote that lists, chapter and verse, corresponding references from the Bible, by which the statement of the phrase is derived. A set of wonderfully clearheaded studies of the Westminster Confession of Faith and the Shorter Catechism has been written by G. I. Williamson,[8] and it seems that wherever I travel I meet someone who has benefited from his books.

Why spend time with a catechism, you might wonder, or the study guide to one? Catechisms contain a distillation of the doctrines the church has articulated over the centuries. There are

Christians who shy as wide from the word "doctrine" as from a catechism. "I just want to know Jesus!" they say, confusing, I suspect, doctrine with dogma defined by a hierarchy. Doctrine merely means "teaching," and Jesus never opens his mouth except to speak doctrine. The Holy Spirit speaks doctrine and the Spirit has been given to the church of our era also, so to shun catechisms or the writings of the Church Fathers or diligent theologians of the past is to deny, at least partly, the working of the Spirit in the history of the church.

To really "know Jesus" it's best to have an overview, like a map to a perilous country, of everything the Old and New Testaments teach of Him, and everything that the church has pondered and taught about those testaments. There is rugged terrain ahead for those who are constitutionally incapable of referring to the paths marked out by wise and spirit-filled cartographers over the centuries.

If you wish to run your Christianity or doctrine of the church from scratch, you may as well disregard the book of Acts, too, and begin all over to invent the wheel on your own. Unfortunately many churches today are doing exactly that, and this is one reason there are so many branches and denominations within the church. On the other hand, there are areas in which the historical church has erred, I believe, as the apostles themselves will err in Acts, and at these points I will note the ways in which I feel the developing church deviated from the pattern set down in Acts—not to mention the notorious wildernesses into which some modern branches have wandered.

Although I've said that catechisms have generally been swept from protestant churches, there are recent signs of a beginning of their return. In some of the materials being offered to families by publishers who are fueling the home-school movement (of which, more later), I have seen references to catechisms, and was surprised to find that a textbook issued under the Bob Jones imprint

reproduced as an appendix the Children's Catechism—scrupu-
lously revised, of course.

There are other catechisms in currency, but the three above
have had the most impact on the church as articles of reformation,
and these are the ones to turn to still, in the hurry of our age,
for instruction. I was raised on the Roman Catholic Baltimore
Catechism, and there was a period in my life when I resented
those years of wearying drill. But if there is an aspect of that
church, now, that I remain grateful for, it is its insistence on catechizing—an insistence that, from what I hear down corridors, is
beginning to dim: too bad.

The title The Acts of the Apostles, though perhaps a later addition
by the church, is our book's best description. It could as well be
called, though not as felicitously, The Further Acts of Jesus Christ,
as Carried Forward through his Apostles, by the Power of His
Spirit. In succinct, dramatic episodes, Luke relates not only the
relevant acts that the apostles found themselves performing, and
so sets down the history of the beginnings of the Church, but he
touches on every theme and conflict that will come to affect that
church over the centuries. This is, I'm convinced, more than pre-
science. Acts is inspired.

That word is used loosely these days. Young writers talk about
being inspired, but the word is current in the sense I'm getting at
in people who imagine they would *like* to write, and will say, "I expect you really have to be inspired to work." To deal with that
quickly, no. Anyone who wants to write should expect to work at
it every day, day after day, like a bricklayer, or at least plan to keep
bankers' hours, and anybody who hopes to get rich at it should
maybe be a bricklayer. There are fewer than a hundred writers in
the United States today who make a living solely at writing, and
there is no way to regularly produce finished work except to sit
and write for six hours, six days a week.

In the midst of that work, when enough words are down so that the interconnections in the metaphor built of language begin to spark at every juncture, something of what a bricklayer means by inspiration—those singing intimations that occur to any laborer in the midst of engaging work—can overtake you. Then the words might take off or soar in a way that it's difficult to catch up to or even get hold of. Inspiration, in its original sense in the Greek, means divinely *breathed out*, or *God-breathed*. I gladly acknowledge that any effect I've been able to bring to my prose is the result of the talents I've been given by God, and that by his grace those talents have added up beyond even my expectations, but I do not believe, like the pagan Greeks, that a god or goddess or muse, or even God, is breathing the words he wants me to write into my brain.

Something of this sort surely happened to Luke, however (along with the other authors of Scripture: 2 Timothy 3.16; 1 Peter 1.21), when he wrote Acts. I suspect that as he walked the roads of the Fertile Crescent, thinking through these events he wished to put into an orderly account, whole pages like assembled jewelry appeared in his mind, staggering him.

Acts is the most wide-ranging, diverse, and populous book of the New Testament, and in order to gather its major themes into a discernible order, I will divide Acts into the three sections into which it has been divided traditionally. This division is suggested in the first chapter of Acts by Christ himself, when he says to his apostles, "But you shall receive power when the Holy Spirit has come upon you; and you shall be my witnesses both in Jerusalem [I], and in all Judea and Samaria [II], and even to the remotest parts of the earth [III]."

I should mention that I usually quote from the *New American Standard Bible*, which I find the most accurate version, verse by verse, in English, but I also refer to the King James, the

Authorized Version, the New Revised Standard Version, and a text in my computer called the Modern King James Version, and I use the lexicons and concordances that most pastors do. No, I don't read Greek, or I wouldn't employ so many English versions, but I'm about to make another attempt to, and there is a further check on me that I will mention later. I have, as you might say, a little Latin and less Greek.

On occasion I nudge phrases closer to what I believe is linguistic accuracy, or let them stand as pared down as they stand in the original, but whenever I suspect the reader might miss the words of the King James, I will use it, in the *New King James Version*. In some passages, it almost duplicates the New American Standard. The NASB is the most reliable, and besides its word-by-word translation, which shuns the pitfalls of paraphrase, its language reproduces a rough poetic growl akin to the koine, or common-language Greek (in contrast to literary Attic Greek), of the original.

There is no translation harder on my nerves than the New International Version (NIV). The committee that produced it must have been immune to the nuances of music in English, or collectively had, as writers and editors say, a tin ear. The Psalms and other poetic passages particularly suffer, and some of the soaring doxologies of Paul are shoveled into elementary sentences. I should also mention that the NIV, which is presently very popular, inclines almost as much as *The Living Bible* toward what is known as "dynamic equivalence," a form of paraphrase that permits the translator's interpretation of a passage to take precedence over possible shades of subtle meaning within a phrase of the text.[9]

When I quote from the chapter in Acts I have reached in its narration, I often do not include a reference, but if I refer forward or backward in the book, or to another book of the Bible, I usually do. I have purposely cast this chapter in the start-and-stop,

ballooning quality that occurs when there is no narrative to bear
the prose along like a river, in order to offer a contrast to the story
of Acts.

Finally, the reader has by now noticed that sometimes in end-
notes, sometimes in the text itself, I recommend further reading. I will continue to do this. The books or articles expand upon
troublesome or complex venues beyond the scope of these reflections, and should help serve as a beginning bibliography for
any reader who is a serious student.

I cite only two or three commentaries directly, and otherwise
say "you will hear" or "some say" or "it's been written," in order
to remove myself from the temptation of personal remarks. The
books I recommend will, I assure you, be well written, not the sort
you must go at with pickax and shop vac in order to dislodge an
intelligible phrase, as those thick tomes of theology we nod over at
midnight sometimes seem. Unless I say otherwise, I've chosen
writers who write clearly and address their areas of study with the
simplicity and ease that arrive from mastery of a subject, if not
wisdom. Their Christian acts in prose have made it possible for
me to presume to step out on my own in Acts.

I
JERUSALEM

and the Descent of the Holy Spirit

2

The Descent of
the Spirit

The season of harvest is my favorite, from late summer into early fall—sometimes extending as far as the end of October. I love the feel of the air and the quality of light then, along with the look of the fields during harvest. Today, in an acreage of oats laid in long lacy windrows on bleached-out stubble, I began harvesting, and after sitting for two hours behind glass in the cab of a lumbering self-propelled combine, eight feet above the windrow shakily feeding into the whirling auger and frightening flying steel feeder-teeth of the combine, the quiet of solid ground was a balm. My son, who is fifteen, drove up on our old red tractor with a baler hooked behind, along with a bale stacker hooked behind that, and we began to bale up the straw that the combine had blown with dust and chaff out its back in the noisy process of threshing the oats clean.

It had been windy, with the potbellied clouds that carry rain rolling past all day. Yet the sun on the field was so unobstructed that a gold haze shimmered above the stubble, and as I rode the stacker waiting for the next bale, I had time to take in the countryside: a great rough-topped butte whose colors seem to change each hour, off to the south, with wallows of blue-tinged brush creasing its presently emerald sides, and a road tinted by scoria climbing past the far corner of our land toward the plain the butte rests upon. In every direction the country swung away in swells and rolls that heaved up into other buttes, some near, some far—an orderly conical trio to my right, like miniatures of the sister peaks of the Northwest, in this mingling of sun and cloud sending shadows of overcast across the interlocking fields of gold and beige, with pastures here and there like brown-green bass notes stunning the ordered countryside.

There were hardly any buildings visible, only the house and barn of our nearest neighbor, a mile off, and, straight ahead, the roofs of our own buildings against a windbreak of trees—the cedar tower at the south of the house higher than any treetop—and for a second I felt in paradise, or near it. Then I pressed a footpedal that released a pyramid of fifteen finished bales, outlined whitegold in a sudden open gate of sun, and thought, as I often do in my height of pleasure at this place, What am I doing here? If anyone would have told me fifteen years ago that I would soon be living in North Dakota, my native state, I probably would have laughed.

I have lived in New York City and L.A., in Wisconsin and Michigan, in Canada and Minneapolis and Chicago and London. The five years in New York City were among my best, three of them 24 carat, with my wife present, but at the time we lived in the city the pollution was comparable, according to one computation, to smoking two packs of cigarettes a day. Though this problem has been alleviated over the years, that glittering international center of the arts continues to have daily, nearly insuperable problems, as all cities do, and my wife and I came to feel after our first child, a daughter, was born, that we did not want to rear her in a city.

For seven years we looked for "the right place," and toward the end of an odyssey that began to turn spiritual, we decided we must live in the West. After touring every western state from Montana to New Mexico, we agreed that the only area that didn't seem invaded or tainted by the East or Hollywood, and still retained a sense of the frontier, was western North Dakota. My wife was the first to walk this farm. I was in the hospital, recovering from a siege of illnesses that were caused, it was finally discovered, by a blood-sugar condition akin to diabetes. So she saw the fields, and she bought them, in the sense that Proverbs 31 commends, knowing she had my approval and payment at hand.

I never would have imagined I would be here, but the spirit of God works in ways we're unable to manipulate, and in this Republic whose constitution guarantees the pursuit of happiness, we have chosen to pursue happiness here. Our quarter-section was homesteaded in 1917 by a family from the same Wisconsin village where my grandmother grew up; the brother and sister who sold us the farm, Ivan and Enid, are children of the original homesteaders. Enid, now in her nineties, sat in a Sunday school taught by my great-aunt, and Enid taught high school with my father in the forties and remembers me as a four-year-old. We didn't know any of this until we started negotiating for the land, and we started looking in this area because a denomination we had recently joined had one church in the state. Using its location as a center point, we drew a circle with a radius of fifty miles, contacted the pastor, and began to hope and pray we would find the right place within that circle.

Two days ago my wife said to me, "I went down to the basement last night and was looking around, and for the first time since we've been here I felt it was my place, not Ivan and Enid's." This is our fourteenth year of ownership. Ivan and Enid live in a neighboring town, and though they're growing frail and cautious, they continue to drive out and look over the land where they grew up, and visit. On the day of their auction sale, a month before we moved in, Ivan was kept busy with the hurry auctioneers demand, but at the end of the day he wanted to demonstrate to me how a riding mower—which I had decided should stay with the place and had bought—worked. To do that he had to move a garden hose, and to do that he had to go down on a knee and disconnect it. It was getting dark and as I stared off at a butte with a sense of experiencing the West for the first time, he rose with a hand to his back and said, "Ooo, stiff." And then he looked to where I'd been looking, and said, "But I guess I should expect that. I've lived here now for seventy years."

One of the first times he drove Enid out, a while after the closing, he started across the acre-wide yard to where I was unhappily mending a fence of his—a tall man in a tweed Scots golfing cap, hands in his pockets, setting each foot down with such casual ease it seemed he knew the placement of every tuft and pebble, and for a second I envied him his sense of place and peace. But he would be as at ease in Scotland or Scandinavia, I thought, since his body had conformed itself to the sense of home by seventy-some years of learning the land he now walked. He stopped at the proper distance to keep from presuming on my neighborliness and smiled, hands still in his pockets, and I saw that he was staring at the trio of conical buttes over my shoulder, five miles to the north. Then he looked at me and said, "Don't those buttes anchor you?"

One of the outbuildings of the farm, a wood granary, had been torn from its footing and tipped on its side by a past tornado, and one of my first undertakings that year was to set it upright on a slab and begin rebuilding it as a place to walk to each day to work, separate from the house. I'm sitting in it now, below narrow windows installed so high I'm unable to see out even when I stand. This wasn't poor design or bad carpentry, but purposeful; the subtle contours of this land lying a little south and east of the Badlands, with its panorama of perfectly unpolluted sky, is as mesmerizing as the sea, as tempting to stare at, and on my desk I always have another world to enter. I rest my fingers on the keyboard, sensitive at each joint from bale twines, trying to put from my mind the thought of this hidden pinpoint on the planet where pyramids of bales stand above a harvested field (safe from moisture, shelter and food for wildlife, bedding for animals) growing dim now in the dark, and then the sudden clatter of keys below is like the onslaught of summer rain.

After Luke's prologue to Theophilus (like mine to a former student), he shifts to the forty-day period when Jesus, after his resurrection, regularly sought out his disciples (see Mat. 28, Luke 24, John 20–21); and by the third sentence of Acts Jesus appears. He speaks and the apostles question him as they did during his earthly ministry, in an early instance of what present-day writers call a flashback. Luke has returned us, we realize, to the moment of Christ's ascension, which is a recapitulation of the close of his gospel, in order to interleave Acts with his "previous account." They're one story, he's saying. Then as dozens of witnesses watch, Jesus is "lifted up."

The point of this is that the Spirit, who has been promised over the centuries in the Law and the Prophets, and in Jesus' own declarations (John 14.26), is about to be given to the apostles. "But you shall receive power when the Holy Spirit has come upon you," Jesus says, naming those geographical areas where his disciples will serve as witnesses to him.

Several curious things have happened at once, besides the recapitulated ascension. In the third verse Luke says that Jesus "presented himself alive, after his suffering, by many *infallible proofs.*" That's the translation the King James and other versions prefer, and the Greek from which "infallible proofs" is derived is used only once in the Bible. Here. For the Greeks of the time it meant, in logic, "demonstrable proof" and, in medical science, "demonstrable evidence." As a physician, Luke means the latter: there is demonstrable medical evidence that Jesus was alive after his death.

This is also the verse in which Luke mentions the forty-day period when Jesus appeared to his disciples, and some commentators feel this is merely another use of a recurring biblical period—forty days, forty nights, forty years—and is therefore a "literary device" rather than a measure of actual time. My reaction as a writer is, Then why mention it? No serious writer uses a "literary device" in this formulaic sense. Every phrase in a closely written book comes to seem inevitable, and it is only the critic afterward who sees the repetition of blue, say, as a literary device, or worse, a symbol, and then teaches his or her students that it is.

Luke is a scientist whose words move in pure clear steps toward the highest goal of what is best in both prose and medicine: accuracy. He is composing factual (what we might call nonfiction) prose, not a villanelle. If he were writing formal poetry or myth, the necessity for factual precision would not pertain in the same way, as he surely knew, knowing the Greek myths and their fabulations. And if this is a myth, why end with forty days? Why not carry it as far as possible, up to the present, as with Zeus, if people go for that? The quality of Luke's prose argues too consistently for scrupulousness to even suggest the fantasies that people unfamiliar with writing try to impose on him.

And then to step back once more in Luke's manner: in his opening sentence to Theophilus, he says that his first account was about "all that Jesus began to do and teach, until the day he was taken up." Then the third verse occurs. If Luke's statement is to have consistency, then each sentence that follows should be explaining what Jesus *continued* to do and teach. It's necessary to keep that continuation in mind as proofs for it begin to pour into Acts. It's important, too, to remember this moment immediately after Christ's ascension: as the apostles are staring up, two men appear among them, wearing the same white robes as the figures exalted with Christ on the mountain of his transfiguration. Those were Moses, the giver of the law, and Elijah, Israel's prophet who was "taken up" in a manner similar to Jesus, in "a fiery chariot" whose makeup Ezekiel 1 further defines.

Whether the men in white are Moses and Elijah attesting again, as on the mountain of transfiguration, the centrality of the per-

son of Christ, about whom the Father says, "This is my beloved
son in whom I am well pleased," I don't think anybody can say
with authority, but if you are familiar with the gospels you can't
help making the connection. Luke wants all Theophili to carry
that image forward from the first of Acts to its conclusion: Christ
clothed in majesty, ascending (or coming on the clouds) to the
right hand of the Father, with prophecy on one side and the law of
God on the other.

The apostles hurry from the Mount of Olives back to Jerusalem, "a Sabbath day's journey,"[1] or less than a mile—a reminder
that the followers of Jesus were devout Jews, always moving over
hallowed, familiar ground: Ivans. In Jerusalem they gather, minus
one, in an "upper room" with a hundred others, including women,
"devoting themselves to prayer."

Just as we begin to wonder about the twelfth apostle, Judas,
Peter rises and says, " 'Brothers, the Scripture had to be fulfilled,
which the Holy Spirit foretold by the mouth of David concerning Judas, who became a guide to those who arrested Jesus. For
he was counted among us, and received his portion in this ministry.' (Now this man acquired a field with the price of his
wickedness; and falling headlong, he burst open in the middle
and all his bowels gushed out. And it became known to all who
were living in Jerusalem; so that in their own language that field
was called Hakeldama, or Field of Blood.) 'For it is written in
the book of Psalms, *Let his homestead be made desolate, and let
no man dwell in it,* and *His office let another man take.* It is therefore necessary that of the men who have accompanied us all the
time that the Lord Jesus went in and out among us—beginning
with the baptism of John until the day that He was taken up
from us—one of these should become a witness with us of His
resurrection.' "

Here, from Peter's mouth, is the authoritative definition of an
apostle: one who has witnessed Jesus' ministry from his baptism to
his resurrection. I have quoted at length to give a sense of Luke's

dovetailed technique, already apparent in the opening that links his gospel to Acts. Luke was clearly a Greek, but his packed concision out-Greeks the Greeks of Greek drama and is a forerunner of the kind of writing we won't witness in its full-blown application until own our stark, purged fiction of the twentieth century.

There is one other element that Luke will emphasize; with the possible exception of Matthew's Gospel, Acts, more than any book of the New Testament, interweaves the correspondences between the Law and Prophets and the new covenant. We will see the apostles engaged in this practice, applying the existing covenant to the one emerging, as Peter does here, and Luke is attentive to these interconnections. This is why Acts is commonly turned to by the church for its teaching of the doctrine that has come to be known, in its broadest terms, as The Covenant.

For the present "covenant" can be partly explained by looking at the origin and meaning of another designation: New Testament. As our scholar, commentator, classicist, and historian Dr. Machen points out, "The English word 'testament' comes from a Latin word." Which should immediately give pause to anyone who knows that the scriptures of the Bible are written in Hebrew and Greek. Machen goes on to say, "As used in the Greek Bible it may mean either 'covenant' or 'testament'. Usually it should probably be translated 'covenant'."

To continue to follow his thought: "The phrase 'new covenant' occurs about five times in the New Testament. In none of these passages does the phrase refer to the 'New Testament' in our sense. It designates a new relationship into which men have been received by God." After a trim discussion of these covenants, the first made with the Hebrew nation, through the mediating person of Moses, the second made with "every tribe and tongue and people and nation, who should through faith accept the salvation offered by Christ," he says, "Perhaps it would have been better if we had started to say 'New Covenant' where we now say 'New Testament.' "[2]

Perhaps if Machen's suggestion had been adopted when it was offered, in the 1920s, Jewish believers might have taken less offense at Christianity, for they have taken offense, and rightly so in this case. The term "Old Testament" suggests that testament is irrelevant, when it's not, while "covenant" implies a new conciliation or addition, since a covenant, and especially one made by God, can be altered or satisfied only according to His terms. Jesus excoriated the scribes and Pharisees for interpreting scripture unfairly or wrongly, not for any regard they may have had for the existing covenant as the word of God. He himself quoted from the old covenant as much as any Pharisee, or more, and throughout his ministry and the rest of the new covenant the decisive argument, as Acts will illustrate, is always "It is written."[3]

To return to Peter's speech, let me note a detail that some who are familiar with the account of Judas in Matthew 27 see as a discrepancy between the two, or a lack of harmony between them: after throwing the thirty pieces of silver on the floor of the temple in front of those who hired him, Judas goes out and hangs himself. Matthew, who wishes to tie his account to the first covenant (specifically Jeremiah), concludes with the same *Hakel Dama,* or field of blood—named so after Judas' blood money. Since these details exist in Matthew, I see the description from Peter as an elaboration, in a sophisticated accreting manner that would please a Robbe-Grillet, on this betrayer's awful end. Once he had hanged himself and grown ripe in the semi-arid atmosphere of Jerusalem and was cut down, or fell from his own ripeness, his bloated body burst and his intestines slithered out.

When Peter finishes his speech, "they" propose two candidates. "They" could refer to the entire crowd in the room but probably means the apostles, since they have been recently mentioned by name (1.13), and they are direct appointees of Christ; it's to their number the twelfth will be added.

The nominees are Joseph, called Barsabbas, and Matthias. Now it's clear that the selection was made by the apostles, for "they prayed, and said, 'You, O Lord, who know the hearts of all, show which of these two You have chosen to take part in *this ministry and apostleship* from which Judas by transgression fell, that he might go to his own place.' "

After their prayer, perhaps surprisingly to some, the apostles in effect flip a coin. They cast lots. For those familiar with the original covenant, as the apostles were, however, even the supposedly random selection of lots is under God's jurisdiction—"The lot is cast into the lap but the whole disposing thereof is of the Lord" (Prov. 16.33)—and casting of lots was used to decide Levitical duty. The lot falls on Matthias. The end of chapter 1.

We never hear of Matthias again. Why? Because he was not properly chosen as an apostle, I believe, and so never fruitfully served as one—and not because of any "sin" in the casting of lots. All the apostles were personally called out by Jesus with that "Follow me" that none could resist:

> I want to understand, if only for the story,
> how a man like this,
> a man like my father in harvest,
> like Bunk Mac Vane in the stench of
>   lobstering,
> or a teamster, a steelworker,
> how an ordinary working stiff,
> even a high tempered one,
> could just be called away.[4]

Jesus says, in John 6.70, "Have I not chosen you, the twelve, and one of you is a devil?" This devil has been dealt with, and the apostles apparently feel they must now take it upon themselves to fill out the twelve, not yet understanding the power of the resurrected Christ and his ability to call another to serve him, as he will.

For the moment, however, all the loose threads of the gospels have been gathered up, including that final detail of Judas' death, in order to prepare us, now that Christ has assumed his place of power and glory at the right hand of his Father, for the single most significant event of the new covenant Church. If you have read the Bible from Genesis to here, the opening of the first sentence in chapter 2—"And when the day of Pentecost had come"—might give you pause. It's the first time *Pentecost* occurs in the canon.

It was a day of religious observance, set aside in the original covenant, commonly called the Feast of Weeks. "It is regarded as the second of three obligatory observances, coming between Passover and Tabernacles (cf. Exod. 23:14–17; 34:18–24; Deut. 16:16; 2 Chron. 8:13)."[5] It was also known as the "feast of harvest" or of the "first fruits," a feast that fell fifty days from Passover. Probably after the destruction of the Temple in Jerusalem in A.D. 70, it came to be called the *Shavuot*, or celebration in thanks for the Torah, still observed in Judaism today.

John Calvin, the much-maligned theologian who is one of the most self-effacing and humble commentators, says it was Augustine's view that "as the Law was given to the people of old fifty days after Passover (*Pascha*), written by the hand of God on tables of stone, so the Spirit, whose work is to write that Law in our hearts, the same number of days after the resurrection of Christ, who is the true Passover, fulfilled what had been prefigured in the giving of the Law." Calvin finds this interpretation somewhat "subtle," and says he feels there is a sounder (or simpler) one: "it was upon a feast-day, when a great multitude always gathered at Jerusalem, that the miracle was performed, that the fame of it might be the greater."[6]

I have another suggestion: that all of the above are true, but that it was also on *the fiftieth day after Christ's resurrection*. In this room, then, where the disciples are gathered in fear from all they've recently witnessed and suffered, "suddenly there came from heaven a noise like a mighty, rushing wind, and it filled the whole house where they were sitting. And there appeared to them tongues as of fire distributing themselves, and they rested on each of them." The arrival of the Holy Spirit in fulfillment of the promises of Christ. Pentecost.

There is a building reference to Christ. This is one of two times in the new covenant when the Spirit becomes visible. The first was when Jesus stepped from the Jordan where John had baptized him, and, to refer now to the King James version, "the heavens were opened to him, and he saw the Spirit of God descending like a dove, and lighting upon him: and, lo, a voice from heaven, saying, This is my beloved Son, in whom I am well pleased"—one of the clearest conjunctions of the Trinity in scripture. And now in this electrifying instance in an upper room in Jerusalem, probably the same room in which Jesus held the Last Supper, the Spirit is manifested to the disciples again as a rushing mighty wind and still flame. Since this is their true baptism, they do not "go down into" the Spirit. The Spirit descends on them, as it descended on Christ when he stepped from the Jordan. And now, so that all their senses are confirmed in the promise that Jesus' followers will be baptized not only with water but fire, the fiery minister appears a final time. They *see* the Spirit as clearly as they saw Jesus, standing over everyone's head in flame, and then "they were all filled with the Holy Spirit, and began to speak in other tongues, as the Spirit gave them utterance."

They raise such a commotion that a curious city crowd draws up. The regions of original habitation of this crowd will soon be given, though for the present they are "dwelling in Jerusalem," an international city. No doubt Calvin is also correct; that many others are present for the feast day, so that this significant moment can be witnessed by many, although the text of Acts doesn't explicitly state this (2.5) except to mention "visitors" from Rome. The immediate response of the crowd is one of wonder, for though the speakers are Galileans, country cousins marked by their garb and accent, yet "Parthians and Medes and Elamites, and residents of Mesopotamia, Judea and Cappadocia, Pontus and Asia, Phrygia and Pamphylia, Egypt and the districts of Libya around Cyrene, and visitors from Rome, both Jews and proselytes, Cretans and Arabs—we hear them in our own tongues speaking of the mighty deeds of God."

This is the crowd's initial response, but the disciples are so elated, and perhaps helpless, too, to control the language pouring from them, that skeptics say in a mocking tone, "Aw, they're full of new wine." They're loaded. Peter tries to disabuse them of this by pointing out that it's only the third hour, or about nine in the morning—an ingenuous explanation that wouldn't deter any modern American drinker. So what is this matter of many tongues? The disciples are identified as Galilean, but the diverse dwellers of Jerusalem are hearing them speak in *their* indigenous tongues.

The key to interpreting scripture is to turn to other relevant passages in it, and if one looks ahead to the incident in the house of Cornelius, when the gentiles are first called into the kingdom, the sign that attests to the validity of their calling is the phenomenon of speaking in tongues (10.44–48). Here the gentiles "speak with tongues and magnify God." In Paul's lengthy disquisition on tongues, beginning in 1 Corinthians 13, and continuing through 14, we read that "he who speaks in a tongue does not speak to men but to God" (14.2a) and "he who speaks in a tongue edifies himself," while one who prophesies edifies the church (14.4).

The weight of experiential conversion, in the form of "gifts of the Spirit" and tongues, along with the concept of a "second baptism," still causes contention in the church, and will be discussed fully when we reach Cornelius and his household. It seems safe for now to say that the apostles are speaking in plainly understood foreign languages.

And now Peter, altered from the person who less than two months ago denied even knowing Jesus (tossing in curses to make his denial stronger), takes "his stand with the eleven" and gives the first sermon—understood by all, we must assume from the above and the sermon's results—of the New Covenant. I don't think this place of honor grants Peter special standing or primogeniture among the apostles; that isn't the issue. Indeed, after the first chapters of Acts, Peter begins to fade from the narrative, which doesn't mean, either, that he must decrease while the others increase; the issue is that the apostles, personally chosen representatives of Christ, are meant to deliver the Truth.

Which Peter does with bright boldness. He quotes from the prophet Joel, "And it shall come to pass in the last days, says God, that I will pour out of My Spirit on all flesh . . ." (2.28), referring to the Old Covenant's knowledge of this arrival of the Spirit, in order to announce the opening of the New Covenant to the crowd. The prophecy from Joel reinforces what is known as a postmillennial view: that these are "the last days," however long their duration, during which the fulfiller of the covenant will be bringing his kingdom to pass. Peter speaks with authority, exegeting Psalms 16 and 110, and sets Jesus before the crowd as their "Lord and Christ"—the anointed one, the Messiah.

There is the charged vivacity of conviction in every turn of his speech, yet its message is complex. He sets in the right balance for his listeners, who are attuned to old covenant theology, the issue of the predestinating will of God in relationship to personal responsibility: "This Man, delivered up by the predetermined plan and foreknowledge of God, you nailed to a cross by the hands of godless men and put to death." Explicitly Peter means the Roman authorities, but he isn't exculpating anyone.

This is Peter's second instance of covenantal exegesis (the first in choosing an apostle, in which his conclusion was correct, though he was hasty in assuming it was his duty to follow through), and in this pattern he follows the example of Christ, who always stated, "It is written." Peter says that when David wrote in Psalm 16 that the Lord would not permit "His Holy One to undergo decay," David wasn't referring to himself: "I may confidently say to you regarding the patriarch David that he both died and was buried, and his tomb is with us to this day. And so, because he was a prophet, and knew that God had sworn to him with an oath to seat one of his descendents on the throne, he looked ahead [to this moment] and spoke of the resurrection of Christ."

Peter mentions, in reference to the psalm he has quoted, that Christ "was neither abandoned to Hades nor underwent decay," which gives a certain credence to those who wish to rewrite *The Apostle's Creed* (and they exist in the church) by deleting "He descended into Hell." Peter's exegesis of the Psalm indeed suggests that the "harrowing of hell," which has received considerable treatment by poets and writers through the centuries, enticing as the idea might be, is an instance of actual myth.

The major portion of Peter's sermon is taken from the psalms, so it would be profane to say that Christology (a pointing to the person and work of Christ) isn't present in the psalms, as some do. And he quotes from them for a significant reason; since they were used in Temple worship, and therefore probably in the worship in synagogues, every faithful member of the covenant had many memorized. So the crowd is able to follow the points that Peter makes about the Davidic prophecies of Christ in the psalms.

It would be remiss not to mention, too, that there are present-day Jewish spokesmen who regard Peter's crucifixion statement, and other new covenant passages (particularly when read in the Church), as anti-Semitic. In this instance those spokesmen are, I believe, off base. Peter was a Jew himself, as the apostles were, as Jesus was, and implicit in Peter's sermon is the proclamation of the fulfillment, in Jesus the Messiah, of the law and prophets—that outward view of hope found in all covenant believers, and expressed in Job's confession: "I know my redeemer lives, and at the last He will take his stand on the earth. Even after my skin is destroyed, yet in my flesh I will see God."

At this point Peter is a prophet, newly anointed by the Spirit, and his words fall in the vein of those spoken by all of the prophets to God's Israel since the time of Moses (Deut. 32.5, 2 Kings 17.20, 2 Chron. 25.7, Ezek. 3.7–9, Amos 9.7, and so forth). It is out of that context, or text and tradition, that Peter speaks, as his hearers—"Jews living in Jerusalem, devout men, from every nation under heaven"—surely recognize. And it is under this aegis, when they are "cut to the heart" and ask what they can do, that Peter tells them to repent and be baptized: "For the promise is to you and to your children, and to all who are far off, as many as the Lord our God will call to Himself."

Three thousand are baptized that day.

The words of Peter, "the promise is to you and to your children," reaffirm the original covenant. For members of the new covenant being called by Peter to be baptized, that covenant can't be seen separate from baptism, so it's necessary to look at the relationship of baptism to the covenant and then turn to a matter of contention in the church for centuries: the mode of baptism.

Whether we view the covenant as a five-point structure with similarities to ancient Suzerain codes,[7] or as a movement from Old to New, in reference to the two Covenants, it begins in the Garden, with God's implied promise of eternal life to Adam and Eve, and thus Eve and Adam's offspring, if they do tend the Garden (the first picture of paradise, or heaven) and do eat all but one fruit—that of the tree of the knowledge of good and evil. That one forbidden fruit they do eat, breaking the covenant, and the repercussions of their fall precipitate the flood, when a further covenanted promise, sealed by the rainbow, is established with Noah and his descendents: life will continue in its seasonal pattern, and humankind never again be wiped off the face of the earth by water, Jehovah vows, casting this in a gentle fall of poetry:

> While the earth remains,
> Seedtime and harvest,
> And cold and heat,
> And winter and summer,
> And day and night
> Shall not cease.

The covenant then attaches, as an "everlasting covenant" with broadening promises, to Abram and his seed after him (Gen. 15–17). Abraham, whose name changes when he is called into the covenant (as names in Acts shall change), is told he will be the "father of many nations" and will inherit, with his seed after him, "all the land of Canaan, for an everlasting possession"—a further picture of paradise. And now a sign of this covenant is instituted: "Every man child among you shall be circumcised." Not just Abraham's offspring, we learn (Gen. 17.13–14), but every child born in his house, whether his or a servant's, and every servant taken in battle or bought—all of his household (Gen. 17.23). This is of utmost relevance as we come to households within Acts.

So members of the covenant do not all share in the same familial or racial or ethnic identity, and not all remain within the covenant or remain faithful to it, though they all bear the sign and seal of it, circumcision. Being brought into the covenant, however, does not imply regeneration; God's Israel can violate their side of the covenant, refusing to accept Him or his terms. Those who will fall away may at first remain in the covenant, as Ham and Esau do (and so a distinction must be made between application of the sign of the covenant and actual salvation, which certain branches of the church seem to telescope) and as King Saul later will, while the covenant moves on, excluding Ishmael, to Isaac, and then past Esau to Jacob, or Israel, father of the twelve tribes or nations of Israel.

Each of these nations keep genealogies so that the duties and inheritances of each remain clear (such as the priesthood limited to the descendents of Levi), and all of them continue to circumcise everyone in their households, whether they travel into Egypt or Babylon, falling not only into bondage but into a further, widening, international community, prefiguring the outreach that will begin to propel the book of Acts outward in every direction. All of the tribes of Israel practiced circumcision through every generation, upon every son and every member of the household, up to and including Christ, of the tribe of Judah, who was circumcised on the eighth day, as prescribed (Gen. 17.12), so that when Peter says "the promise is to you and to your children," his auditors hear: *The Covenant. My household.*

Proselyte baptism began to be practiced at some point within the covenant, to symbolize the cleansing of an adult outsider before he was circumcised. Proselytes are listening to Peter (2.10) as they will listen to Paul (13.43), and there will soon be a proselyte, Nicolas, chosen as one of "the Seven" in an act within Acts. When Christ submitted to the baptism of his cousin, John, he initiated the sign and seal of the new covenant: baptism. But the familial or household nature of that covenant never changed, as you will see over and over in Acts.

This covenantal pattern, enforced by Acts, is the reason so many otherwise diverse branches of the church baptize infants. These baptized members may or may not remain faithful members of the covenant, just as adults who receive a "believer's baptism"—as some branches of the church call it, as if to authenticate it—may or may not remain faithful. Or as Geoffrey W. Bromiley, a former professor at Fuller Seminary, puts it, "The faith by which Christ's righteousness becomes ours is not primarily or independently a human decision. It is the gift and work of the Holy Spirit.

Certainly this gift and work of the Holy Spirit is a miracle in infants. But it is equally a miracle in adults."[8]

As for the mode of baptism, any mode is acceptable, I venture, since it is unlikely there was enough available water in the semiarid, mountainous region of Jerusalem, with aqueducts providing even the drinking supply, for three thousand to be immersed by, say, fifty in one day.[9] Or sufficient water for immersion in a jail and other locations throughout Acts. Immersionists often look for the verbal equivalent of "going down into" water, in order to validate immersions, but as I've pointed out, the true baptism by the Spirit has come down from above, through no church's or person's mode or cultic correctness.

I would permit myself or my children to be baptized by sprinkling, pouring, cupping and patting—and even immersion, perhaps, unless the claim was made that immersion alone was acceptable, since that insistence seems to suggest the mode itself is effectual. Baptism is a sign and seal of the regeneration we hope for in all members of the covenant, but is not the working of the Spirit.

To put at ease, if one may, however, those who remain reluctant to baptize infants, Professor Bromiley says, "Parents are not disobeying any clearcut command if they withhold baptism from their children. On the other hand they are assuming that the extension of the covenant promise to the nations has brought a discontinuity with God's mode of covenant dealings with families and peoples. No evident support can be found for this in the New Testament. Indeed, all the evidence that we have points the other way. Christians still live within a family structure and a church structure. The one covenant of grace still obtains."[10]

I step out of the converted granary where I work, telling myself it holds a certain store of harvest, and in the quiet dark of beginning sunrise I notice the morning star, wobbling its way up the sky like a distant sparkler, trailing streamers of light. Off to the east, past a line of toothed and rounded buttes, the sky is orange-crimson, and for a second I feel I'm viewing the hills of Jerusalem, where this account has taken me—that stark outline on the horizon where Acts unfolds. An owl hoos to the north, and a startled bird, perhaps awakened by it, shrills twice in a far-off field. Then in the morning silence that can saturate this landscape so wholly that generations of the earth seem to lie stilled, listening, I give thanks that the same Spirit who descended with power on the apostles has called me across these vast distances of time into faithfulness to Him on this particular point on the earth.

I give thanks for my family, and turn away into blackness—except for outbuildings bearing orange light at their edges—and decide to climb the tower past the room where my son lies asleep and watch the hills of Jerusalem resume the shape of the buttes of my neighbor. As they will, soon, with this fiery sun arriving in yet another promise kept by God.

3

MIRACULOUS EVENTS

ON THE WORST of those days when nothing seems to go well, either in the fields or on the fields of pages on my desk, I feel pinned and hemmed by the question local people often ask: "Still writing books?" I might as well ask them, I think in my uncharitable moments, if they're still living. The sense of pleasure a writer derives from getting a book or a story or a paragraph right is perhaps best communicated by the writing itself, and it's mostly that pleasure, as profound as any I know, that keeps me going. But under the momentum of every writer is the memory of a book or two, usually read at an early age, bearing an aura of the nearly miraculous.

An editor once mentioned, in a letter to me, that a well-known writer had just read a book and said it affected her so much she wasn't sure she would ever be the same. "And that, my friend," the editor wrote, "is what this business is about." A laureled prime minister of Holland, Abraham Kuyper (1837–1920), came across an English romance when he was at his lowest ebb; he had made an all-out effort to win an academic prize, and had won it, but then suffered a breakdown. Up until then, he had been a model student and a sometime Christian, drawn to the higher criticism (which essentially assumes that scholars have a better sense of what is taking place in a text of the Bible than the Bible) that was then emerging from German universities. Broken, barely able to read, Kuyper picked up *The Heir of Redclyffe*, a novel that doesn't appear to be included in the canon, by the British author Charlotte M. Yonge.[1]

The six-hundred-page novel follows the friendship and rivalry of two young men—one spiritually needy and retreating, the other assured and scintillating, a nobleman—whose lives come into conflict, or are brought into conflict by the nobleman. Kuyper sided with him. By the end of the book, however, the roles are reversed, and the dynamic young nobleman, older and wiser, understands he isn't worthy to enter the room where the man he maligned lies dying. Then in a moment of repentance brought about by a woman quoting to him from Psalm 51 ("A broken and a contrite heart, O God, you will not despise"), the nobleman enters, resolving to speak about his repentance, but finds "neither an accuser nor a judge, not even one consciously returning good for evil but a friend. . . ."

Kuyper was alone when he finished the book, and later wrote, "What I lived through in my soul in that moment I fully understood only later, yet from that hour, after that moment, I scorned what I formerly esteemed, and I sought what I once dared to despise." The drama of that novel, rawly romantic as it might have been, was used to draw Kuyper over the threshold into conversion. The right book at the right time has that potential. It can teach us to live, or make it possible to live, or render incarnate through its characters the lived life of a Christian, or simply draw us out of bed and set us on our feet again. This can seem nearly miraculous when it happens, and this is the moment we seek, writers first of all, when we enter the first sentence of a novel: a way to live.

The apostles and the thousands drawn into the church on the day of Pentecost hadn't fully found "the way." But they didn't hold themselves separate from Judaism, a miracle in itself if the original covenant had been dismantled. They considered themselves the inheritors of that covenant. An existing community based on pentateuchal standards continues into Acts, and some converts probably even kept on worshiping as they had, in the temple. In any case, at the opening of chapter 3, it is clear that Peter and John, now filled with the Spirit, know how to locate those who should view Jesus as the source of every story of the covenant, their Messiah: by going to the temple near the center of Jerusalem.

If there had been an end to the Old, they would stay away. But now, at the time of prayer before the evening sacrifice (Exod. 23.39), when they know a crowd will be gathered (most of whom probably have heard about the commotion caused by the Spirit), Peter and John head for the temple. They're confronted by a man who has been lame from birth and each day is carried and set down "at the gate of the temple which is called Beautiful." This may have been the Golden or Corinthian gate, which led to the Court of the Gentiles and was fashioned from Corinthian bronze overlaid with gold and silver artwork, according to the historian of the era, Josephus. When one considers the progress of Acts, the gate seems an enameled path of God's purposes—its luxuriant detail opening onto the Court of the Gentiles.

This beggar asks Peter and John for alms. "Look at us," Peter commands, suggesting the attentiveness we owe a messenger of the gospel. "Gold and silver have I none," Peter begins, in the phrase now a song, "but what I do have I give you: In the name of Jesus Christ of Nazareth, rise and walk."

If you had been lame from birth, it would be tough to take that seriously, I suspect, as it seems tough for the beggar. Peter has to take him by the hand and haul him to his feet. You will read commentators and hear preachers (a good number of the televised ones) say that because this man had faith he was healed. There is no such indication here, as there is none in most of those instances when Jesus worked his miracles. But it is in his name, Jesus of Nazareth, the Christ, as Peter confesses, that miracles occur.

Could Lazarus, who was dead, exercise the faith some will say is necessary for a miracle? The man whose son is perhaps epileptic (Mark 9, Luke 9) or perhaps possessed, but clearly afflicted by a spirit who wants him dead—"he has often thrown him both into the fire and into the water"—this man in tears cries to Jesus, "I believe! Help me in my unbelief." He's having difficulty believing, which is the authentic confession of most believers: I believe, now help me believe! The power of a person's faith can bring assurance, stability, dynamism in a scintillating life of faith, or peace, but it's not the teaching of scripture that the degree of your faith can cause a miracle.

Miracle anyway doesn't mean what many take it to. I recently heard a man say that the circumstances that led to his buying a new house were miraculous. We often use the term to designate an extraordinary event, a sudden suspension of illness, or an event so intricately woven it seems part of a divine plan. As it is: God's sovereignty and providence work through people and events in ways that are infinitely organized, since His person is infinite (spatial) and eternal (temporal), so that His will is ultimately done on earth as it is in heaven. Healing in a person can take place through His mercy and providence; resurrection from the dead cannot.

A miracle presupposes a suspension of the usual operations of nature, such as the parting of the Red Sea or, as C. S. Lewis puts it, "interference with Nature by supernatural power. Unless there exists, in addition to Nature, something else which we may call the supernatural, there can be no miracles."[2]

So disbelievers, too, should watch the way they use the word. In one of the works of providence, the author of Acts is a physician; the lame man's disability receives, in Greek, a medical description. "The words used to describe the seat of the lameness tend to show that the writer was acquainted with medical phraseology, and had investigated the nature of the disease under which the man suffered."[3] The man is lame with paralysis in the base of his feet, at the socket of the ankle. It is a congenital paralysis that the course of nature could not cure.

Jehovah alone has the power to work miracles, and miracles are a confirmation of His rule over His created world. Christ as God incarnate (John 1) worked miracles while he walked the earth, and now in the case of this lame beggar, so that it will be indisputable that Christ's apostles have had His power conferred on them by the Spirit, Peter pulls the man to his feet.

The beggar stands, he walks, unable to believe this either. He leaps! He must be laughing with the relief we feel even when a foot fallen asleep returns to normal. Then from the Court of the Gentiles the beggar enters the temple with Peter and John, "walking, leaping, and praising God." A stir is caused, of course, and another crowd gathers. To this crowd Peter delivers his second recorded sermon, similar in content to the first but with the telling observation that God raised up Jesus for the Jews: "You are the sons of the prophets, and of the covenant which God made with our fathers, saying to Abraham, '*And in your seed all the families of the earth shall be blessed.*' To you first, God, having raised up His Servant Jesus, sent Him to bless you. . . ."

The effect of Peter's message is twofold; the number of believers grows to five thousand, as we learn soon, but at this exact juncture the Sadducees and priests and temple guards show up, "greatly disturbed," and clap Peter and John in jail.

Now, in Luke's characteristic backstep, we will look at the local government in Jerusalem. It was first of all under the authority of Rome. Hebrew was no longer the everyday language; an Aramaic dialect was spoken. Since the time of the conquests of Alexander the Great (300 B.C.), Greek had infiltrated the area, and by the time of Luke it was the language of trade. The old covenant had been translated into Greek, also around 300 B.C., and was known as the Septuagint, meaning seventy (you will see the Septuagint denoted *LXX*), presumably after seventy scholars who worked on the first translation of the Pentateuch. When Torah was read in the temple, translations followed in Aramaic or Greek.

Judea was governed by a Roman procurator, but the Sinai peninsula, like Gaul, was divided into three parts. These were governed by tetrarchs. "The Christian movement came into existence soon after the fifteenth year of the Roman emperor Tiberius Caesar when, according to the evangelist Luke (3:1–2) 'the word of God came upon John the son the Zechariah in the wilderness.' In Luke's view the date was so significant that he also mentioned the rulers of the various parts of Palestine. Pontius Pilate was governor of Judaea; Herod (Antipas) tetrarch of Galilee, his brother Philip tetrarch of Ituraea and Trachonitis, and Lysanias tetrarch of Abilene."[4] These heads of state have shifted by the time of Luke's second account, as we shall see.

At least as important to the apostles and their growing number of followers was local Jewish rule. In the affairs of Jerusalem, the holy city, a certain autonomy of residual Mosaic rule was retained, dispensed by a council called the Sanhedrin. The Sanhedrin had its own police force, or temple guards, as we see when Peter and John are carried off, and the head of the Sanhedrin was the high priest. Other members were chief priests, "of the aristocratic families from which the actually officiating high priest could be chosen, 'scribes', that is, men learned in the Mosaic law and in the oral interpretations of it, and 'elders'. The Sanhedrin was not only an administrative assembly, but also a court."[5]

Within the Sanhedrin were two principal parties, the Pharisees and the Sadducees, who were often divided on issues, a failing that Paul will later use against them. I can do no better than the trusted cartographer Machen:

The Sadducees were the wealthy aristocracy. From their ranks the high priests were chosen. They occupied the positions of worldly authority. As men of wealth and high position they were content with the existing order of things. They were supporters of the Roman government, and hospitable to Greek culture. They accepted the Mosaic law, but favoured the laxer interpretation of it, rejecting the traditions of the scribes.

The Pharisees, on the other hand, were strict in their interpretation of the Mosaic law, and bitterly hostile to foreign influences. To them belonged most of the 'scribes', or professional interpreters of the law. In order to insure the keeping of the law the scribes had put about it a 'fence' of oral tradition, which in the guise of interpretation really imposed new legislation of the most oppressive kind. To keep the Sabbath or to observe the distinction between ceremonial cleanness and uncleanness according to the requirements of the scribes was an art which required the minutest attention to endless details.[6]

Those extralegal details were what Jesus upbraided the Pharisees for, not their zeal in upholding the law. The two parties sound strangely like the parties in modern American churches, though now they're called liberals and conservatives. Similar party structures exist in that para-church, the academy, in its handling of the "law" written across the shelves of its libraries and known, in sly imitation of scripture, as the canon. But now the dark is fading in Jerusalem where the apostles have spent the night in prison, and we must step back to the point where we left them.

A bustle rises in Jerusalem as the Sanhedrin convenes, the rulers and elders and scribes in their robes, along with Annas, the high priest, "and as many as were of the family of the high priest"— again the familial nature of the covenant. They bring Peter and John before them and get right to the point: "By what power or what name have you done this?"

"Then Peter, filled with the Holy Spirit, said to them, 'Rulers and elders of the people, if we are on trial today for a good deed to a helpless man . . . let it be known to all of you, and to all the people of Israel, that by the name of Jesus Christ the Nazarene, whom you crucified, whom God raised from the dead—by this name this man stands here before you in good health." When the members of the council "saw the boldness of Peter and John, *and perceived that they were uneducated and untrained men,* they marveled."

Luke's concluding statement—my emphasis—records the usual response of a hierarchical authority or the educated elite to matters of the spirit (for it's through the Spirit that Peter and John speak): a baffled denigration bordering on prejudice. What can these country rubes know? What will that muleheaded monk from Wittenberg dream up next? How can a fundamentalist who actually believes the word of God applies to politics presume to question a Ph.D.? But the Sanhedrin also marvel, not quite sure what to do with the healed man standing there, proof positive of Peter's words, on feet that support him. Finally they order the apostles not to speak or teach any more in Jesus' name.

"Whether it is right in the sight of God to give heed to you rather than to God, you be the judge," they say. "For we cannot stop speaking what we have seen and heard."

Still bold. As with many such councils, the Sanhedrin's decision rests on the prudence of covering its own. The local populace is noisily glorifying God for the miracle they're well aware of, since the former lame man is, after all, forty years old and a fixture at the temple, perhaps a personality of sorts, as long-standing (or sitting) beggars in New York come to be. The Sanhedrin threatens the apostles further and finally lets them go.

When Peter and John return to "their own" and report what has happened, we witness what seems a worship service; as the gathered believers receive the news, they raise "their voice to God *with one accord,*" and say or sing excerpts from the psalms. Then they speak, still in unison as it seems from the text, a short history of how Jesus was turned over to death, adding a prayer for "your servants, that with all boldness they may speak your Word, by stretching out your hand to heal, and that *signs and wonders* [further works] may be done through the name of your holy Servant Jesus." Then the place where they're assembled is shaken, as they're filled with the Spirit, as I've heard church buildings in Scotland and America shake when the psalms given by the Holy Spirit are sung under the Spirit's reaffirming power.

Remember that most of the apostles are country boys like Ivan, not city boys, like me, on Ivan's land. Many came from the area near the Sea of Galilee (or Lake Gennesseret) when they received the call from Jesus that believers now receive through his Spirit. In concluding the poem quoted earlier, Roland Flint says of the men called to apostleship, "I'd pass up all the fancy stunting / with Lazarus and the lepers / to see that one." So he views the call as *miraculous*. Because they were common men? Only one is designated as having a publicly recognized occupation or bureaucratic connection: Levi, or Matthew, the author of the gospel, who was a tax collector—more despised than our own IRS agents, since he was extracting local money for Rome.

The prevailing attitude toward the apostles in their time (present even in Flint's poem) is an attitude you might come across nowadays if a young upstart from Maine or, better, Iowa got in trouble with higher-ups in Washington, D.C. Yet Jesus called such as his apostles. Once Peter and John are free of the Sanhedrin, Luke almost immediately adds: "And the congregation of those who believed were of one heart and soul; and not one of them claimed that anything belonging to him was his own; but all things were common property to them. . . . For there was not a needy person among them, for all who were owners of land or houses would sell them and bring the proceeds and lay them at the apostles' feet, and they would be distributed to each, as any had need."

This certainly puts most contemporary branches of the church to shame, or it should. Can any church say in honesty, *There is not a needy person among us?* What is more common is a scene I have witnessed in more than one church after a worship service, as members gather around coffee or in the vestibule, and two or three of them, perhaps elders, are comparing the merits of real estate or combines before they close a deal, when a scruffy-looking person who may be homeless, or a rather tattered elderly couple that happens to be existing on social security, steps up tentatively, trying to get past, and those who are comparing prices glance at them with a look of perturbation or embarrassment, and then turn away and keep on talking.

It's merely another variation on the Sanhedrin syndrome, but shouldn't be ignored by people who take Christianity seriously. If any disciple at the time of Acts happened to be involved in our sort of vestibule apostasy and wondered whether the Holy Spirit was of the same Lord God Jehovah who had opened the earth under Korah, Dathan, and Abiram after their rebellion against Moses, and had consumed 14,700 at the time with a plague (Num. 16), or had sought out Achan, when he had concealed the spoils from Jericho under his tent, and had had Achan and his family burned by fire (Josh. 7), then they were about to witness the case of Ananias and Sapphira, husband and wife, tenders of a mutual lie.

This couple, along with many of the Jerusalem disciples, sold a piece of property for the common cause. I can find no teaching in Acts, or anywhere in scripture, that suggests they were compelled to; this seems a further working of the Spirit. The rich young ruler of Matthew 19 (cf. Mark 10, Luke 18) shouldn't be seen as a standard of warning to those who possess wealth; what he is refusing to forgo is his dearest idol, the one that bars his entry into the kingdom, not wealth per se. If there weren't a steady infusion of capital into the church, it would soon be unable to minister to anybody, and the ability to gain wealth and use it wisely is a gift like any other (1 Cor. 12; Luke 16.1–11, 19.11–27).

Ananias and Sapphira have sold a piece of property and Ananias comes and lays "a certain part" of it at the apostles' feet. Now watch the power that these feet assume:

"Ananias," Peter says, "why has Satan filled your heart to lie to the Holy Spirit and keep back part of the price of the land for yourself? While it remained, was it not your own? After it was sold, was it not in your control? Why have you conceived this thing in your heart? You have lied not to men but to God."

A further supernatural work of the Spirit permits Peter to see into Ananias' intentions, as Jesus could see into every person's and "then Ananias, hearing these words, fell down and breathed his last." Much as many Christians might wish to deny it, here is another miracle: immediate judgment. Miracles are not always happy events, as Pharaoh's army, if it were able to speak, would testify. The action in both Exodus and Acts takes place through God's Spirit and attests to His power over every realm He has established on earth.

Miracles do not bring about belief if one isn't prepared to believe. Jesus says that anybody who won't listen to Moses and the prophets won't be persuaded even if a person is raised from the dead (Luke 16.31), as Lazarus was. And Jesus. For the present, in this instance of miraculous judgment against Ananias, "great fear fell upon all those who heard these things. And the young men arose, and wrapped him up, carried him out, and buried him. Now it was about three hours later when his wife came in, not knowing what had happened."

Peter confronts her. "Tell me whether you sold the land for so much?"

"Yes," she says, "for so much."

"How is it that you have agreed together to test the Spirit of the Lord?" Peter asks. "Look, the feet of those who have buried your husband are at the door, and they will carry you out." And so they do. Whether this work of God through his Spirit to purge His Son's church is a further teaching of the Trinity, or whether it is "just," in the sense that people argue against the justice of Jehovah, it does suggest the continuity of His character and confirms that the apostles' power wasn't their own.

The proceeds held back were for the common coffer, the establishment of which certain branches of the church assume is a new element of "the apostles' doctrine." I don't think so. In Leviticus (chapter 25) and Deuteronomy (15, etc.) and Proverbs (14, 29, etc.) and elsewhere (Mat. 25.34ff.), there are commands to provide for one's own, and not to turn away the needy in their hour of need, and since the apostles' followers have grown from a hundred to over five thousand in days, perhaps a common coffer was the only way in which to meet, in all sincerity, the needs of those followers.

And there is a further area that few modern commentators address; a form of eschatology (a term not found in scripture that means a view held about the end of existence as we know it) that is termed postmillennial. The postmillennial view was held by the majority of the church until this century. Over the history of the church, when history was attended to with a scrupulousness that our age lacks, and there wasn't a craze of premillennial eschatology (Jesus is returning in 1988!), as now, commentators took to heart Jesus' prophecy that Jerusalem and its temple would be razed within the lifetime of those he was addressing (Mark 13.1–23, Luke 21.5–24), and they saw in Josephus' history of the terrible and entire destruction of Jerusalem in A.D. 70 the fulfillment of that prophecy.

The events prophesied by Jesus *did* happen in the lifetime of those who heard him; the events that are to come even he couldn't date, he said. They will come *without* a sign, like a thief in the night. Those commentators who are knowledgeable about history and hold, intellectually anyway, a postmillennial view, see the apostles' consolidation of resources as a way of liquidating what would have been lost when Jerusalem was razed (besides being a preparation for the coming famine, 11.28–29), and so a form of stewardship applicable to their situation, not the perdurable model for the church. How tithe without property or income? Or remain independent of the tyrannical Roman Empire without funds to meet the contingencies of a rapidly growing church?

It's largely the failure of the contemporary church to provide for its own that causes its members to turn to the federal (or state or local) government as benefactor. I'm sensitive to the concern for foreign missions and foreign missionaries, considering the "Great Commission" (Mat. 28.19–20, Mark 16.15) and the unfolding of Acts itself, but I think it's inadvisable for a church to send monies to a denominational or diocesan office for a foreign field if local members are in need. I don't believe missionaries should be sent out from a denominational level to begin with—a teaching so central to Acts it has to wait for its proper place.

To allow the needs of that homeless man or the raggedy elderly couple to remain unmet is to allow the Social Gospel or "democratic" or liberation theology to gain ascendance, as it were, not only in impoverished countries, but in your own community and church. Unless the local church is taking care of its own, a commission demanded by this portion of Acts, it's presumptuous to imagine its concerns lying farther afield. Could it be that the daily, sometimes disorderly demands of needy members are too trying to deal with and the call of foreign cultures too exotic to resist?

Three-fourths of the church has ignored the demanding middle portion of that great commission, which states, after the command to make disciples of all nations, to teach the disciples "to observe all things whatsoever I have commanded you." This would include all of the law and prophets and the entire new covenant. Quite a task.

So I would say that unless the local church is daily or weekly engaged in teaching the fullness found in Christ, in order to insure that its members are being cared for and fed ("Feed my sheep," Jesus says to Peter, in John 21.17) in this essential spiritual realm, then that church shouldn't presume upon its ability to carry its teachings into a foreign culture. I've watched almost every branch of the church become overextended, more thin in its teaching, and more divided by internal troubles over the last ten years than in decades before, and at least a part of these troubles begin with overspending on foreign missions.

Finally, however you interpret the action taken against Ananias and Sapphira, please note that the property isn't communal, as Peter defines it to Ananias himself: "After it was sold, did it not remain under your control?" This isn't the socialism that certain theologies propose, but a kind of corporate holding. Peter reveals the canny greed beneath Ananias' and Sapphira's untruthfulness; though the proceeds from the sale of the property had been put in a common coffer, it remained under their control, but they wanted a bit more on the side for themselves, just to be sure.

A contemporary commentator suggests that the action against Ananias and Sapphira—by the Holy Spirit, note, who is God— was a necessary form of discipline in the small but burgeoning (five thousand members were added in a matter of days) new church. This inaugurates another realm in which the modern church is remiss: discipline. In many denominations disciplinary actions such as censure and excommunication are practiced so seldom they're nonexistent, which is to the detriment of the church. Discipline is the only means of maintaining healthy membership (1 Cor. 5), yet delinquent pastors, even, escape censure nowadays, and the world outside properly cries, *Hypocrites*.

The discipline of Ananias and Sapphira comes from above, which is the real source of church discipline, as we see in Matthew 18.18, and has its effect. Within two verses we learn that the number of believers keeps growing daily—so fast, in fact, the high priest and the Sadducees, "filled with jealousy," clap the apostles in jail. Again. An angel of the Lord releases them, in an act instructive of Acts' source, and tells them to teach in the temple—so it can be safely said that this was the reason Peter and John went there to begin with. When the Sanhedrin sends for the apostles and discovers they're not in prison but in the temple, they call the apostles in front of them once more to explain this. The boldness of the apostles hasn't dimmed and their response is even more pointed: "We must obey God rather than men."

How does this council of spiritual rulers deal with those who oppose it? They want to kill the apostles. Gamaliel, a Pharisee (the Pharisees believed in the resurrection from the dead), intervenes, however, in the first tie in Acts to Saul—a nearly hidden thread in this book so closely woven it yields increasing detail with each reading. Gamaliel sends the apostles out of earshot and cites the instances of men who have risen up, claiming to be somebody, yet have come to nothing. His pragmatic advice is the kind you hear daily from every businessperson attempting to cover his or her own. And finally he concludes, "And so in the present case, I say to you, stay away from these men and let them alone, for if this plan or action should be of men, it will be overthrown; but if it is of God, you will not be able to overthrow them; or else you may even be found fighting against God."

The apostles are flogged, whipped with leather thongs which often had pieces of metal attached to their tips that embedded themselves in the skin and muscle of the back on impact and then were jerked to tear things up; and are told never to teach again in Jesus' name. The chapter ends, "And every day, in the temple and from house to house, they kept right on teaching and preaching Jesus as the Christ."

The apostles have not yet moved beyond Jerusalem, and chapter 6 relates the choosing of "the Seven," an act that the church has historically interpreted as the institution of the office of deacon. I'm

not sure I agree. The term *deacon* is never used to identify any of
the seven, while *evangelist* is (21.8). Whatever the office, it rises
out of a squabble; Hellenistic Jews complain that their widows
("the stranger, the fatherless, and the widow among you shall be
fed"—Deut. 14.29) are being neglected by native Judeans in the
daily meals. So the apostles call together their disciples.

"It is not desirable for us to neglect the word of God in order to
serve tables," they say. "But select from among you, brothers,
seven men of good reputation, full of the Holy Spirit and wisdom,
whom we may put in charge of this task."

Psychology would probably suggest that since the problem
originated with women, it would be wise to appoint women for
this office, but the "statement found approval with the whole congregation." The Seven are brought forward, and the apostles pray,
and then lay hands on them, as the Levitical priesthood laid hands
on sacrificial animals. The laying on of hands in Acts first is the
means by which the Holy Spirit is conferred, and later will signify ordination to an office in the church—a sacrificial giving over
to God. Ask any pastor.

Stephen, "full of faith and the Holy Spirit," is one of the seven,
and straightaway we learn he isn't merely going to wait tables. He
performs "great wonders and miracles among the people." Again,
miracles; the power of apostolic signs, given through the Spirit,
has been conferred by apostolic hands, directly. If the seven are indeed deacons, then acts of apostolic dimension proceed from the
deacon Stephen. His works of wonder gather such momentum
that false witnesses from the Freedmens' synagogue (a congregation of slaves, circumcised into the covenant, and since freed) are
suborned into saying he has been speaking blasphemies against
Moses and God. So Stephen is called before the Sanhedrin.

In the mixture of misunderstanding and untruth stated by the
witnesses, this appears: "We have heard him say that this Nazarene,
Jesus, will destroy this place." Jerusalem, they mean, which is yet

another reference to the prophecies of Christ that were fulfilled in A.D. 70.

The high priest asks if the accusation is true, and Stephen gives the council a recapitulation of Jewish history from the canon, beginning with Abraham, moving to Moses—some of whose acts he explicates in a new light, adding luster and dimension to Moses' calling as Israel's prophet; and then in an apostrophe past David and Solomon, Stephen concludes in the language of Moses: "You stiffnecked and uncircumcised in hearts and ears, you are always resisting the Holy Spirit, just as your fathers did. Which of the prophets did your fathers not persecute? And they killed those who previously announced the coming of the Righteous One, whose betrayers and murderers you have become."

What Stephen has done in his lengthy sermon (as it might be seen) is to retell the story of the covenant, the redemptive history of God's Israel. And what he is stating before this highest council of the still-existing church of that covenant is that their history can't be disconnected from the descent of the Spirit, but should be brought to bear in application to the Spirit's arrival, as Peter has done on Pentecost. Stephen's model sermon and "testimony" is the perfect study for modern church members and pastors to heed.

Then Stephen looks up and says, "Behold, I see the heavens opened up and the Son of Man standing at the right hand of God." The supernatural work of Christ in the book of Acts is revealed directly to Stephen, Christ not reclining in rest, but on his feet, poised for action. How does the Sanhedrin react? They drive Stephen out of the city and start stoning him, the punishment prescribed by Moses for blasphemy—perhaps at a place constructed for such an end, as pictured in an etching by Doré. As the stones strike home, Stephen calls out, in signification of the new covenant the Spirit has initiated, in a variant of Christ's cry from the cross, "Lord Jesus, receive my spirit!"

Then, sinking to his knees under the punishing stones, another variant: "Lord, do not hold this sin against them!"

Luke concludes, "And having said this"—and it can hardly be said less vindictively—"he fell asleep."

The first martyr since the giving of the Holy Spirit, the first martyr of the Christian Church. Only after this action is past and beginning to subside, one hopes, does it register that the robes of the witnesses, who by old covenant law were compelled to cast the first stones, have been laid at a young man's feet.

This man is Saul.

Before turning to Saul, however, I sense the exigencies of the community in Acts spread against a background as black as that last early-morning sky, before the idea of seeing my neighbor's buttes reassume their contours drove me past the bunk where my son lay asleep and on into the tower he and I had built, where I climbed a shaky stepladder into a suffusion of orange light, and then climbed another ladder to the ceiling at the tower's peak to stare down and see the sun's first edge emerge in a blinding scorch.

4

COMMUNION AND

COMMUNITY

What I do wish to affirm is that the whole of modern literature
is corrupted by what I call Secularism, that it is simply unaware of,
simply cannot understand the meaning of, the primacy of the supernatural over the natural life: . . . I anticipate a rejoinder from the
liberal-minded, from all those who are convinced that if everybody
says what he thinks, and does what he likes, things will somehow,
by some automatic compensation and adjustment, come right in the
end. "Let everything be tried," they say, "and if it is a mistake then,
we shall learn by experience." This argument might have some value,
if we were always the same generation upon earth; or if, as we know
to be not the case, people ever learned much from the experience of
their elders. These liberals are convinced that only by what is called
unrestrained individualism will truth ever emerge. Ideas, views of life,
they think, issue distinct from independent heads, and in consequence
of their knocking violently against each other, the fittest survive, and
truth rises triumphant. Anyone who dissents from this view must be
either a medievalist, wishful only to set back the clock, or else a fascist,
and probably both.[1]

Though the above might sound like a conservative senator addressing the National Endowment for the Arts, they are the words
of T. S. Eliot, with no embellishments, from 1935. We are not,
as he says, always the same generation on earth, and any writer

writing about our generation is aware that truth does not rise directly from his or her own head, or should be. Certainly the Christian writer must acknowledge this. For the Christian, whether writer or rancher, the entire truth as found in both covenants is embodied in Christ.

To be in *communion* is to declare your belief in Christ and his teachings and to be accepted as a member of His body, in a church with scriptural standards. You are then allowed to participate in the sacrament of communion, or the Lord's Supper. In the context of Acts, it is best seen this way:

> The new Christian community did not at first regard itself as distinct from Judaism. The disciples continued in diligent observance of the temple worship. Though in reality Christianity was from the beginning a new dispensation, it appeared to the careless observer to be nothing more than a Jewish sect. Even the disciples themselves were unaware of any break with their ancestral religion.
>
> From the beginning, however, the disciples of Jesus were conscious of the bond that united them with one another and separated them from all others. Their unity found expression in various ways.
>
> In the first place, the authority of the apostles, which was derived from Jesus himself, led to a community in belief.
>
> In the second place, 'the breaking of bread' symbolized the benefits received from the crucified Lord. Every meal that the disciples ate together was a reminder of the fellowship of Jesus with his disciples. One form of meal was particularly sacred.[2]

This meal is the Lord's Supper. For a member of this body or communion, the definition of *community* is rendered rather complex by one of the apostles recently jailed, John, in his first epistle to the church,

> That which was from the beginning, which we have heard, which we have seen with our eyes, which we have looked upon, and our hands have handled, concerning the Word of Life (v. 1) . . . we declare to you, that you also may have fellowship with us; and truly our fellowship is with the Father and with His Son Jesus Christ . . . (v. 3b). If we

say that we have fellowship with Him, and walk in darkness, we lie and do not practice the truth. But if we walk in the light as He is in the light, we *have fellowship with one another . . .* (vs. 6–7a).

and by 1 Corinthians 10, in the prelude defining the proper practice of communion,

> Therefore, my beloved, flee from idolatry (v. 14) . . . the things which the Gentiles sacrifice they sacrifice to demons and not to God, and I do not want you to have fellowship with demons. You cannot drink the cup of the Lord and the cup of demons; you cannot partake of the Lord's table and the table of demons (v. 20–21).

and finally by 2 Corinthians 6.14–16:

> Do not be unequally yoked with unbelievers. For what fellowship has righteousness with lawlessness? And what communion has light with darkness? And what accord has Christ with Belial? Or what part has a believer with an unbeliever? And what agreement has the temple of God with idols? For you are the temple of the living God.

This temple of the living God should be a reality to Christian writers. They have been given particular gifts to think in metaphor and work with words within that temple. They're daily walking the tightwire of each sentence, with no safety net, toward the perfection found in Christ. Thoughts are formed with words, so as a person arranges words to expose with increasing clarity his or her thoughts, that person becomes a writer. Narrative, however else we think of it, is primarily an extended thought. The writer is inviting a reader, an island community, to think these same thoughts along the same lines. Writing, then, is a form of teaching (not preaching), and a narrative or any form of writing that places us inside a metaphor, as the parables do, is one of the most potent forms of teaching available.

This is the most sobering aspect of the business for me, when I consider the communion I belong to, the community I hope to reach, and those I might affect, whether I want to or not. If Eliot in his opening statement seems abrupt, it might be because he believed the temple of God was being displaced by idols. I do. What always brings me up short about the present displacement is that the largest share of it has taken place in my lifetime, in the past twenty-five years. I have had to reconsider everything I've written, and thus taught, and have to confess to having served, more than once, Belial. When I examine myself to figure out why, I usually end up at a single central point: my education.

I haven't had as much formal education, I'm sure, as many readers, but I received enough of it so that after four years of college I'm still, at the age of fifty, trying to disentangle its ropes and vines from the temple where God should dwell. I learned at least as much from reading (in relative safety, able to pause and sort matters) and more from a dear mentor, an editor. Then I was called to faith, then into the Christian community, and then into a communion. This was fifteen years ago, and soon I began to understand that my perspective on writing, and on everything else, for that matter, was skewed. My allegiance to the source of authority over the highly personal materials of my writing and the problems it posed was, I saw, misplaced. That allegiance could no longer be to professor X or Y, one of whom was excellent, or to these books or writers, nor to that dear editor, much as I loved him, but must be to Christ—and to others to the extent to which their teachings were faithful to His truth.

In college I was taught to think critically, but not to discern spirits. There's a difference. I attended the University of Illinois, which then had a student body of 37,000. It's not a Christian college, but my experience of Christian colleges is that they're teaching approximately what I was taught in the sixties. By study, by tutoring, by the sharpening of my dullness upon particular members within my communion, I began to see that Christ embodied not only the way of life, but Truth. The ultimate reality is him, and all of our realities are true only in the degree to which they conform to his reality, since the substance of reality is him (Col. 1.16–20). And by reality I mean every element of existence that his Truth confirms.

For the epigraph to one of my novels, I used a sentence from Erik Erikson, " 'Reality,' of course, is man's most powerful illusion; but while he attends to this world, it must out-balance the total enigma of being in it at all."[3] I still believe this statement is true, as far as it goes. Reality must outbalance the total enigma of being and living in the world or we're helpless against the world's machinations. For the world, though, if the world would attend to it, and for Christians, if they would, the hard-edged definition of reality is found in the person of Christ. It's only when we study him and the world of his creation beyond our noses that reality in its complexity begins to appear. It's the reality of this world, after all, that everyone alive has to deal with, discern, and ultimately bear responsibility for.

The more I studied both covenants and came to understand Christ, the more reality and the relationships within it (including those spaces between, which scripture doesn't always speak to explicitly) were revealed. I understood that Christ was God, a spirit infinite and eternal, and that as much as I was able to, in my finite and sinful self, I should be serving him—a more dependable master than, say, *The New York Review of Books*.

I wrote to friends, trying to communicate the tenor and joy of this service. Few, as you can imagine, wrote back. I spoke with some when I had the chance and saw them cringe. The offense of the cross, I thought (though hurt myself, of course), and kept on writing. I'm referring now to the broader writer's community, which I'll return to; in the Christian community in general, and within my own communion, some of the responses were: Write? But what do you do for a living? I see. Does your wife support you?

Still writing books?

Or: This won't be like those others, will it?

Some of this stung, as it should, but I kept on writing, and the pleasure of working as a servant was so inexpressible that at times I had to sit back from my desk in tears. If some of my work took longer then, that's one of the reasons—besides the rearranging of those allegiances. But joyful weeping, as with anything, doesn't last; the next day it turns to sorrow.

Which happened, and it wasn't just the reviews. The more I attempted to do what scripture asked—understanding that even if I was able to do everything, I was to consider myself an unworthy servant, since I was merely doing what it was my duty to do—the more it seemed other Christian writers were heading in the opposite direction, if not bailing out.

See for example the title story in John Updike's *Pigeon Feathers* and his "Seven Stanzas from Easter," both from the same period, and then his novels *Roger's Version* and *S.* My perception of writers bailing out was partly illusion, perhaps, since I was now seeing Christianity from the inside, from the viewpoint of obedience rather than supercilious scorn, but it was also partly true. It has been helpful, recently, to have come across a paragraph from a book I read then, *That Hideous Strength*, the final volume of C. S. Lewis's space trilogy:

> If you dip into any college, or school, or parish, or family—anything you like—at a given point in its history, you always find that there was a time before that point when there was more elbow room and contrasts weren't quite so sharp; and that there's going to be a time after that point when there is even less room for indecision and choices are even more momentous. Good is always getting better and bad is always getting worse: the possibilities of even apparent neutrality are always diminishing. The whole thing is sorting itself out all the time, coming to a point, getting sharper and harder.[4]

It's of interest to me now (though I wouldn't have known it at the time) to see how close this follows the thought of a philosopher and Christian apologist who was a contemporary to Lewis, Cornelius Van Til. Van Til left Princeton in the thirties to help found Westminster Seminary in Philadelphia, and the essence of his teaching is that your presuppositions not only color your thought but dictate its conclusions. The truth that any Christian must begin with, to truncate Van Til terribly, is that a trinitarian God created the universe. If you work toward this up steps of natural law or empiricism, or ride to it on the pure elevator of Platonism, or the whirligig of Kant, then you have at best a synthesis that will take you somewhere other than where Christ would prefer you come to rest. You have not thought God's thoughts after Him, beginning at the beginning, down past every revelation through Revelation. There is no neutrality, or even apparent neutrality, for the Christian or anybody else, Van Til says. Either you're for me or against me, Jesus says. Whatever is not of faith is sin, St. Paul says.

Van Til explains, to condense him again, that no fact exists without an interpretation of it. If we say a tree needs water, for instance, that is meaningless unless we know what a tree is, how it exists in nature, and so on; and our interpretations of its being and existence depend upon the presuppositions we begin with, and will lead the Christian, one hopes, to a conclusion different from the chaos-theory Tao physicist. A brute fact is a mute fact, Van Til says. To put it another way, extending a paraphrase of Van Til: finite human beings reason and move in circles, either vicious circles, which end in violence and death, or in covenantal circles, bound within the communion of the body of Christ.

The world and the church are at the edge of a new decade, and as a Christian and a writer, I believe this is one of the best times to be alive. I'm not sure good is getting better and bad worse, but there is less room for indecision, and many Christians seem to sense that their choices, even daily, are becoming more momentous. They will become even more so soon, as Lewis says. Things

are indeed growing sharper and harder, because all of the modern
world, not just literature, is corrupted by secularism, is simply unaware of, simply cannot understand the meaning of, the primacy
of, the supernatural.

Each of us has a list of the stunning events of the last few years: the
war in the Gulf, the crumbling of the Soviet bloc, the attack on
students demonstrating for democracy in Tiananmen Square, the
resounding voice of "the masses" of Russia and Central America
actually heard in elections, the signing of a new document by the
Oxford Committee on Christian Economics, the dismantling by
the state of Kentucky of its public school system—you may add
your favorites.

    These events took people in the Christian community by sur-
prise, because in their reluctance to conform to the way of Christ,
they didn't really believe that formulations and theories and prin-
cipalities and powers outside Him were empty, void, vanity of
vanities. "All those who hate me," the Spirit says in Proverbs 8.36,
"love death." Christians, too, had come to believe that these prin-
cipalities were pretty much what the media presented them as; not
so bad, and probably about as *valid* as Christianity.

    Fifty years ago, in elaborating on those ideas rising from indi-
vidual heads knocking against each other, Eliot wrote,

> It is not only that the reading individual today (or at any day) is not
> enough an individual to be able to absorb all the "views of life" of all
> the authors pressed upon us by the publishers' advertisements and the
> reviewers, and to be able to arrive at wisdom by considering one against
> another. It is that the contemporary authors are not individuals enough
> either. It is not that the world of separate individuals of the liberal dem-
> ocrat is undesirable; it is simply that this world does not exist. For the
> reader of contemporary literature is not, like the reader of the estab-
> lished great literature of all time, exposing himself to the influence of
> divers and contradictory personalities; he is exposing himself to a mass

movement of writers who, each of them, think that they have something individually to offer, but are really all working together in the same direction.[5]

Eliot defines a community here. It's difficult for writers who confess to be Christians to separate themselves from the direction of that community, when most of them are supported by universities. The university system, a monolith untouched by scripture, has taken Christian writers captive. It not only numbs them to the dullness of an Associated Writers Project (AWP), but enters the church through them. The university is the center of that other community: the AWP network and reading circuits, state and federal grants, prizes and awards, and the literary politics necessary to administer them—besides the indentured servitude of six to eight years in an assistant professorship until you knuckle under and are ruled on as acceptable for tenure by the reigning hierarchy, often an old-boy network.

Sixteen years ago, at America's most revered university, Harvard, Aleksandr Solzhenitsyn told America to wake up and return to its moral roots, to recognize that the basis of Soviet communism was emptiness, lies, coercion, and a totalitarian need to bring everyone under its dominion. For this he was labeled reactionary, banished from intellectual consideration in any university—a view enforced by the oligarchy of the media—and looked on with shame by many Christians who had hoped he would speak reasonably of détente, as they were. At about the same time Solzhenitsyn said that the single most powerful source of hope for Russia was its Christian underground. Then he stepped into yet another exile, American style, and kept on working.

Communism and forced communal living represent another community. The Soviet politburo obviously didn't listen to Solzhenitsyn any more than American writers did, and when the Soviets instituted a glasnost they expected to be able to control, they unleashed an unstoppable tide, that Christian underground.

What should now be remarked upon by those in universities who only two years ago were promoting Marxism (and will be again next year) is the lack of life lost in this truly democratic revolution from the ground up. Few generations have witnessed a more graphic illustration of the verse in Psalm 2: "You shall break the nations with a rod of iron." Even Gorbachev and Yeltsin stood helpless as His will worked through the lives of millions. All this happened not like the Crusades that some in the university still harp on and not like the Glorious Revolution of 1917, when millions more than were killed in all the Crusades were slaughtered (not to mention the Gulag that continued into the nineties), but by the working of the spirit of the Prince of Peace.

Solzhenitsyn knew that Christian Marxism is an oxymoron. Dialectical materialism and Jesus Christ don't mix, as any Marxist will tell you—except the ones who use the symbols or iconography of Christianity to manipulate the people they want to control. The cure for the inequities that Marxism said it would cure is Christ, but few Christians were confessing this. Universities had taught the church that this wasn't so, and writers and intellectuals in the church had absorbed that teaching and passed it along to their community and local communions, paralyzing the church. Its paralysis began with the separation of social works from the complex teachings (a writer knows what it's like to have a sentence lifted from a closely written page for inclusion in a review) present in the rest of the gospel. It began with an incorrect supposition to effect the cure.

My wife traveled to Nicaragua just before the elections that removed Ortega and the Sandinistas from power. She was part of a Christian group ministering to the people not in symbols, but with the gospel and a catechism in Spanish and eyeglasses and sewing machines and plans for self-supporting businesses, and a Christian curriculum for Nicaraguan schools. She was there only a week, moving among the lower classes, although her main contact was with a member of the Sandinista Department of Education, and after her short stay she said that if a fair election were held the Sandinistas couldn't win—something I never heard from the media. "Look what we've come to in only ten years," Nicaraguans said to her. Or, "The operating force now is fear." A current of change, as she sensed, was spreading from a Christian underground, a community united in Christ.

In Paul's account of reprobate communion taking in First Corinthians he cites violations of *community*. When people gathered to worship on the evening of the first day of the week, since Sunday was then a workday, they brought their evening meals, and some of them, instead of sharing their food, kept it from those who had less (reminiscent of Acts 6), causing divisions among them. So after Paul gives the words of institution for the Lord's Supper, he goes on to say:

> Therefore whoever eats this bread or drinks this cup of the Lord in an unworthy manner will be guilty of the body and blood of the Lord. But let a man examine himself and so let him eat of that bread and drink of that cup. For he who eats and drinks in an unworthy manner eats and drinks judgment to himself, not discerning the Lord's body.

He says that this is the reason many are weak and sick and asleep, or dead, among them. "Therefore, my brethren, when you come together to eat, wait for one another. But if anyone is hungry, let him eat at home, lest you come together for judgment." Not "discerning the Lord's body" can refer to theological heresy, or failure to hold to the doctrines of Jesus' life, work, atoning death, and resurrection, but the failure to hold to these doctrines can be everyday practices as well.[6] Everyday specifics are a writer's *Gloria*.

In this case Paul is referring to a specific body or community that is not acting like a family of believers. They don't understand (discern) that the body of Christ includes people of every level of society. So they reject some and refuse to share their food with them. Wherever the church fails to be a community, then, and when any member of it is negligent of his familial responsibilities to other members—the central biblical metaphor is the family—this passage states that it is there that the body of Christ is not discerned, and communion is taken in judgment.

Theologically and intellectually, we might claim to know Christ as few do, but if we are incapable of recognizing (discerning) the needs of those who make up his body, we stand in danger of hearing, "Depart from me, you cursed, into everlasting fire prepared for the devil and his angels, for I was hungry and you gave me no food; I was thirsty and you gave me no drink; I was a stranger and you did not take me in, naked and you did not clothe me, sick and in prison and you did not visit me." And if we wonder how this can be, as his disciples did, he answers, "Inasmuch as you did not do it to the least of these, you did not do it to me."[7]

The problem, as always, begins at home. It begins with me, within my local communion, first, and broadens into my community. The problem with the church is that it has not taken care of its own, nor the downcast, disfranchised in its unbelieving community, before it has launched a new missionary campaign or set a global agenda. For the past decades the church has been running on theory as much as on scripture, and those theories, once lived out, have proved to be as empty as Marxism. They arrive, as it were, from the hallowed ivies of the East and reach into other colleges and universities, then into Christian colleges and the church.

What is amazing, considering the precipitousness of the spiritual decline in the last twenty years, is that matters aren't much worse. In his mercy God has preserved America due to a faithful remnant at its center. A few years ago I heard a Marxist deconstructionist deliver a paper, a broadside, really, but a well-documented one, against the humanist monolith of the American University System. There are Christian administrators who have told me that no such monolith exists, though from my university experience I know there are organizations of humanists in every state and a monthly publication, *The Humanist.* Regardless of whether it's a monolith or not, or a Humanist Monolith, the Christian should be able to confess one thing for certain, even as a university shelters him or her: *its basis isn't Christian.*

That is the heart of the drama of *That Hideous Strength,* a truth Lewis taught our community in 1946.

In response to the relativism of early-American Unitarian social egalitarianism, Randall Stewart, in his book *American Literature and Christian Doctrine,* wrote:

> Now there *is* such a thing as Christian equality. It is an equality of humility: all have sinned, have erred, have strayed from Thy ways like lost sheep. And this kind of equality has the advantage of safeguarding certain radical, necessary distinctions: between good and evil, heaven and hell, salvation and damnation. For Christian doctrine recognizes, paradoxically, a hierarchical principle, a scale of values: there are thrones and dominions, principalities and powers. There is inclusion and exclusion: "Not every one that saith unto me, Lord, Lord, shall enter into the kingdom of heaven." Excellence cannot exist in a distinctionless world.[8]

Christian writers and critics must be ready to say that something doesn't measure up, that it falls short of the mark, that it's no good, that it's terrible or fundamentally *bad.* They must be willing to say that it's evil. The teaching of the next decade is destined to rise from committed writers and teachers, those who form thoughts for others to think after them, and these people will be members of faithful local communions. There is a growing Christian underground in America, too.

Some readers by now are looking for my theory of the way to produce Christian art or write Christian fiction, since theories are what people believe govern the world. They don't, and I have none. I am working out my aesthetics (and perhaps salvation) with each book—with this one—and each book poses unique problems. But I can assure you that you will not begin to form your own aesthetics or way of writing unless you first belong to a church that teaches you fellowship and unity within Christ, and then begin to see writing as your daily humble job within that community.

No writer is able to write a book that bears any authority, even speculative fiction set in Antiterra, unless the writer understands the working of the relationships within a community. Our presence as writers in a communion is more quintessential; as members of a body we understand that our most inconspicuous members are the most essential. The supposition behind each of their thoughts is often more correct than that of a professor from the best university. And if such people aren't the mouths or eyes or ears of the body of the church, perhaps they are the brain stem or adrenal cortex or the liver (some are even the bilious gall), but every part of this body, from its organs and sinews to its bones and outer tissues, is working together for one purpose: to instruct and edify (or build up at each connection) every other part in love.

I say this knowing that I'm supported by the members of a communion necessary to my existence. I know there are readers of my fiction, even Christian readers, who believe that I am somehow able to write what I write in spite of my beliefs, so I feel I must say that if it weren't for those beliefs, which are the unspoken undercurrent in even my earliest work, I would have written next to nothing by now or, worse, written volumes without a spark of relevance. If it weren't for those beliefs, I wouldn't be here; I wouldn't have a reason to live. Recognition and rewards only amplify the emptiness of one already emptied of the spirit of Christ.

"O Lord, deliver me from the man of excellent intention and impure heart," T. S. Eliot wrote in part 5 of "Choruses from 'The Rock' "—"for the heart is deceitful above all things, and desperately wicked."

> Preserve me from the enemy who has
>   something to gain: and from the friend
>   who has something to lose.
> Remembering the words of Nehemiah the
>   Prophet: "The trowel in hand, and the
>   gun rather loose in the holster."
> Those who sit in a house of which the use
>   is forgotten: are like snakes that lie on
>   moldering stairs, content in the sunlight.
> And the others run about like dogs, full of
>   enterprise, sniffing and barking: they
>   say, "This house is a nest of serpents, let
>   us destroy it,
> And have done with these abominations,
>   the turpitudes of the Christians." And
>   these are not justified, nor the others.
> And they write innumerable books; being
>   too vain and distracted for silence: seek-
>   ing every one after his own elevation,
>   and dodging his emptiness.
> If humility and purity be not in the heart,
>   they are not in the home: and if they are
>   not in the home, they are not in the
>   City.[9]

The time has come for Christian artists in their communities to begin building that City on a hill again, and I hope that one young student, or even a middle-aged one, will understand what I'm saying and perhaps at this moment sense the stirrings of a first novel. If that student takes scripture seriously, he should know that the more he immerses himself in a particular communion and comes to understand the ways in which each person within it is essential, the more distinctive and original his writing will be. And I hope that some young woman has begun to visualize her lifework, a shining series of interlocking narratives that will provide the material to repair some of the buildings of the centuries-old tradition of Christian writing. These were left unfinished when the writers of my generation turned aside to imitate our culture rather than turning first to the community that always should be available in Christ.

I have sinned, yes, I confess with no joy, but a broken and a contrite heart, I'm assured, God will not despise.

II

JUDEA AND SAMARIA

and the Calling of Saul

5

THE WORD

IN THE WORLD

SAUL, WHO WILL TAKE the name of Paul in Acts, remains the most controversial character in scripture. Of all sinners, he says, he is the chief, and people who resonate too fondly with that or wonder whether they aren't about as bad are often less contrite than ready to impress on others a sinfulness that might elevate them to his status. I'm familiar with the temptation. I have said that books can persuade you to live, or a book's characters embody an applied life, and in this sense they are instruments. The separate writers of scripture, like Paul, are also instruments. Every instrumentality under heaven is the work of one author, and it isn't Shakespeare.

When I began to read scripture as other than an object of interest, it was Paul who freed me into the poetic intricacies of thought that I, as a writer, seemed to believe I deserved. I'm not a Paulist nor a Pauline apologist. Paul is not the bearer of his own words, but of the good news given by the Spirit. Three-quarters of the epistles to the church are his. If you read these straight through you will come away shaken, or perhaps shrugging, though you can't help but be impressed by his combination of logic and searing directness. And because of the tarnish on his early life, he is a daily encouragement to those of us who finally admit we're less than perfect.

Acts and the book of Galatians are the places to go to find the Saul whom Paul condemns. In both books he says that he was so zealous for the law he persecuted the church in its infancy until he almost smothered it in the cradle. My redaction. He had a say in people's deaths and tortured some to get them to blaspheme (26.10–11). He was perhaps a passive but willing participant in the stoning of Stephen.

His epistles, which contain his "testimony," reinforce our fears about our worst tendencies. We are sinners who have gone astray and opposed the gospel—as passive or active enemies—by the flapping of our mouths or the rashness of our intellectual reflex to judge. And so, in the paradox that Paul makes more and more clear through each epistle, we are precisely the ones who ought to be able to speak with the most authority about the transformation wrought in our lives (and so our acts in the world) through Christ.

Equipped with his knowledge of the Law and the Prophets, Paul is the best exegetical commentator on scripture the Church has had. It is he who reaffirms that scripture comes by inspiration of the Holy Spirit (2 Tim. 3.17–18) and that it is by the Spirit, who is God, that it is applied to us. It is of God and is God. Jesus was that Word made flesh, and *is;* he is the embodiment of the words of the entire canon, and the consummation and fulfillment of them. He was the word walking the earth and is still, as in the vision revealed to Stephen (also see Hebrews 10.12), actively interceding for his people and applying to them, through his Spirit, the words of scripture.

In another sense, as Paul tells it, that Word is the fullness that fills all in all (Eph. 1.23)—it has entered and is reconciling the cosmos, the created universe (Col. 1.17–20), and the church should be the first to confess its cosmological fullness. Our local communions should represent the church as a body in all its diversity, and the only way to achieve that is by faithful worship and fellowship with its members, while giving your own body over to the acts of life as a living sacrifice (Rom. 12.1).

This is each separate member's *reasonable* service.

To attain a service of such selflessness you must come to know the law and the prophets, so that every new covenant benefit bows fully to its Author. The arena of the word where details interlock will then touch on infinity, in the way that the word in its application to the world is, in essence, infinite. A dutiful student of Acts, for instance, will notice Luke's use of feet. Yes, feet, as in the feet connected to the anklebones of the beggar who was healed.

This focus of Luke renders incarnate the prophecy of Isaiah in chapter 52, "How lovely on the mountains are the feet of him who brings good news," a theme recapitulated by Saul himself, as Paul (Rom. 10.15), in that echo foreseen at the Corinthian gate: "How beautiful the feet of those who preach the gospel of peace!" In Acts, Luke's use of feet points to both the beauty and the power of peace inherent in those moved by the Spirit to convey that gospel by the most common and humble means of transportation, footpower, into the fields that widen from Jerusalem to encompass the world.

Whether Luke purposely intended the connection to Isaiah or is employing a literary device—well, such speculation pales beside the content of his inspired context and its shine. It is clear that the literary gifts of Luke the physician (writing is closer to science than any of the arts) are being employed to the utmost as the Spirit speaks what the Spirit wishes through Luke. Each prophet and poet and apostle had a designated portion of the canon to bring to the world; none was trying to outdo or overstep another. Those feet always travel in the way of Christ. No human mind could channel or arrange the structure and patterns that at certain moments in Acts step off through whole tracts of the old and new covenants while applying to a situation you noticed only this morning.

For me, a writer aware of how much more complex each book becomes with each sentence added, it was the clarity of these patterns and structure in scripture and their ability to intermesh with one another through as many levels as I could imagine that convinced me that the Bible couldn't be the creation of a man or any number of men, and was certainly not the product of separate men divided by centuries, but was of another world: supernatural. I was forced to admit, under no pressure but the pressure of the text itself, that it could be only what it claimed it was, the word of God. Do I believe that?

I do. Do I believe in it? I do indeed, since it was its complexity itself that drew me so far inside I was left resting in belief.

What I have found surprising since is the vague interest in scripture, when indeed it's present, of contemporaries who confess to be Christian—as if Christianity derives from any other source. Are linguists or historians, or even eminent theologians, as wise as scripture? Some seem to assume so. A writer recently wrote to me, "I love these writings but they are not an idol to me." For any writer, a book, and especially the writer's own, can become an idol, and no book is ever a solution to a writer's quest; each one only proves there is that much more to do. It may be true that you can't teach an old dog new tricks, but over time you can teach one of most any age to break bad old habits. That's the trick.

Scripture is the text for the universe, full and in the round, and warns us not to add to or diminish it (Deut. 4.2, 12.32; Gal. 1.8–9; Rev. 22.18–19). Money and a position in the world and women and men and images (Rom. 1.21–25) and cathedrals and Baal and television can become idols for a Christian, but not single-minded attention to the Word. It is Christ complete. It's only through the words of scripture that you can come to a knowledge of him, and he isn't an idol.

But, this writer writes, I don't find anywhere in the Bible an ordinance for the sacrament of matrimony or see this sacrament anywhere urged in the new covenant, and I know that it didn't become a sacrament until the church, assuming responsibility, instituted it as one in the Middle Ages. So then I answer, first, that this is one of the instances in which the historical church erred, as Peter did in his proposal to choose an apostle. The only sacraments the church should celebrate are those instituted by Christ; the first being baptism, the sign and seal of the covenant, which He underwent to establish its precedence over the covenant's original sign, circumcision—so that women and children of every age and race could be baptized.

That's one. The other sacrament is communion, or the Lord's Supper—in commemoration of that Last Supper we're to remember him by until he manifests himself at the end of time. Marriage is an ordinance established by God in the beginning (Gen. 1 and 2) for the orderly propagation of the people of His covenant. This ordinance arrived with the creation of human beings, as Jesus reminds the Pharisees when they question him on divorce: "Have you not read that He who made them at the beginning *'made them male and female,'* and said, *'For this reason a man shall leave his father and mother and be joined to his wife, and the two shall become one flesh'*?"[1]

The teaching of marriage as "one flesh" is referred to over and over by the writers of the new covenant.

These two sacraments are the only sacraments that most branches of the protestant church have recognized since the Reformation—the Reformation being that period from the late fourteenth into the sixteenth[2] centuries when proponents of the church, from within the church itself, began to question some of the traditions and hierarchical demands that were beginning to wander wide of scripture in the Roman Catholic and Greek Orthodox churches; these branches had already split. The spirit of the Reformation was not necessarily to break the yoke of Rome, as some have put it, but was an attempt to purge the church of the vestigial paganism remaining in it.[3]

Nor was the attempt at reform new. "The Reformation leaders went back to the Apostolic Church, as described in the New Testament, to find there the spirit and practice of the Church as they believed it should operate. The republishing of the works of the early Church Fathers—Jerome, Cyprian, Origen, and Athanasius—was a great aid to them. . . . From these men they learned the simple character of the early Church and found it widely different from the adorned service of their own day."[4]

It is exactly this character of simplicity that we discover in Acts.

In the 1370s, or nearly two hundred years before the advent of John Knox, the Scots Reformer who defied Mary of Lorraine and Mary Queen of Scots, John Wycliffe, a scholar and fellow at Oxford, first complained against the political elements in the papacy. Wycliffe eventually came to disbelieve in the transubstantiation (the teaching that the bread and wine of communion become the actual body and blood of Christ, not officially adopted as a teaching of the Roman Catholic church until the Council of Trent, 1545–1563), and his *De officio regis* anticipates the inauguration of theocratic kingship as it was formulated during the Reformation.[5] Hus, the morning star of the Reformation as he has been called, came from Bohemia and suffered a martyr's death (largely for denying that Peter was the head of the Church), in 1415, a hundred years before Martin Luther posted his ninety-five theses on the door of the Castle Church in Wittenberg.

Luther was not an obscure rural monk,[6] as often depicted, but held Masters of Arts and Doctor of Theology degrees, and was professor of religion at the University of Wittenberg—Hamlet's alma mater, as it were. He was prior of his monastery and vicar over eleven other monasteries, and was responsible for buildings, accounts, legal matters, and brotherly discipline. He had traveled widely and been an emissary to Pope Julian II in Rome by the time he was thirty-four; then he posted his theses—a common practice of the day in order to bring about debate on a specific topic.

"Here I stand," Luther said, referring to the authority of scripture four years later, after being pursued by both church and civil authorities. "God help me. I cannot do otherwise." *Sola Scriptura*, scripture alone, was the legacy of Luther and is the means by which the church has been able to keep to the path of Christ. Not just in doctrine but in the matter of the sacraments, too, since the human tendency is to devise permutations of an ordinance or command, as with matrimony or Extreme Unction, in order to cover every contingency. At some modern seminaries, for instance, lesbianism is taken as the highest sacrament. So the ordaining and naming of sacraments in the new covenant was, for the church that emerged from the Reformation, left to Christ.

But the genius of the Reformation was that it dislodged scripture from the hierarchy of the church, which tended at the time to treat itself as an elite, and put it into the hands of the working person. Yikes! that's the problem! some will say. All this disputatious mishmash! I won't dismiss the view as totalitarian (there are times when I've felt it myself), but it represents the attitude some governments take toward "the people." During the Reformation, translations appeared in the vernacular throughout Europe. Before this, Bibles in Latin were chained to pulpits; the church was their custodian. Scripture came to be seen to apply to every area of life and every occupation, from the shoemaker and farm family to the tradesman and housewife, all of whom were viewed as servants in the kingdom, equal to any clergy.

Faith was not a suitcase you picked up on Sunday to carry to church, as now, but the source of vibrant application of scripture to every task. The Reformation's dark side was that separatist groups such as the Anabaptists[7] withdrew further into sheltered communities, and there was a proliferation of what came to seem endless branches, offshoots, and sects of the church, many apparently endlessly at odds. The number of schisms, or divisions or breaches or separations, suggests the depth of the church's sin, now two thousand years of it and growing, as addressed here:

It is to be admitted that the fragmentation and lack of co-ordination and solidarity which we find within strictly evangelical and Reformed Churches create a difficult situation, and how this disunity is to be remedied "in the unity of the Spirit and the bond of peace" is a task not easily accomplished. But what needs to be indicted, and indicted with vehemence, is the complacency so widespread, and the failure to be aware that this is an evil, dishonouring to Christ, destructive of the edification defined by the apostle as "the increase of the body into the building up of itself in love" (Eph. 4:16), and prejudicial to the evangelistic outreach to the world.[8]

I would not deny the working of the Spirit within the church through history, as I've said, but unless the church turns to scripture for its direction, like the Bereans we will meet, then every person's "leading by the spirit" is equally valid. The act of christening as valid every opinion that anybody can possibly hold ("we welcome bigots," one university's policy statement reads, "for what we can learn from them") is exactly the sacramental of the secular world, and the reason for our culture's present decline.

No doubt I am word oriented, but I'm also a fairly representative modern, as much at home in New York City as in the country or the academy, and what I find particularly surprising is that those who study scripture to formulate their beliefs, if not their theology, will exclude passages that disagree with personal views or go against present trends rather than wrestling with the passages as further portions of the source of their belief, as Jacob wrestled with the preincarnate Word, present in his arms as an angel.

Scripture itself doesn't claim it will be easy, and once you dismiss portions of it, for whatever reason, you can't deny others dismissing their portions, and then it's all dismissible. This leaves you without Christ, or the Christ of scripture, anyway, who kept quoting from Genesis and Leviticus and Deuteronomy and Isaiah and the law and prophets to substantiate his teachings to anyone who would listen.

"He who has ears to hear," he said, "let him hear."

Either it's the word of God or it isn't, I'm inclined to think, and I sense the red flags of fear of the Falwellian go up. My view is actually more Augustinian, in that I believe I should study the whole counsel of God, precept by precept, in order to understand the heavenly city He has built—and is building here on earth, through the instrumentality of the acts of His apostles, first, and then through the Holy Spirit who applies the acts and the teachings of those apostles to the present-day church. It's through the application of scripture by the Spirit that the church is set free of the inventions of human beings, and I don't want to reinvent the structure of the church any more than I want to reinvent the wheel of doctrine. At one or another of the partings of the Reformation each must take a stand.

The Spirit inspired and is present in all of scripture (2 Tim. 3.16; 2 Peter 1.20–21), and scripture is the blueprint for the church in its ensuing acts. I'm sensitive to those who wish to follow the leading of the Spirit, since I believe the Spirit has led me into a knowledge of myself and my work I never possessed, but I don't need to look to that leading to decide which necktie to wear, much less let it lead me to establish neo-Nordic teachings.

"Know this first," Peter says in the verses cited above, "that no prophecy of Scripture is of any private interpretation. For prophecy never came by the will of man: but holy men of old spoke as moved by the Holy Spirit." This Spirit has spoken directly to every essential any believer needs to know (2 Tim. 3.17), and so, à la Augustine, it seems more fruitful to me to study what stands than to follow the airiness of leading.

The pitfalls inherent in that attitude were addressed by T. S. Eliot, again years ago, in a statement that seems also to cover the temptations inherent in the neo-orthodoxy of Karl Barth, wherein if the Spirit doesn't illuminate the reading, say, of a certain passage of Acts, you may apparently conveniently ignore it, along with any other troublesome scriptural texts. In the essay "Thoughts After Lambeth," T. S. Eliot writes, "Certainly, any one who is wholly sincere and pure in heart may seek for guidance from the Holy Spirit; but who of us is always wholly sincere, especially where the most imperative of instincts may be strong enough to simulate to perfection the voice of the Holy Spirit?"[9]

There has always been a branch of the church, monastic or separatist, that withdraws from the world, viewing it as rank evil, as the Anabaptists did during the time of the Reformation, and sets individual internal experience with the Spirit above the texts of scripture. This often causes a dualistic tension; such separatists tend to hate the world, though they're dependent on it for sustenance, and mistrust civil government, though they turn to it for protection, and their hate and mistrust inhibit them from carrying the acts of scripture outside themselves.

They often refuse to take or make vows, and so the term "affirming" on a Bible has been adopted by the American judicial system to accommodate them—though I think few have compunctions about signing a contract with an institution or employer in the world. And after working for that employer in the world to pay their way, they will, during private meditation and worship on Sunday, cherish their personal experiences with the spirit. This attitude has overtaken a major portion of the church, in tandem with another that seems to run counter to the mutual regard for members in the growing church in Jerusalem: "What I do during the week is *my* business." So the world in which Christians are to act as the preserving salt evolves further into decay. And then that world presents worse problems for retreatists' children.

The internal experience with the spirit is similar to the "inner light" of the Quakers, also separatists, who are not necessarily higher residents in the peaceable kingdom, as some think. During their formation in England and America they violently interrupted worship services, and the inner light of their experience

quickly led them past the basic teachings of scripture, such as original sin, for which Christ's death on the cross alone has paid the
price (1 Cor. 12.21–45). When a person or a sect sets aside scripture as the rule of faith and the practice of that faith in life, then
other agendas have to be established, and I don't find it odd that
not many years ago, during the war in Vietnam, Quakers were
supplying food and medicine and other essentials to what would
become one of the most venomous killer armies in history: the
North Vietnamese and Pol Pot's Khmer Rouge.

The one who chides me not to make an idol of scripture will now
chide me for condemning some who can't live up to every jot and
tittle of it, though I'm not. I am trying to open the eyes of
Christians to some of the ways in which the historical church was
drawn aside from the teachings of the apostles we find in Acts. I'm
not suggesting that every Christian shouldn't exercise scrupulous
personal judgment in every area of his or her life; on the contrary, I believe, along with C. S. Lewis, that one of the greatest
(and often most neglected) gifts given to members of the church is
the brain. The most enduring and meritorious talents of even the
finest athlete reside there, and the stewardship of our intellect is
the one Christ will perhaps examine most thoroughly before he
calls us good and faithful servants. If he does.
    In order for that intellect to be able to operate in matters of the
teaching of the church or for us to be able to be actually guided
by the Spirit, we must know as much of both covenants of the
canon as we can. Now that chider will bring up the fallibility of the
canon, perhaps, mentioning the "flawed human filters"—or some
such term—of the writers who received it from the Spirit.
    Certainly the authors of scripture were flawed with sin like
everybody, but when they spoke or wrote as they were moved by
the Spirit, their flaws were overwritten by God. If you begin to
try to pick out verses you feel are tainted in this way, the ten-

dency is to make an idol of your ability to discern where Paul or Luke went wide—of what mark? Yours. Then you will suggest the possible errors mere copyists may have made in transmitting scripture, whether accidental or purposeful, and what about that? Or you will mention debate racking the church over its inability to settle the matter of the canon within itself.

First, in all the manuscript discoveries and all the variants unearthed over the centuries, there has never been one that alters any teaching of scripture. The same for every copyist's error, a few of which have surfaced: the plethora of manuscripts have cleared these up—flyspecks in pepper. *The Book of Q,* reconstructed "by scholarly consensus," is not supported by hundreds of manuscripts and fragments, as the gospels are, and is based on some imagined consensus of scholars two thousand years later. There have been too many manuscripts and copies found in too many locations for the arguments about *The Book of Q* to serve the church any more than balloons flatulently losing air.

This is a debatable passage: "For thine is the kingdom and the power and the glory forever." This may have been added to Matthew's recording of the Lord's Prayer, but it doesn't change its meaning or alter other scripture; it conforms to it. The same for the last twelve verses of Mark, which also might be a later addition.

Not all of the ancient manuscripts contain the account in the first part of chapter 8 of John's Gospel, about the woman caught in adultery, but to question its canonicity from this distance is to choke on a gnat and swallow a camel. The passage contains nothing new or contrary to scripture; the Pharisees, custodians of the law, want to trip Jesus up for opposing the law, as they assume, so they bring him a woman caught in adultery ("in the very act") and remind him that Moses commanded she be stoned. Now, what do *you* think, they ask. Jesus stoops down and writes "on the ground with his finger." He could be reminding them that the Mosaic law was written on tablets of stone by the finger of God, and that this law states, in the matter of a capital offense, the need for at least two witnesses. So far there are merely accusations. Who was she caught with? Have any of these men known her? Is their forgoing of judicial law a way of removing someone common to them all?

Jesus is presented with mob rule, and with no witnesses forthcoming, the one who must obey the law in every particular appeals to their consciences, that inner state that no external adherence to law can cover, as he does throughout the gospels. He says, "He who is without sin among you, let him cast the first stone." You know the rest; the crowd of men disperses; and since no witnesses have appeared to condemn the woman, Jesus doesn't condemn her either. Nor does he say, Go, live as you wish; my grace and love will cover all you possibly can do. He says, "Go and sin no more."

Respond to mercy with repentance, he says, a turning away from your former course in life.

As for the integrity of the canon, the Roman Catholic and the Greek Orthodox churches have accepted the Apocrypha, as it is termed—books not included in the canon when the Septuagint was translated, three centuries before Christ. These books are also known as Deuterocanonical, or of secondary stature in the canon, and I can find no serious debate in any protestant church over the last four centuries for including Bel and the Dragon, for instance (one of the apocryphal additions to the Book of Daniel), into the canon.

Nor do I believe that you must know and believe every verse of the canon in order to be a Christian, or that members of churches that accept the Apocrypha aren't Christian—a stand adopted by some. If false teaching is taking place, those who remain sitting under it won't be blamed as much as the instigators of the teaching, as Jesus mentions in Matthew 5.19, 18.6–7, and the parallel passages. Nor do I believe we need to follow every verse (Saul hacked Agag to pieces in Gilgal, friend), but if we know the rest of Scripture, we will know how single verses relate to the whole.

I'm only going to believe what Jesus teaches, you say, and in saying so accept the writings of Matthew, Mark, Luke, John, and Paul as authoritative and canonical. They are the ones who transmitted the words of Jesus. He didn't set down with pen any book of the canon, though by his Spirit he is author of it all, Leviticus and Deuteronomy as well as the Sermon on the Mount, which recapitulates and parallels those two books.

Many of the problems with the canon originate in modern scholarship—that "scholarly consensus." Anyone who has experienced literary criticism in a university knows that professors believe their criticism is of a higher order than the text, even if it's L. Woodhead on Shakespeare. In the church, this is the view that higher criticism takes—that one's suppositions supersede the received canon—and in the following that view is presented by an Episcopalian, whether purposely or not, as a five-point covenant model for the higher critic:

> First, he *assumes* that the books of the Bible are textually jumbled. Second, he tries to *prove* that the books of the Bible are textually jumbled. Third, he *assumes* that through creative myth-making, he himself can produce a meaningful reconstruction of what the ancient authors ("redactors") really wanted to convey to all mankind, despite each one's short-term goals of political or bureaucratic manipulation. Fourth, he tries to present a *"deeper" message* for modern man that transcends the Bible's unfortunately jumbled texts. Finally, the higher critic offers *his version of the Bible's true transcendent ethical unity.* Somehow, this newly discovered transcendent ethical unity always winds up sounding like the last decade's political manifesto for social democracy. . . . [10]

Abraham Kuyper lost faith in higher critics in 1861. He was a seminarian in Leiden at the time and had listened a few years earlier to the august Scholten, whom he loved, argue that "provided you elided a few verses, the Gospel according to John definitely and clearly proved its own genuineness. Now, in 1861, Scholten issued a writing in which he stated that this Gospel contained no word by John himself."[11] The ethics of such scholarship ended it for Kuyper.

The major divisions in the church, that age-old rock it has always broken upon, the cornerstone ignored by the builders, subsumes every division. Spirit vs. Word, Grace vs. Law, Liberty vs. Obedience, Love vs. Judgment—these are not warring contraries, but concepts woven into unwindingdom. That the majority of the modern Church declines to understand this is apparent in the recurrence of the divisions. People don't wish to submit to the word, as they haven't since Adam, and whether you say you're resisting the law or the gospel, it is the same rock. The law was filled out in Christ (the Greek *play-roo*); it was filled to full, to the top, the brim; it was caused to abound; was brought to complete realization —"I have not come to destroy the law, but to fulfill it," Jesus said. He filled out the decrees of God as revealed in His law and obeyed that law as it should be obeyed, so that the promises of God, given by the prophets of the covenant, would receive their fulfillment to the full. His perfect filling out of the law applies to every lawbreaker and justifies (see p. 14) lawbreakers according to the standard of perfection demanded by God in Christ (Mat. 5.48).

What then? Every Christian knows it's not by obedience to the law that salvation or righteousness before a righteous God is achieved. We are saved by grace (his unmerited favor extended to us) through faith alone, but even the trembling faith we're able to summon to accept God's grace is a gift from him. Should we sin then to receive more grace, as the Manicheans did? God forbid we should follow the route some of our media preachers have. We're to bring our lives into line with the life lived by Christ, the servant of scripture, who was obedient to the dotting of every *i*, tempted as we are, yet without sin. And thus servant to our greatest need: freedom from the bondage to death. Though he was God, the mightiest supernatural power, he humbled himself in obedience; through suffering he learned further obedience, and in obedience he bowed his head in death.

If Christians intend to follow his way rather than give it lip service, they must obey him. His grace is sufficient to cover every hidden sin and open outrage we perpetrate along the way, and is sufficient to enable us to endure, but is not sufficient to reconcile any who taste the gifts of the covenant and then turn away to live as they please—Hebrews 6.4–6. That warning from Hebrews is one of the most solemn in scripture and is directed to the branch of the church that continued to suspect they could secure righteousness by adherence to ceremonial law.

Once Christ broke down the middle wall separating Jew from Gentile, man from woman, slave from master, husband from wife, mother from child, all children from their fathers and mothers and every other source of authority and comfort, he instructed his followers to come and lay the weight of their works and the self-righteous justification of all their liberties on him and to learn to accept the greater weight of his glory. His spilled blood can't be wiped away for a night of license without offense to the life He lived in order to receive the reward we deserve. Death.

This is the glory and power and terror of the covenant; once in, never out. Its blessings and curses fall as they will over those who are or are not in conformity to Christ, while those who wish to live as if a written covenant never existed, even if they're able to cast out demons in His name, stand in danger of hearing, in that exegetical statement at the close of the Sermon on the Mount, "Depart from me, you who practice lawlessness. I never knew you."

The ethical nature of Christianity can't be blurred by saying it's all grace, and the effect of a lot of textual and literary criticism, even when practiced in good faith, blurs those ethical roots. The term for a person who shies from even the word "law" is antinomian—against law, more specifically, against *the* Law. This is the real line along which all of the divisions in the church fall into place, and this division has made its way so deeply into the church that it has affected the work of every modern Christian writer.

Early in his career, John Updike began to read the work of Karl Barth, a native German who felt the full effect of higher criticism as it developed in that country. Barth epitomized the divisions in Christian thought that were manifest since Emmanuel Kant, though these divisions were present in religious thinking since Plato: the Ideal (as undefinable as mist) reflecting the Idea—a Hellenism alien to Saul the Pharisee, as we shall see. In an effort to evade judgment of the kind that Jesus (in the quote above from Matthew 7) claims will come, you must presume his word to be disconnected from the ethics of the covenant and to be, to pit Episcopalian against Episcopalian—"incoherent, unclear, and limited to the individual conscience, rather than coherent, clear, and universal in every human conscience."

> Karl Barth was a defender of just such a radically individual ethics, an ethics which matched his thesis of a radically dialectical, incoherent, creed-denying, God-man encounter—a noumenal encounter beyond nature and history. . . . Barth thereby proclaimed the triumph of Kant's noumenal trans-historical realm of randomness over Kant's phenomenal historical realm of scientifically predictable cause and effect, all in the name of a higher ethics and higher critical insights. This was Barth's assertion of the triumph of historical and ethical relativism over the Bible.[12]

Updike, silver eminence of American letters, whose body of fiction communicates the elegant resonance of a Bellow but tends to shun the often fussy intellectuality that can clog a Bellow narrative (Updike has a fine intellect himself but downloads as it were his ideas into his essays and book reviews), has written out of a vision unlike Bellow's or any other's: *In the beauty of the lilies Christ was born across the sea* sums up the mystery that all his work has attempted to capture, he has said.[13] Updike is the only living writer of his stature in America who has consistently confessed to be a Christian. He has woven Christian doctrine and iconography into his fiction in *Pigeon Feathers, Rabbit Run, The Music School, Of the Farm, Couples, Marry Me, Roger's Version,* and other short-story collections and novels. In his recent autobiography, *Self-Consciousness,* near the end of the last section, titled "On Being a Self Forever," Updike, who was reared a Lutheran in Shillington, Pennsylvania, but is presently a practicing Episcopalian, writes:

> I found a few authors, a very few—Chesterton, Eliot, Unamuno, Kierkegaard, Karl Barth—who helped me believe. Under the shelter . . . that I improvised from their pages I have lived my life. I rarely read them now; my life is mostly lived. God is the God of the living, though His priests and executors, to keep order and to force the world into a convenient mould, will always want to make Him the God of the dead, the God who chastises life and forbids and says No . . . Imitation is praise. Description expresses love. I early arrived at these self-justifying inklings. Having accepted that old Shillington blessing, I have felt free to describe life as accurately as I could, with especial attention to human erosions and betrayals. What small faith I have has given me what artistic courage I have. My theory was that God already knows everything and cannot be shocked. And only truth is useful. Only truth can be built upon. From a higher, inhuman point of view, only truth, however harsh, is holy.[14]

If we confess to believe in God, as Updike has—stating that a Christian is one who can confess the Apostles' Creed—the next step is to examine the source in which God has chosen to reveal himself (other than his Incarnate Son), the texts of scripture. In these he reveals himself to be infinitely more intelligent than any human being. So indeed nothing can ever shock him—not the paragraphs of a glorious or disenfranchised or meek writer any more than the motives of the person who appears in a fast-food restaurant firing an automatic pistol. That does not mean, however, that He doesn't hold the originator of each action accountable for his or her actions, as he held kings Saul and David accountable.

Updike's reference is to Matthew 22.21, and when the incarnate son at that point in the Gospel refutes the Sadducees, the aristocratic sect who did not believe in the resurrection and who had confronted him with the gross and joking proposition of a woman who has married seven brothers, under the pretense of asking him who, then, would be her husband when all of the many parties are resurrected, Jesus points out that God has said He is the God of Abraham, Isaac, and Jacob. He is the God of those members of the covenant who are renewed to life by faith— "the God of the living"—not the God of those who out of their deadness pose the entrapping paradigms that the Sadducees and Pharisees were prone to.

Otherwise I approve of Updike's "inklings," even where I disagree with his theology. I approve of them much more than those of that set of Oxford dons who had a bent for Hellenic and Norse mythology and so dramatized for their age its predisposition toward a pietistic retreat into frozen, murky, movies of internal fantasy. And rather than assume the role of executor, I will only repeat with emphasis, *From a higher, inhuman point of view, only truth, however harsh, is holy,* and point out that this is exactly what scripture teaches, and why scripture claims to be, on its self-attesting terms, authoritative and holy.

So when I say, "It's either the word of God or it isn't," I mean what Peter and Augustine and the Church Fathers meant, and for me or others to pass over whatever might seem, from a human standpoint, unhappy or "culturally irrelevant" (a dispensation of convenience) would be to adopt a raison d'être as blind as the one that will formulate an entire theology and world-view on the basis of a favorite verse or two. And so to refute such views I have employed the theology of the central character of the book of Acts, Saul.

6 ————————————

SAUL

I DOUBT THAT ANY WRITER has ever enjoyed an unkind review, except perhaps the Marquis de Sade. And by unkind I don't mean negative, but one that goes for the jugular of the person of the writer so fast there's hardly a chance to mention the book at hand. The book is merely a springboard for the act, releasing into reality the sad truth that there are people you've never met who would as soon you weren't around. So there is that about this business, and there is another aspect I find almost as unprofitable: the dust jacket photo. Is this really necessary? I tend to wonder—and wondered even before I got old and ugly.

A picture certainly can't convey a sense of your self if the writing hasn't. And photographers have a tendency to project their conception of "the author" (daunting or offhand or sensitive or scurrilous or whatever) into their photos. There can even be a kind of political scrum over *which* photographer will do it. I once spent a week in New York in sessions with three different photographers, and every finished proof sheet was like an unreeling series of cheap shots. Not one was used. No picture, anyway, represents the way one looks just then, although an editor or a publicist will usually disagree. The ones that you like appall them, even though your mother always said you had good taste. So you

leave it to the editor, and he or she, in conjunction with the publicist, and perhaps even the publisher, selects the one in which you
look like a camel. The consolation is that one of those reviewers
wouldn't know you from Adam if the person ran into you head
on. Best have your spouse send along a Polaroid.

When I see myself, however, sitting in the embracing, scruffy
chair in which I've settled for the last twenty years to read ("That's
the most comfortable chair I've sat in," my brother, a man of comfort, once said to me, unsolicited, as he rose from it), or lying at
my side of the bed under a spindly beam of light that attracts
those floating hairs that look like bee hairs, and notice that I'm
opening the back cover of a book for a glance at the writer, I can
understand the attraction or allure, I guess. But would it exist if
publishers hadn't started using photos in the first place? Or was it
a scurrilously sensitive yet daunting camera-hungry author who
did? Like that Dreshout, you know, he said, of Willy the Shake. I
have a sense that readers would read more deeply into a text if they
weren't suspended or satisfied by that one-dimensional represen-
tation of a writer who never in the world looked like that, believe
me, while at work.

One of the astonishing accomplishments of scripture, from a
photographed writer's point of view, is that for the length of the
entire canon, including all of the gospels and epistles, there is
never a physical description of Jesus, not one. Think of it: twelve
apostles and hundreds of disciples who came to cherish him as the
source of life, many of them magnificent writers, and in the hundreds of pages written about him from a variety of perspectives
there isn't a detail of description, not an eyebrow, nose, lips, chin,
beard, hair color; not even height or weight. Astonishing. This is
in accord, of course, with the commandment not to make a
graven image nor bow down to one. Only an overseeing Spirit
could restrain the writers who wanted to set down Christ as he
was, or merely pay homage to the impact of his presence.

The oversight is so entire, I suspect few Christians are able to accept it as purposeful—wooed as they are by the production of artists from every era of likenesses and images of Jesus. Even fewer could accept this as one of the most profound teachings of scripture (for writers it should be the final proof of its supernatural source), since it operates entirely by silence and absence. This, as any good Jewish theologian will tell you, is exactly as it should be, when dealing with the person of God. That Jesus was also a man, but not one to depict, has been settled by church councils over and over; his person is inseparable from Jehovah's. No artist can portray the shekinah glory in a human face; no living artist has seen the face of Jesus.

A further astonishing matter is that the same oversight has been exercised toward the apostles; not one of them is anywhere physically described. At points in his ministry, Jesus suggests inner details—"I am lowly and meek"—a telling way of teaching that his concern isn't with externals but with implanting his word in the *heart*. Paul in his epistles reveals similar inner detail: he is the least of the apostles, the chief sinner, not much to look at, weak, tearful at times, and beleaguered by a "thorn in the flesh."

We're never told what the thorn is, and you will find otherwise sober commentators speculate from headaches and troubles with his eyes (once blinded) to kidney stones and a spiritual problem. He was a Pharisee of Pharisees, which may mean he had a wife, so that when he says, "I would that all men were as I am" (1 Cor. 7.7), he might mean he is remaining faithful to a wife who died, rather than endorsing bachelorhood, which he endorses nowhere else. He probably had a beard; not only because he was a Pharisee but because at times he appears to take Nazarite vows and is referred to in Acts as a Nazarene (24.5). Nazarites let their hair grow until they completed a vow, then shaved it off. Nobody knows any of this for sure and nobody will until we're translated, if then. Such details may be so meaningless (like why God made mosquitoes) that we'd be appalled to think they occurred to us. We do know Saul was a terror to the church.

After the stoning of Stephen, chapter 8 opens, "And Saul was heartily in agreement with putting him to death," precisely be- cause of Stephen's teaching of the history of redemption from scripture. We should notice, too, the artful way in which Luke is used by the Spirit, considering the overseeing mentioned above; Saul's presence is like heat under the page: the adversary, the one who would curtail or restrict the word as preached by Stephen, stands before the reader, breathing heavily. This firebrand is also an intellectual, a member of the local academy—he has studied "at Gamaliel's feet" (22.3)—and now he joins the Sanhedrin in op- posing the disciples in Jerusalem.

"Beyond measure I persecuted the church of God, and wasted it," he declares in Galatians 1.13, "and I profited in Judaism above many of my equals in my own nation, being more exceed- ingly zealous for my ancestral traditions." Saul did not at first appreciate the joining of the new covenant with the old, either. The church in Jerusalem is "scattered abroad," largely through his persecutions, we learn, and with the sometimes omniscient eye of Acts we follow fleeing Philip, one of those ordained with Stephen, into Samaria, the next area of ministry mentioned by Christ.

Again, considering the "signs and wonders" attributed to Philip while in Samaria, you have to wonder, or I do, about the histori- cal propriety of the church in naming the seven deacons. It might be possible that the seven held an office derived directly from the apostles that doesn't appear again in the church, as the apostolic office does not.

The church, as it came into being, was laid on "the founda- tion of the apostles and prophets, Jesus Christ himself being the chief cornerstone," according to Ephesians 2.20. The offices of the church can be seen as fitting within one another in order of hierarchy, as those Russian dolls of descending size nestle inside each other. Deacon inside elder or bishop or presbyter (all three titles designate this office in Acts and the epistles), elder inside, perhaps, the Seven, and this office inside the apostle, each apostle clothed in the power of Christ and under his head. And as any builder knows, once you've laid the foundation, you don't dig it up to build a belfry. Apostolic powers have ended.

The Samaritans, who were not exactly Gentiles but Jews of mixed heritage who rejected portions of the old covenant (and would not worship in Jerusalem), were abhorrent to orthodox Jews. This is why Christ's parable about the Good Samaritan arrived with such impact—that an outcast Samaritan would aid the injured man, and not a priest or a Levite. Samaria is where Philip's teaching flowers, and as he performs a series of healings and begins to gather adherents, including Simon, a former sorcerer and magician, the source of the church's power and the interrelatedness of these offices becomes clearer.

When Peter and John arrive, as they do, Simon sees them administer the Holy Spirit by the laying on of hands. Having received the Spirit, the apostles are able to confer it directly, as Christ has from above—as they have conferred it on Stephen and Philip, by the application of their hands. This is a power that Philip apparently does not possess, because when Simon, the sorcerer who has been so taken by Philip's "signs and wonders" that he has become an adherent, sees the apostles' further power, he offers them money, saying, "Give me this power also, that anyone on whom I lay hands may receive the Holy Spirit."

"Your money perish with you," Peter says, forthright as always, "because you thought the gift of God could be purchased with money!" Which should also remind us of Peter's confrontation with Ananias and Sapphira, when they wished to sell the Spirit short, and might remind those more conversant with church history of one of the practices that accelerated the Reformation and thus protestantism: the sale of indulgences that Luther, among others, objected to. Or of James Joyce's *simony.*

"Repent of your wickedness," Peter says to Simon, an effect of the gospel that nobody likes to hear. "And pray to God that the thought of your heart"—a deeper thought Peter has discerned through the Spirit as he did with Ananias and Sapphira—"may be forgiven you. For I see that you are poisoned with bitterness and bound by iniquity." This, of course, our other Simon (Peter is also "Simon") has not revealed.

"Pray to the Lord for me, that none of the things which you have spoken may come upon me," Simon asks, dodging the central spiritual issue, repentance. Should Philip have been more discerning? He was as discerning as he was able to be, given the powers conferred on him—which has direct relevance to the matter of adherents in the present-day church. How can a board or a session of elders be discerning in the way Peter was? They can't. They can't be any more discerning than Philip, and must take the words of an adherent's confession as the truth. They don't have apostolic gifts.

The apostles start back for Jerusalem, and you will observe at this point (8.26) a new turn in Acts: "Now an angel of the Lord spoke to Philip, saying, 'Arise and go toward the south along the road which goes down from Jerusalem to Gaza.'" At each important juncture in Acts, as we shall see, this angel of the Lord appears, to keep insisting into the consciousness of those of us still dull of learning that the reality of Acts is being governed by the administration of Christ.

The route that Philip is instructed to take is succinctly described: "This is desert." After all the followers Philip was accumulating in Samaria, how could a lonely desert road seem fruitful? Yet he takes the road, as directed by the angel, and while traveling there he sees an Ethiopian eunuch, the court treasurer of Candace (queen of Ethiopia), rolling along in a chariot, reading from Isaiah. This man, who is of course black, has perhaps been in Jerusalem for the fairly recent feast day and is presumably a follower of Judaism, since he is reading from Isaiah. His appearance, however, would not suggest to Philip that he is an orthodox Jew.

Philip runs and catches up, and hears the eunuch, who is wonderfully imperturbable, reading from the prophet Isaiah. Philip asks if he understands what he is reading. "How can I, unless someone guides me," the eunuch says, reminding us that every church member must rely on at least one other person to hear the gospel. Or as Augustine put it, he never would have known God as his father if he hadn't known the church as his mother.

"And Philip opened his mouth and beginning from this Scripture he preached Jesus to him." Here the Spirit conferred upon Philip provides him with the ability to preach Christ incarnate from the original covenant. The reality of Christ's presence in that covenant was propounded in another maxim credited to Augustine, which illustrates the inseparable nature of the two: "The New is in the Old concealed; the Old in the New revealed."

Isaiah teaches that all nations and all races on earth will be called to worship the Messiah, the lamb who was led like a sheep to slaughter; and the Ethiopian eunuch, who is not only black but physically deformed (unclean; Leviticus 21.20) by the castration he has undergone for Queen Candace at the moment he receives the gospel, cries, "Look! Water! What is to prevent me from being baptized?" So although the eunuch might be an adherent or a proselyte, he has not yet received a proselyte's baptism. Has he been circumcised? There is no textual evidence either way, so it is safe to suspect not.

To confirm that the shadowy ceremonial forms of worship of the original covenant (these forms are what have passed away) have found perfect expression in the new, and that there is now no opposition to his baptism, Philip says: "If you will believe with all your heart, you may."

"I believe that Jesus Christ is the son of God," the eunuch declares, a declaration as substantial as Peter's: that Jesus was the anointed one, the Son of the living God (Mat. 16.16). The chariot is brought to a halt, and both the eunuch and Philip go down into the water, where Philip baptizes him. Was the water of sufficient depth in the desert to immerse? If they "go down into the water," does that mean immersion, and if they both go down into it, as the text reads, does that mean Philip is immersed? Mere quibbling, perhaps, for in the strangest turn of this strange encounter, as the two step from the water Philip is "snatched" by the Spirit to Azotes, some twenty miles off—literally "spirited away," in the idiom our language has adopted to accommodate the event. We're not told how this is accomplished, merely that Philip is suddenly in another place.

The eunuch, unperturbed, rolls along on his way in his chariot, rejoicing. The supernatural is now incarnate in him.

Then back to Saul, whose wrath keeps building until he starts "breathing threats and murder against the disciples of the Lord." He hurries to the high priest and asks for letters to dispatch him to the synagogues in Damascus, commissioning him to arrest any of the Way (an early name for the adherents of Christ: the Way, the Truth, and the Life) that he might possibly find in Damascus. He wants to bring them back, bound, to Jerusalem, to stand trial. Apparently he's heard that some of the disciples have fled as far north as Syria to escape him, into a country a hundred and fifty miles from Jerusalem, and now he's saying, *Let me at 'em!* He heads off with a group of men whose identity and number we never learn, probably a set of temple guards, toward the city of Damascus.

And now Luke's account becomes so novelistic it might be instructive to turn the tables and observe that the genre of the novel, which is indebted to every storyteller of the canon and owes much to the artful compression in Acts, is often the best way to get at the truth. There has been so much Christian writing of the imaginative sort in the last century the church has forgotten that the novel was once viewed as the vehicle of "manners," or ultimate societal truth, not a rocket ship into a stratosphere of fantasy. Luke could have recorded "mere facts," as nonfiction writers are touted to do (some of these are the theologians we nod over at night), but as Luke well knew, truth does not always arrive by a logical statement of fact with all the necessary footnotes attached. Truth often *happens*. Truth is an act.

The greatest enactment of it was the appearance of Christ, his birth in a stable, with cattle breathing on him while he was wound with swaddling clothes to designate being now enwrapped in flesh, and then laid on boards that prefigured the cross he would hang from. The church needs to exhort its members to return to this moment by turning to the literature of its writers from the past, who know better than other writers the ways in which to robe characters with aspects of Christ or employ characters that embody the way to live. The act of the incarnation is the single greatest power at the center of every work of fiction, Christian or not; it enacted the *way* in which words take on flesh. Contemporary Christian writers have neglected the source and power of their heritage by adopting the Hellenistic tendency toward "pure thought" or, worse, the mystical and syncretistic retreat into fantasy.

Christian fiction is a way to live the life Christ calls us to live on earth, using as a measure the example of his life and the writings he committed by his Spirit to the church. The church should not, like the university, dig for its truth through the fragmented scraps that remain after deconstructionists have detonated in rage the Christocentric monolith, as they call it, the rock that still coheres in spite of their abuse and insistence that the center cannot hold. And instead of turning to increasingly antipathetic scholars to discover what's up in literature or what literature should be up to, the church and its writers should study the truth of the incarnation available in every word of scripture.

If you're sufficiently nimble to be able to say that God is the source of this truth, so that any truth that appears, in whatever context, is really *His* truth, then you've read the Puritans, I suspect, but misconstrued them. And you've opened yourself to the question Pilate poses, "What is truth?" Truth of course stood in the flesh in front of Pilate's eyes. "Put aside science falsely so-called," Paul says, and "Beware lest any man corrupt you through philosophy and empty deceit, after the traditions of men, the rudiments of the world, and not after Christ" (Gal. 2.8). For the consistent Christian, truth exists only as it is embodied in Christ and revealed through his word.

So watch. As Saul and his cohort near the end of the last part of their trip to Damascus, and probably come within smelling distance of the city, a sudden impact of light from above strikes and envelops Saul. He falls down, stunned, and hears, "Saul, Saul, why do you persecute me?"

"Who are You, Lord?" he asks, using the Greek term for Jehovah, aware of the majesty of the one who has struck him down.

"I am Jesus whom you are persecuting."

What? Isn't this God? How is Saul persecuting Jesus? That the members of his church are united under his head is the first revelation Jesus delivers to Saul, answering his cry to Jehovah by introducing I AM before his name. The Angel of Acts has appeared in the state he was translated into by his resurrection: *his head and hair white as wool, as white as snow, and His eyes like a flame of fire; his feet like fine brass, as if refined in a furnace, and his voice the sound of multitudinous waters.*

He has laid the fire of his hand on Saul to choose him as his twelfth apostle. This shearing of reality through his blinding presence is a miracle beyond the imaginings of Peter and the rest of the apostles. He has outreached their imaginations by extending this direct apostolic calling to Saul. He does not persecute Saul, scholar of the law and prophets, who will be his most significant writer of the new covenant, or say how mistaken Saul has been. In this bolt of light that none in the present should be able to blink back, he is signifying that there is no disjunction between the original covenant and the new, and no prejudice involved in his calling and choosing.

"Arise," he says, "and enter the city, and you will be told what you must do."

Saul is now His servant on earth. The soldiers, who have also seen the light and hit the ground, do not have to endure the voice that is like oceans breaking against each other, or at least they don't hear what it says (22.9). And as Saul gets to his feet, further revelation comes; he can't see. He's been blinded. Nobody can look upon the glory of Jehovah without being undone, as any reader of the covenant knows. The soldiers have to take Saul by the hand and lead him like an infant into Damascus, his former worldly powers reduced to nothing in one stroke.

He lies in bed three days, helpless and blind, refusing to eat or drink. *What have I done?* is a thought bound to occur to a person of Saul's vigor and intellect who is suddenly, helplessly disabled, and there are moments in the epistles that register his remorse: "I am the least of the apostles, who am not fit to be called an apostle, because I persecuted the church of God." But perhaps he also receives a sense of the words Jesus will later speak, "My grace is sufficient for you; my strength is made perfect in weakness." Everything he had fought for to the point of inflicting death, everything he opposed and abhorred, he now feels himself becoming in the transformation into the person he always was meant to be, or even always was (Eph. 1.4).

Something as remarkable as this is taking place, because in a later letter he says about this Damascus moment that seems instantaneous, that "when He who had set me apart, even from my mother's womb, and called me through His grace, was pleased to reveal His Son in me, that I might preach him among the Gentiles, I didn't immediately consult with flesh and blood" (Gal. 1.15). The call is seen as seamless. What a journey that trip to Damascus came to be! Saul, inside the city now, in the dark of blindness, feels infinity enter, unfolding all the way back past his birth. And he sees that it has been ordained for him to be set apart to serve the One he hated, the One standing now at the door to eternity.

That door opens and God enters through the instrument of a member of his body, Ananias, a "disciple at Damascus," by coming to Ananias in a vision. The Lord who gives to his beloved even in sleep, tells Ananias to go to a "street which is called Straight" (Mat. 7.14); there Ananias is to ask for Saul, who is praying and who in a vision of his own (in this perfect conjunction of Old and New) has seen Ananias arrive and lay hands on him in order to restore his sight. All of the acts of the apostles, then, since they are not always carried out by the apostles themselves, must be viewed as the acts of Jesus Christ through God.

But "Lord," Ananias says, as reluctant as any modern believer, "I have heard from many about this man, how much harm he did to your saints at Jerusalem."

"Go, for he is an instrument of mine, to bear my name before the Gentiles and kings and the sons of Israel; for I will show him how much he must suffer for my name's sake."

Saul is to bear the name I AM, the Messiah and Savior, to kings and gentiles, as he will, and to *the sons of Israel,* as he first and foremost will: "I am not ashamed of the gospel of Christ, for it is the power of God unto salvation to all who believe, to the Jew first, and also to the Greek." And he will suffer, from physical ailments, a buffeting by "Satan's messenger," that thorn in the flesh our language has also adopted, and suffer, too, from persecution of the kind he has inflicted on others.

Ananias, in an access of courage, surely, since he is facing not only Saul but every authority persecuting the way, obeys. He goes to the house where Saul lies and lays hands on him and, already having accepted the words received in the vision, says, "Brother Saul, the Lord Jesus, who appeared to you on the road by which you were coming"—Ananias' outside confirmation of the incident—"has sent me so that you may regain your sight, and be filled with the Holy Spirit."

How could Ananias confer the Spirit if only the apostles can? The power of the apostles was, from all the evidence, transferable from them alone, not from others. But in this instance the Spirit has been conferred directly by Christ, in his searing calling of Saul as an apostle—in that blaze of light descending as the tongues of flames did from above—and the act Ananias now performs teaches Christians, no matter how important they suspect they might be, to submit to the human hands the Savior reaches to them from his church each day, from this day to the end of history.

As for Saul, we read that immediately "there fell from his eyes something like scales"—another phenomenon covered by an English idiom. Then Saul "arose and was baptized." No matter how many times you read these verses, you won't find that anybody leaves the room, so available water must have been used; and rather than the formula some seek, to *go down into the water,* Saul instead rises up. Was there a ritual bath present in the house? It would have had to have been the house of a wealthy person for such a luxury to exist,[1] and the text doesn't suggest any of this; it's a far-flung possibility you must pull in from the outside.

If immersion is the sine qua non for membership in the new covenant church, then it would be worse than unusual that this significant apostle, who has undergone a dramatic adult conversion, wasn't immersed. If you argue that the passage doesn't specifically say he wasn't, you open an argument against the apostles being the enduring typology, the foundation, of the present-day church. If immersion were the sine qua non, the one to make that point with would be Saul.

The central sentence itself, in its construction of directness rather than elision, argues against a trip to a reservoir or river: "he arose and was baptized; and he took food and was strengthened"—this last a household act. Daily sustenance is never neglected by the physician writer of Acts, nor are the larger implications of it as the "bread which came down from heaven," as Christ literally has come down in power to call and claim his newest apostle.

Saul begins to visit the synagogues, those same places he was going to plow through to locate and persecute more of the way. But now he meekly seeks those people with preaching, although his preaching, like his zeal for persecution, is unequivocal: Jesus is the Christ, the Son of God, he says. His hearers wonder what he's up to, since they know that in Jerusalem he destroyed those who called on Jesus' name, and this only increases Saul's zeal; he "confounded the Jews who lived in Damascus, proving that this is the Christ."

But Saul soon learns about his persecution of the church from the other end of the stick: a plot is hatched to kill him. Somehow, although we're not told how, Saul hears about the plot, and a number of Damascus disciples lower him over the city wall in a basket—a not-so-subtle reminder of the giver of the Law, Moses, and his escape as a fledgling covenant child from Pharaoh. Was it ignoble of Saul to escape in this way, while others, like Stephen, stood and took what he was dishing out?

He was following an injunction of Jesus in Matthew 10.23: "But when they persecute you in this city, flee to another." Then why didn't Stephen flee? Was he being unwise, or ignoring that injunction? From the evidence, he wanted to confront the established authorities on home ground, as Peter and John confronted them. If Saul had vowed to remain in Damascus, as he will later make a vow, it would have been different. Each portion of the church (and every member in it) has a purpose in God's providence, just as each is given individual gifts.

Saul is off into the night.

And now the seamless weaving of time in Acts becomes apparent. In the first chapter of Galatians, we learn that at this point in his life Saul spent three years in Arabia, while Luke communicates a sense of events taking place one after the other, for now in the text Saul travels to Jerusalem and attempts to associate with the disciples. They're afraid of him. They have heard, surely, of his zeal, if they haven't felt the sting of it, and perhaps they have received word of his conversion secondhand; then he was in Arabia for three years.

It should act as a sweet bit of a comfort, actually, for those who have been brought into faith late in life, to see that even the apostles mistrusted a convert (and not just a convert but one called to be an apostle), since the modern church seems to distance itself, dancing on its toes, from a convert with a past, as if to say, How can this person expect to be part of us? Aren't such converts the ones the church is looking for, as with Saul? I can't think what ulterior motive a new convert might have—what profit would there be in it?—but the church often seems to suspect a motive, as with Charles Colson, in the first years after his conversion. Or, more apt, that raging writer of sexual assault and revolution, Eldridge Cleaver. Eldridge a *saint?*

Barnabas, a Cypriot and perhaps somewhat of an outsider himself (he was singled out for his generous giving—4.36–37), befriends Saul and becomes, in a sense, Saul's advocate to the apostles. Barnabas brings Saul before them, and Saul declares to them how he saw the Lord on his way to Damascus and has been preaching in his name ever since. Why should they believe Saul? The Holy Spirit, which they have received, testifies in them to the truth of his report. After this he moves "freely in Jerusalem," opening up a further phase of missionary work within the city: to the Hellenistic Jews encountered earlier, when the Seven were chosen.

There are neo-Marcionites who will say Saul was a Hellenist who invented a new religion by removing Christianity from its old covenant roots in ethical law; some will even go so far as to say that it was this invention that made the Christian faith palatable to an international audience, a truly anti-Semitic statement if I've heard one. Scripture, however, teaches the opposite, for in this tenth chapter of the book of Acts, we read that Saul "spoke boldly in the name of the Lord Jesus and disputed *against* the Hellenists, but"—changed his mind later?—"they attempted to *kill him*" (10.29).

He refuted them so soundly their only recourse was to kill him. His impetus from the beginning was the antithesis of inventing a new religion. Kill the guy! Do away with this wiseacre protégé of Gamaliel if he's going to tell us enlightened Hellenists that the Messiah of our fathers has arrived! But Saul is now the member of a body: "When the brethren found out, they brought him down to Caesarea and sent him out to Tarsus."

So Saul returns, undoubtedly downcast, to his birthplace in Cilicia, the hardest place for a convert to crack: the hometown folks, the family. It will be fourteen years, as we learn in Galatians, before he appears again in Jerusalem. The sovereign intent of God was clearly to have Saul absent for the next major movement in Acts, so it could never be said at any point through the ages that Saul had the smallest part in it. The quiet of a caesura comes with a summary statement that could end this chapter of the book of Acts: "So the church throughout all Judea and Galilee and Samaria enjoyed peace, being built up; and going on in the fear of the Lord and in the comfort of the Holy Spirit, it continued to increase."

But it doesn't, for now the omniscient eye of Acts turns to Peter, who at the moment is in Lydda, where there are "saints." None have been officially named saints by any apostolic authority, and they need not be; this is merely another word for believers, as in "To the saints who are at Ephesus and the faithful in Christ Jesus." In Joppa, Peter finds a man who has been bedridden for eight years with paralysis, as observed by our physician author, and says to him, "Aeneas, Jesus the Christ heals you. Arise and make your bed."

Which Aeneas does. There is none of the emotional drama of a modern faith healer, nor has Aeneas traveled great distances to be brought into the presence of the healer. Through the supernatural acts that Jesus continues to perform (to recall Luke's prelude), Peter locates Aeneas and tells him to rise. There's no equivocation; he isn't maybe partly healed: "And immediately he arose." Such acts are self-attesting to the power invoked, that of the Christ, and the effect is as it should be in apostolic hands: "So all who dwelt at Lydda and Sharon saw him [Aeneas healed] and turned to the Lord."

Then Peter is informed of the death, in nearby Joppa, of Dorcas, a woman "full of good works and charitable deeds." Peter goes to the room where she is laid out, "and all the widows stood beside him weeping, and showing all the tunics and garments that Dorcas used to make while she was with them." Peter sends everyone from the room, as Christ did in similar situations, to reduce the drama, perhaps, or perhaps to protect the privacy of a helpless individual, and for the first time since the ascension of Christ, the momentous miracle we might have expected on behalf of a mighty man of the gospel like Stephen is touchingly extended to this lowly but diligent seamstress. Peter kneels and prays and then turns "to the body" and says "Tabitha, arise." Then he reaches out and raises her from the dead.

7

GENTILES AT THE GATE

I GLANCE UP AT MY HIGH WINDOWS that face north and east and see the colorlessness of an overcast after rain. This corner of the state is so arid we have ground cactus growing across our yard, and the rains, when they come, can be so local that we receive two inches and our nearest neighbor, less than a mile off, hardly a drop. It can be soaking wet on one side of our road and dusty on the other. But from the look of the sky this morning, the rain that came earlier and was accompanied by cannonades of thunder that seemed to split trees has been general. Rain was not falling faintly through the universe and faintly falling, but splattering down in a local soaking wash that left puddles in seconds.

I'm sometimes surprised by the misinformation I carry about people and places (the light at my windows is already brighter, delivering a feel of heat), and I was surprised even as a native to discover that the snow in this part of the state seldom stays and that some winters there is hardly any. The next time I look up I might see a panorama of clouds in such perfect formations against cerulean that my windows take on, as they do, the eerily new-minted appearance of freshly hung paintings, postage stamps by Magritte; as shocking as those panels of water lilies by Monet you encounter in the concrete bunker of the Modern. Water is the essence of life—even our bodies are composed mostly of it—and here people not only wait on the rain, but pray for its arrival.

You don't have to be blind or misinformed to be a Christian, as I once supposed; and, no, it doesn't help to be. The more intelligence you bring to your faith, in fact, the deeper scripture takes it, until the tail-ends of the far reaches of your most ambitious thoughts open into a spaciousness that is the first door to infinity. The sensation is usually reinforced by having been pulled at some point from a bed that smelled of death. I've said that certain books can do this, although the central one that has proliferated the others (Psalms 40.5, Eccles. 12.12, John 21.25) is scripture.

But if you work on books until you sense that of the making of them there is no end, books have the ability to assume the face of death. At stages in my life, doctors have recommended (or prescribed) that I not read or write any more of them, at least for a while, which appears to be the further experience of the preacher of Ecclesiastes, when he says "excessive devotion to books is wearying to the body." And mind. I don't mean to diminish the satisfaction I receive from the making of them, but I confess as a parent would both portions, joy and sorrow, of an offspring brought up.

One of the times when books were beyond the pale of even contemplation was before we moved here, when the load of drugs prescribed for the already mentioned multitude of illnesses, which seemed legion, had caused a muscular tension that made it an effort even to walk, although another drug was supposed to remedy that. My contact with the land, its look and contours, enabled me to jettison the drugs. A local implement dealer loaned me a tractor (a little Allis Chalmers C, for aficionados, with a belly mower) to mow the hay that hadn't been taken from our farm for years, in exchange for hay for his daughters' horses. It was October, and as I recall my state it seems I kept shedding layers

of clothes until I was bare to the sun—that fall it stayed in the seventies until November—and then in a final agile outbreak of joy
that has the feel of adolescence from this distance, I was free of my
grave wrappings, alive again. The most elementary work of creation was used to reach out to me like Peter and jolt me from the
last of those wrappings: the land.

The light at my windows has already brightened so much that
it has, in this north country that many suspect is akin to the
Arctic, the stinging brilliant heat of desert light.

Now it's apparent why we're with Peter. Another pair of visions,
as with Saul and Ananias, begins to merge, to bring about a call
from death that will send disciples across the world. For a moment
the eye of Acts moves to Caesarea to focus on Cornelius, a centurion, or Roman commander of a hundred soldiers, "a devout man,
one who feared God with all his household, and gave many alms
to the Jewish people, and prayed to God continually." So this
Italian soldier worships Jehovah and is probably a proselyte to
Judaism; he may be a proselyte of the gate, one who has access to
an outer court of the temple, or a spectator's place in the synagogue, but he probably hasn't been immersed as a proselyte and
surely hasn't received the sign of the covenant, circumcision.

On this day, at the ninth hour, an angel (or *the* Angel) appears to
him in a vision. Cornelius the soldier is at first afraid, as anyone is
when the glory of God, directly or indirectly, is revealed, as Joshua
the general and Isaiah or Zacharias were—overcome by unworthi-
ness in the blaze of perfection that confronted Saul head on.

"Your prayers and alms have ascended as a memorial before
God," the angel says; or Jehovah isn't deaf. "Now dispatch men
to Joppa, and send for a man Simon, who is also called Peter; he
is staying with a certain tanner Simon, whose house is by the sea."

No heavenly fantasies here, but unadorned, unequivocal directions that will lead the men (see the previous chapter, 9.43) directly

to Peter. Accurate directions, as the military well knows, save lives. Cornelius summons a pair of trusted servants and "a devout soldier" and explains matters—in a more credulous age, clearly—and sends the entourage off.

The next morning, as these three approach Joppa, the scene shifts in mid-sentence to Peter, who is going up to a rooftop to pray. Peter gets hungry, and as a meal is being prepared in the house below, he falls into a trance and sees heaven open and something like a sheet, held at four corners, descend. In it he can make out "all kinds of four-footed creatures, and crawling things of the earth and birds of the sky." Then a voice says, "Arise, Peter, kill and eat!"

Peter, obviously appalled at the implied contradiction of the dietary laws of Leviticus and Deuteronomy, says, "By no means, Lord"—aware that this is Jehovah—"for I have never eaten anything unholy or unclean."

"What God has cleansed, no longer consider unholy."

This happens three times, a way of God's attesting to Himself, in conformity to His word: that every fact must be established by two or three witnesses. Thus Joseph says to Pharaoh, "As for the repeating of the dream twice, O Pharaoh, it means the matter is determined by God, and God will quickly bring it about." This is a pattern that Peter has suffered personally, when the resurrected Christ, without stating openly that Peter denied knowing him three times, says in three variants to Peter, after asking Peter if he loves Him, "*Feed my sheep.*" Which is what Peter is being called at this moment to do: feed those sheep. This is a hunger from God that no food will appease.

Peter is the kind who gets wound up, gets carried away, gets flustercated, as Southern country people put it (Peter is from rural Galilee), and then bursts into decisive action that is either exactly right—"You are the Christ, the Son of the living God!"—or absolutely wrong—"You shall not die!"—and will even expostulate and curse if the situation calls for it, as he did to emphasize his denial of Christ on that night of betrayal. Now he's "greatly perplexed," and as he tries to figure out the vision, the men from Cornelius arrive at the gate of the house and call for him.

"Behold," the Spirit says, in a further conjunction, "three men seek you."

This Spirit is Christ speaking directly to Peter.

"Arise," he says, "go downstairs, and accompany them without misgivings; for I have sent them Myself."

The men from Caesarea repeat Cornelius' story, and after Peter invites them inside in Christian hospitality, they rest. The next day Peter and six disciples (three trios plus Peter make ten; see 11.12) travel back toward Caesarea. The trip is a distance of forty miles along the coast, or a walk of eight hours, say, if they keep steadily at it in this footpower of the gospel. In order to deliver that gospel in our age, you have to walk up to somebody, even if you've arrived earlier on a Concorde, and there is no proof that the spirit a Christian carries, or the Spirit who applies the gospel to a congregation, is transmitted over television. In Acts the delivery of the gospel is a personal act.

I acknowledge that God can use whatever means he wishes to call those he wishes to call, but the disciples who continue to do and to teach what Jesus began always apply the personal touch epitomized by Christ. There are many tales of evangelists, often unflattering and perhaps apocryphal, that suggest a detachment from the personal directness found everywhere in Acts. One is of a fellow who feels called to evangelize in Africa, and so stows away in a commercial airliner and arrives without a passport, an illegal alien, illuminated by not one word of the native tongue, so he's unable to explain to the authorities why he's there, much less evangelize. Another heard on good authority is of a young American who appeared in Athens and explained to a local pastor that God had told him to travel to Greece and do evangelistic work in the pastor's church. The pastor said, "As soon as I get the same message, you can start."

This answer conforms to the pattern we see in Acts, as Peter and his cohort head for Cornelius. Both sides have received the same message, parts of it triplicated, with no variants. The spirit that "leads" is all too often on the leash of personal motives, as Eliot notes, and if heartfelt concern instead of "leading" led to the neighbor next door, or the man who approaches in need (and if we're not afraid to dirty our hands or have our social standing tarnished, and don't turn aside with a sigh to let him pass in the vestibule as we calculate what a second missionary to Belize will run), then Christianity might not have the reputation it has among people with sense for encouraging the folly of fools.

We're given a preview of the scene ahead as Peter's cohort approaches: Cornelius, an adult foreigner, has gathered friends and relatives in his house. Besides being hospitable, he is taking a public stand among those who know him best, and it's he who has assembled the gathering. The Church has in no sense lured them. When Peter arrives, it seems Cornelius hasn't learned the correct etiquette each branch of the church demands of a potential convert; he falls at Peter's feet and worships him. Does Peter consider this proper obeisance to the rock on which Christ promised he would found his church?

He pulls Cornelius to his feet. "Stand up," he says. "I myself am only a man." Only a man, yet an apostle, Peter is first gently corrective, and then again forthright, as he studies the gathered crowd: "You yourselves know how unlawful it is for a man who is a Jew to associate with a foreigner or to visit him; and yet God has shown me that I should not call any man unholy or unclean."

The Spirit has supplied the meaning of the vision that Peter was trying to puzzle out for himself. It had nothing to do with unclean food, as the hunger of Jehovah for the growth of his people had led Peter to believe, but was a picture meant to validate this moment. In his forthrightness Peter might have overstepped or, more probably, echoed a tradition of the Pharisees; no specific prohibition against *visiting* outsiders exists in scripture, I believe, and Jesus certainly visited and talked with them, as Philip has. It's this propensity for tradition in Peter that will later get him into trouble, as recorded in the book of Galatians.

Cornelius relates the story of his vision with a slight variation— "a man stood before me in shining garments." This is the third time the story arrives in this chapter of triads, a pattern whose purpose will assume more than literary trinitarianism, when it applies to Saul's account of his encounter on the Damascus road. Why does Cornelius say it was a man in shining garments instead of an angel? Angels in Scripture, to render their glory bearable to human beings, assume the form of men, so this is how Cornelius *saw* the angel. It's his first recorded testimony of the visitation, and actually he adds a new detail: *his garments were shining*.

The exceptions to angels assuming the shape of men are the cherubim or seraphim of the prophets (Isa. 6, Ezek. 1, John's Revelation), and these are not angels. The prophets were given glimpses of the glory of Jehovah through these many-faceted figures that pictured attributes of His being. Now, as the appearance of the Angel of Acts to Cornelius falls into place a third time, over and above the concurrences mentioned, you should sense that the trinity is signalling from above, in this, the lengthiest section of Acts (through 11.18), to alert us to the most important turning point of the church about to occur.

At the conclusion of Cornelius' story, Peter opens his mouth and out comes the interpretation of his vision in an even clearer application—"Of a truth I now understand that God is no respecter of persons"—a truth of particular relevance to our author, Luke. Then Peter begins to preach, an act that doesn't have to take place in an auditorium. "But in every nation the man who fears Him and does what is right is welcome to him. The word which He sent to the sons of Israel"—the scriptures to his covenant people—"preaching peace through Jesus Christ."

The connections are inseparable; these potential gentile believers, too, understand this, as they hear the story of God's redemptive history, the full counsel of the gospel: "Of Him all the prophets bear witness, that through His name whoever believes in Him shall receive remission of sins." As Peter states this, Jeshua himself, the one able to save them from their sins, suddenly makes his presence apparent; the Holy Spirit falls on the entire assembly, "and all the circumcised believers who had come with Peter were amazed, because the gift of the Holy Spirit had been poured out on the Gentiles also. For they were hearing them speaking with tongues and exalting God."

This Spirit was to be the sign of redemption by the Messiah of *their* church. And to hurry briefly through the important points included in this household sermon, under the noise of the ecstatic voices rising now from every nation, Peter underlines the importance of scripture by quoting from it as he expounds upon the centrality of Jesus as Savior and Lord of All; that the Holy Spirit anointed Jesus with power; that there are witnesses able to testify to His signs and wonders, and to the death that he endured on the cross and his bodily resurrection—people who ate and drank with him after He rose from the dead; that he is the Righteous One appointed by God as judge of the living and the dead, and that his righteousness (and by implication his sacrificial death of atonement) applies to every one who believes in him, as the "prophets bear witness."

Get that into a sermon.

A change as radical as the one Saul undergoes is a mere step ahead for Peter, once he's set in the right direction, and his bluntness, even if it stuns, is always touching, for now he says, "Surely no one can refuse water for these to be baptized who have received the Holy Spirit just as we did, can he?"

Surely the disciples with Peter are as amazed at this as the phenomenon of these gentiles speaking in the language of Joel's
prophecy, but they are probably being taught as rapidly as Peter by
the Spirit. Peter is speaking to them, asking for their helping hand,
when he orders the assembly "to be baptized in the name of Jesus
Christ."

The first universal call of the gospel is proclaimed by Christ
through his apostle Peter, *not Paul.* And the whole household receives the sign of the covenant in its fullness, the baptism by water
that Jesus underwent. This baptism comes after the assembly has
received the Spirit, so baptism by water can't be called regenera-
tive; nor are there any sanctifying steps of progression that lead
to a "second baptism" by the Spirit. The baptism by fire arrives as
it always does, by the power of God alone, yet the family members
and close friends (and their children, too, we have to assume; "the
promise is to you and to your children," as Peter earlier said) receive the sign of the covenant to mark them as members of the
church, God's Israel.

Peter and the disciples are invited to stay on at the house of
Cornelius for several days.

Now Peter has to report this event to the rest of the apostles, and
when he returns to Jerusalem, "those who were circumcised took
issue with him, saying, 'You went to uncircumcised men and ate
with them.' "

They have not received the revelation Peter has and are holding to the figurative, ceremonial aspects of the law ("Circumcise
your *hearts,*" Moses and other of the prophets enjoined, "not your
foreskins") as continuing necessities.

Ratiocination here won't take the day. So what does Peter do?
He tells a story. He recounts his version of the entire event "in
orderly sequence,"[1] an extended recapitulation to a purpose, because as you observe his adherence to every detail (including

Cornelius' vision of the angel), you begin to understand the real meaning of "faithful witness." It is one who can tell a story in orderly sequence, without embellishments for dramatic effect or designs to draw attention to one's self. Which is how holy men of old spoke when they were moved by the Spirit (2 Peter 1.21), and the way in which Jesus spoke in parables. Here it happens before our eyes, in one of those moments in scripture when we are able to watch scripture testifying to its authenticity as it takes place.

This sort of witness was necessary before scripture was recorded, yes, but it's a model, too, of the way in which scripture has accreted. How does it affect the apostles who listen? "When they heard this, they quieted down, and glorified God, saying, 'Well then, God has granted to the Gentiles also the repentance that leads to life.'"

The Spirit has testified in their hearts to its truth, scripture's final test of authenticity, and this silences them. It's one of the few calms in this book that unfolds in act after act—a moment of resigned reconciliation. The apostles have had to acknowledge that the sweeping prophecies of Isaiah (chapters 42, 49, 54, 55, 60, etc.), and others of the prophets who foretold this moment, have come to pass. The blasted bunch of mixed beasts in that sheet—the Gentiles of every nation on the earth—have been added by an act of God to his Israel, the church throughout the ages.

The covenant has opened, the walls of division between every faction being broken down, and the new kingdom is not the political one of the days of David and Solomon, as many had suspected. In the kingdom of God, the *covenant* is sustained, and Christ administers grace through his disciples, all of whom will be held responsible for every idle word that comes out of their mouths. For the moment they're silent. They understand that the administration of grace makes no sense except against the immutability of the law. Though obedience to that law can never be achieved and won't earn them the first point of merit in God's sight, and circumcision did not save them (but the grace applied by Christ), it is by the standard of the law that their actions from now on will be measured, and that standard can't be removed without rendering the majesty of grace meaningless.

Francis Schaeffer has written, "Once we have come to God in the proper way, we stand in unconditional blessing. There is an unconditional portion to me and to you. It reaches all the way back to the beginning of the Bible and is emphasized in the Abrahamic covenant. If we come in the way that God has directed—namely, through the work of Christ—we will never be lost again." But he adds in his next paragraph:

> While this is true, the New Testament makes plain that for the Christian, as for the Old Testament Jew, there is also a conditional aspect. The moral law is the expression of God's character, and we are not to set it aside when we become Christians. Our obedience to it will make a difference in what happens to us both in this present life and in the believers' judgment in the future. So much of Jesus' teaching emphasizes the importance of keeping the law of God! So much of the New Testament emphasizes that we should *think* and then *live* in a conditional as well as an unconditional framework![2]

The ceremonial aspects of the law that pictured Christ as sacrifice and scapegoat, as the unclean beasts pictured the admitting of the gentiles, have been fulfilled in full by the lamb slain from the foundation of the world. There is no need to return to ritual and symbolism (see the book of Hebrews), and Jews in the nearly two thousand years since have tacitly accepted Jesus as the ultimate sacrifice and great high priest by abandoning ritual sacrifices in the temple, which has not been rebuilt since A.D. 70.

While the chapter rests on this quiet note, I want to mention two intertwined themes that its actions prompt: charismatic gifts and Christian fantasy. The arrival of the Spirit and the visible effects of its appearance have troubled the church in different eras. The second-century Montanists said that the Spirit hadn't fully arrived, partly because of political and secular corruptions that were beginning to appear in the church. There are modern charismatics who express similar reservations about most of the established church.

Traditionalists (as we might call them), in contrast to this, maintain that the gift of tongues was for a given time and purpose, so that the gospel of Christ, which was still oral, not yet inscripturated, could be spread with alacrity in this early phase of the church, throughout the Roman Empire with its polyglot of tongues. A later view was that the phenomenon of tongues was merely a facility for languages or dialects, sometimes given to foreign missionaries—which sounds too rationalistic even to me. Acts supplies support for the traditionalist view, if we note the specific purpose in each instance of the use of tongues. They aren't employed for personal, pietistic ends, but are either the signifier of the Spirit received, as in the house of Cornelius, or, when the crowd gathers after Peter's sermon on Pentecost, a means of enabling rural disciples to grant peoples of diverse languages immediate access to the gospel.

In the present-day Church, in both Roman Catholic and protestant branches, there is a charismatic movement that has gained in force and adherents, for whatever reasons, since the advent of Vatican II (1962 to 1965). Charismatics hold that the "gifts" of speaking in tongues, interpreting tongues, prophesying, and the rest, continue to this day, and in most cases they call the appearance of these gifts "baptism by the Holy Spirit." Many refer to this as a "second baptism."

The definitive discourse for the church on tongues is in First Corinthians, chapters 12 through 14. Although the apostle Paul tells the church at Corinth not to forbid speaking in tongues, he tells them that "though I speak more in tongues than any of you, I would rather speak five words of understanding than ten thousand in tongues." And he directs the church to make sure the use of tongues *in worship* takes place in a proper and orderly way (14.40)—"proper and orderly" being the single most important instruction for every church matter. Tongues also must be interpreted, if used in worship in the church, Paul states.

In his notable chapter on love (1 Cor. 13) he notes that even if he speaks in the tongues of angels but doesn't have love, he is nothing, and goes on to say (13.8) that *"tongues shall cease."* In Acts tongues are conferred only by an apostle, and by the time of the Corinthian epistle, with fewer apostles living, tongues (one of the apostolic gifts I will cover later) were already on the way to diminishment. And without apostolic control over them, as in Corinth, when they had begun to disrupt worship, they were already having to be curbed, or anyway set to proper use. They were being superseded by the canon, one part of which is Paul's letter to the Corinthians, and by the end of the first century the canon, for all intents and purposes, was closed.

I have talked with charismatics who view church members who haven't experienced this "second baptism" as halfway Christians, or anyway ones who need to "graduate." They argue that since God is eternal and unchangeable, He wouldn't end something he began, and I agree with the premise but would add that at different times he has employed different means of expressing his immutability, such as the flood, which he promised not to use again. In Ephesians 4.5, we read that there is "one Lord, one faith, *one baptism.*" This truth is enacted over and over in Acts. Baptism, the sign and seal of the covenant, performed by men, takes place before or after actual conversion, which is by the Spirit.

That is why Peter orders the household of Cornelius to be baptized *after* the assembly is already using tongues, and regenerated by the Spirit. In the case of the Philippian Jailer (16.23–34), his whole household is baptized without any outward manifestation of the Spirit, merely on the basis of the jailer's confession of faith.

The work of the Spirit in conversion is the "one baptism," and the many gifts that believers might manifest after this (enumerated in 1 Cor. 12 and Gal. 5) don't have to be those that charismatics cherish. And nobody, or nobody that I've heard from, has yet claimed the Spirit's special gift to Philip: bodily transport (not just in one's mind) to another location miles away, Azotes.

Or was that Christian fantasy, the genre of popular appeal in most of the modern Church? I have appreciated the work of C. S. Lewis, particularly his essays. *Mere Christianity* was placed in my hands at a time when I don't know what I would have done without it. If Lewis hears in heaven I hereby let him know how much it meant to me. Except for the space trilogy, however, I've never been a fan of his fiction, and I mostly appreciated the final volume, *That Hideous Strength*, when application was made to the institutions that have become as corrupt as Lewis predicted they would. I admire his scholarship in sixteenth-century literature.

But I have never been able to read the Narnia books and perhaps never will.[3] In an essay on literature, in a tone unlike his usual trenchant reasonableness, Lewis writes, "It is, therefore, an absolute rule: the more completely a man's reading is a form of egoistic castle-building, the more he will demand a certain superficial realism, and the less he will like the fantastic. He wishes to be deceived, at least momentarily, and nothing can deceive unless it bears a plausible resemblance to reality."[4]

I'm not sure how to translate "superficial realism," unless Lewis is referring to those transparent cutouts called characters I encounter in works of fantasy; and in spite of his own *Screwtape Letters*, which I also enjoyed, Lewis in this essay seems to overlook the ability of Satan to assume any semblance to deceive. In *From Poe to Valery*, T. S. Eliot wrote:

> That Poe had a powerful intellect is undeniable: but it seems to me the intellect of a highly gifted young person before puberty. The forms

which his lively curiosity takes are those in which a pre-adolescent mentality delights: wonders of nature and of mechanics and of the supernatural, cryptograms and cyphers, puzzles and labyrinths, mechanical chess-players and wild flights of speculation. The variety and ardour of his curiosity delight and dazzle; yet in the end the eccentricity and lack of coherence of his interests tire.[5]

I don't know that it's possible to revamp a reader's tastes, or that one should attempt to, but any discussion of writing should arrive, for the Christian, from a Christian point of view. It's no secret that many self-regarding and solipsistic, if not egoistic, writers such as Poe engage in imaginative work. The trend gained ascendance with the Romantics, who wanted to unleash imagination from the mundane—which also meant from morality. See Byron.

The average reader seems to assume that imaginative writers create whole worlds out of rough burlap, when they're often recording their most intimate fantasies, whether of the Stephen King horrific kind or of a Utopian otherworld more bearable than the one we daily bear. The unchecked libido runs off with the ego—to give a nod to the Viennese who validated for our century the minute examination of full-blown fantasy as an occupation. Because a "realistic" writer like Cather might transfer some of the actual details of a lifestyle or occupation she was familiar with over to a character, or transfer events analogous to her own experience into a character's life, her work is called autobiographical. That means limited and unimaginative.

When Lewis in "On Realisms" states that the tradition from *Oedipus* and *Beowulf* was an author saying, "'The strangest sight I ever saw was—', or 'I'll tell you something queerer even than that', or 'Here's something you'll hardly believe'," and adds: "Such was the spirit of nearly all stories before the nineteenth century,"[6] he doesn't acknowledge that his examples are nearly all drawn from polytheistic cultures or from those that Christianity hadn't yet reached through its acts. The response of readers to *The Old*

Wives' Tale, he says, would have been, "'But this is all perfectly ordinary. This is what happens every day.'"

Chaucer was the first great Christian realist. In "On Realisms" Lewis makes no mention of the Bible, or the art of the story as it is found in scripture, or Jesus' use of story in his parables. "Escape," Lewis writes, ". . . is common to many good and bad kinds of reading. By adding -*ism* to it, we suggest, I suppose, a confirmed habit of escaping too often, or for too long, or into the wrong things, or using *escape as a substitute for action where action is appropriate*."[7] I've emphasized the last because I believe Lewis has hit the nail on the head for the conscientious Christian. In Acts we find the beginnings of a tradition as old as the church itself: the separatist tendency to withdraw from the world, refuse to relate the gospel to it, and anticipate Christ's return to transport us to a fantasy realm.

From the time that the Law and then Christ established a standard for measuring the reality of truth, I believe that every writer has been striving for (besides accuracy and clarity) a substantiality of detail that causes the reader to say, "This is *true*." This sort of accuracy is easy to blur if you're writing about Saturn. All writing is imaginative, as any writer who has worked at it realizes; the question is in which world do you wish to exercise your imagination?

I wouldn't write, for instance, about a Zimbabwe native, not only because I feel I'd be intruding into a world in which I'm probably unwelcome but because I know I couldn't depict the Zimbabwean daily life with even a semblance of accuracy. Research might help—I've done research for all my fiction—but no amount of research can render experiential substance to a page. When a writer like John Gardner talks about the "great lie" of fiction, he doesn't mean the writer is perpetrating a lie in order to pull the wool over a reader's eyes, but that the reader is able to enter a fictional world so fully he takes the metaphor constructed of words to be a reality as substantial as the one in which he just dropped that book to the floor.

I might essay to write about a teenage Eskimo, since the rigors of the North Dakota winter have taught me something about Arctic experience; that he's a teenager would absolve me of a mature apprehension of the Arctic. I'd keep him in an igloo or on a sun-stunned white plain. Only connect, E. M. Forster has said in one of his credos for the writer, but you can't connect even dots if you don't know the sequence (in this world we occupy) that establishes the regularity of numerals. The best stories unfold in the orderly fashion in which reality imprints itself upon a consciousness minute by minute.

Accuracy occurs when proper weight is given through the metaphor of words to an act or process or object within that reality. Truth is reality in all its precision and fullness (containing molecules structured like solar systems), often bearing the idiosyncratic tinge of the narrator or observer—in a radical example, Van Gogh. "Realistic" writing is at least as artful and arduous as chess, since everybody is familiar with its rules and boundaries. My disconnected *imaginings* as I attempt to sleep or assess the effect of pages sent off (a fruitless occupation), juggling images from a dozen directions at once, are at variance to the actual life that each one of us, sinner and saint, has to contend with each hour.

When I think of the great Christian writer Shakespeare, of his histories and tragedies and comedies, a few of which are imaginative, I sense that what enables even semifantasy in his work, as in *The Tempest* or *A Midsummer Night's Dream,* to register as not so fantastical in its application to me and my role in this world is the quality of his people. They are palpable, individual characters: *people.* Writers are not mini-Creators, as the Romantics viewed it, who operate on the vertical to create glittering worlds of their own design. They are often grappling with every talent they have to present horizontal truth.

The tradition in fiction that attempts to portray this world as it exists (and would have been a bore to previous generations, according to Lewis) is largely the Christian tradition. Its power is that the best of its characters convey the breathing reality of members of the household of God. We couldn't otherwise meet these people and extend the hospitality of our hearts to them in the edification that builds up the Church in love.

This is the "enlightening brush with other peoples, other cultures," as the academic world defines such reading, on its terms. "Suspension of disbelief" is not only an awful Coleridgian jawbreaker but a binary confusion you never have to wonder about when you feel another person take your hand. Characters in the best fiction enter your life with that directness, and the more they conform to the image of Christ, the more they provide a means for a young man, for instance, to walk at the side of a father he never had. And with those characters who don't conform to Him, since they aren't actual people who can do us physical harm but metaphors for people and the states we sometimes find ourselves in, we can always walk the extra mile along their way and learn from them before bidding them good-bye.

We can let the gentiles in; we can open up to unbelief, knowing it can't overthrow us. This is an area in which perhaps parents worry the most, for the sake of their children. How are young people affected by what they read? What do they learn from fantasy—which is not necessarily a child's choice of genre but the one adults choose for them. Is it a better genre? Can they translate what those bears and lions are up to in a way that could be called, generously, even imaginatively, constructive? In realistic fiction they could learn how to start a car, but would they steal one? At least the discussion could be brought up. In realistic fiction they could learn to honor their parents, not a vague concept of honor transmitted from the stars.

In an essay entitled "Big Ideas and Dead-End Thrills," the imaginative science fiction writer Thomas M. Disch laments the present quality of the cyberpunk tales overtaking his genre, because of their violence. But as he recalls his early work in comparison to some of the awfulness of, in his own example, Edgar Allen Poe, he says "the same compensatory mechanism is at work"—a mechanism that is a means of coping with adverse circumstances: "Perhaps it is no accident that the plot of my tale, like Poe's, features a tragic romance of a sort that only young men of pristine inexperience and perfected amour propre have ever imagined. And who should their readership be but other such young men, for whom the authors' inauthenticities are more solacing than a lifetime subscription to *Connoisseur*"[8]—where the young would learn, in reality, how those in better circumstances actually live.

Earlier in his essay Disch mentions a talk on "The Embarrassment of Science Fiction" that he gave in 1975, "in which I developed a notion I had first advanced in 1970, in the bulletin of the Science Fiction Writers of America: that science fiction should be accounted, and can best be understood as, a branch of children's literature. I noted how often a taste for SF is acquired in early adolescence—the golden age of science fiction, our tribal wisdom has it, is thirteen. . . . I deplored, at some length, the limitations that resulted from the genre's demographics."[9] What he laments now is the way the genre has been "dumbed-down" even further by Hollywood and television. Summing up, he says, "The final and most excruciating callowness of youth is what SF readers particularly prize: Big Ideas. . . . To a certain degree SF provides a natural playground for the harmless exercise of Big Ideas, even those that are radically unsound." He points out that the "tendency is always to venture toward the current ideological limit"—and mentions one well-known SF writer "who promotes the return to a Native American never-never land." He concludes his essay:

> Ideological silliness is an affliction more tolerable in the young, and, for reasons I've tried to lay out, exactly the same may be said of a taste

for science fiction. This is not meant to be my way of abjuring the field or declaring that I am not now nor have I ever been a science-fiction writer. I have been and I continue to be. I will even go on reading and reviewing the stuff, as long as some small portion of what is published continues to suit my taste. But I won't act as a booster for the genre as a whole, which has become, as a publishing phenomenon, one of the major symptoms of, if not a causal agent in, the dumbing-down of the younger generation and the lowering of the lowest common denominator.[10]

I regret to have to report that no Christian writer has spoken on the subject with Disch's candor. In fact, you will probably find the most resistance to reexamining imaginative writing, which includes science fiction and fantasy, within the Christian community. That community seems to want to live in an ideological never-never land, in which it takes at least two transpositions—translating the fantasy into a recognizable truth and then attempting to transpose that translation into the life we know—to bring the fiction home. If you look at the genre's lifeline (any Christian publishing house's list of fiction), you are forced to come to the conclusion that members of the modern church want to be drawn out of the life they're to attend to, or dumbed-down, if not deceived.

But I also sense a fragrance of hope for contemporary writing, and Christian fiction in particular. In recent years I've seen students grow more interested in accuracy, in the many-layered dimensions of reality, and in the importance of people over recycled Big Ideas. Many are turning from the speeded-up imagery and violence of TV, that great promoter of the fantastic, which always aims for the lowest common denominator, to books. A new generation of readers is emerging, many of them educated at home or in conscientious parochial or private Christian schools, and they are able to read critically. They aren't satisfied by genres that mimic another medium, either film or television, and search for the truth that arrives only when the world as it exists is examined in a scientific sense to convey those "five words that instruct," as Paul exhorts, and so help each of us bring further aspects of existence captive into obedience to Christ.

Though the apostles accept Peter's story, a division rises among their disciples. Some do not believe God has done what he said he would through his prophets and apparently refuse to follow what the Spirit has taught the apostles, through Peter, to teach. They want the Messiah to be available only to their own, for we read that some go off to preach to Jews and Gentiles, and some "to Jews alone."

King Herod (Agrippa I), as though taking advantage of this division, has James, the brother of John, one of the sons of Zebedee, "put to death with the sword." Herod doesn't do this directly, but the statement naming only him codifies—as our modern law, following suit, also does—his guilt, not that of the nameless hireling who wielded the sword to behead John (which doesn't mean this person wasn't at least partly culpable), and so Saul's part in Stephen's stoning is slammed harder home.

The family of Herod, which was from Idumea, south of Judea (we encounter Herod I, Herod Antipas, and Herod Philip in the New Testament, and will encounter Agrippa II), rose to power during the Hasmonean reign, from about 100 to 75 B.C.

Because the Idumeans were forcibly converted to Judaism by John Hyrcanus, the family was officially Jewish.[11] They were artful political manipulators who always seemed able to stay on the right side of Rome while keeping in the good graces of the spiritual rulers of the people, the Sanhedrin, but they don't seem to have endeared themselves to the local populace. This was perhaps partly due to their extravagant living and sexual conduct; Herodias was married to two of her uncles and begat Salome, who married another.

So when we read that Herod's act of putting James to death "pleased the Jews," we should probably read "the Sanhedrin." They had been after these disruptive public preachers for some time, and by my count there are about ten thousand baptized members into the new covenant in Jerusalem and its environs at this point, most every one Jewish. When Herod notices the pleasure he's brought to the spiritual establishment (the group that probably suggested the beheading, as it surely was, as with John the Baptist), "he proceeded to arrest Peter also." The original troublemaker.

This is "during the days of the Feast of Unleavened Bread," leading up to Passover, and Herod intends to hold Peter in jail and execute him after Passover, probably not wanting to desecrate the high holy days and so turn the populace against him—or perhaps it's the Sanhedrin who have helped him decide. Since they knew the emotional and spiritual state of the people in Jerusalem, the tactics, again, suggest their hand. The general populace, as you recall, has been glorifying God at the miraculous acts that the apostles have been performing—the main reason Peter and John were set free before.

Herod delivers Peter over to four squads of soldiers who are to guard him, a significant detail, and he's kept in prison until the appointed time. "But prayer was made without ceasing to God for him by the church," we read. A squad of soldiers is a small tactical group that arranges itself in square formation; here a quaternion, or four sets of four soldiers, to make sixteen. Luke adds further details; Peter is kept unclothed and, even when he sleeps, is bound by two chains to two soldiers. There are guards outside the door watching the prison itself, in two separate sets.

Herod or his henchmen obviously don't want to see Peter escape. But that's not the entire reason for Luke's careful detail. On the evening of the end of Passover, as Herod is about to "bring Peter forward," an Angel of the Lord appears beside Peter, and light shines through the prison. Striking Peter's side, the angel lifts him, saying, "Rise up quickly!"

The chains fall off Peter's hands.

"Gird yourself and put on your sandals," the angel commands, and when Peter does so, the angel says, "Throw on your robe and follow me."

From these patient parental urgings we begin to get an idea of Peter's confusion (and can imagine the soldiers lying stunned the way Saul did) and a sense of how close Peter and the apostles must have been, day by day, to the visionary world while having to maintain a sure footing in this one. We read that Peter, though participating in the moment, "did not know that what was being done by the angel was real, but thought he was seeing a vision." In other words, he wonders for a moment if he isn't being deceived.

Out in the street, he comes to himself, and thinks, "Now I know for sure that the Lord has sent forth his angel and rescued me from the hand of Herod and from all that the Jewish people were expecting." On this Passover, the testamental bridge of Peter's thought is extraordinary. The Angel of Death who passed over the lintels marked with blood in Egypt, in order to spare the first-born of the Israelites has passed over this firstborn of the church, for the sake of the spilled blood of his Christian brother on the prison floor. The Angel of the Lord has arrived to lead him from the hand of Herod, out of bondage of death, as the Israelites were led from bondage to Pharaoh by the pillar of fire each night. And the angel first strikes him on the side to raise him from imminent death, as Christ was struck through the side by a spear, his heart's blood spilled for his church.

This is the Simon, now called Peter, the rock on whom Christ said He would build his church, one of the stones of its foundation through his apostleship, and indeed the one on whose basis and solidity the gentiles have entered the Church. In the act of releasing Peter, the Lord has validated what Peter said to the

Sanhedrin; that he must obey God rather than men—an apostolic statement about church and civil authority. Now that God has rescued Peter from prison, He has added His confirmation to the statement, and in the same stroke has freed Peter from those authorities who not only expected him to die but doubted his Messiah's life. Jesus is the Angel of Acts.

Peter is off into the night.

He somehow makes it to the house of Mary, mother of John Mark, and much of the following information is supported by Peter's flight to this refuge he knows best. John Mark is generally conceded to be the author of the Gospel of Mark, and he was, according to good authority (elders of the first-century church who knew the apostle John, brother to James just martyred),[12] Peter's amanuensis. So the gospel of Mark, with its headlong, newsy breathlessness is the gospel of Peter. The house of John Mark is probably the house where the upper room of the Last Supper and Pentecost is located,[13] and we learn that many are gathered together there, praying—in the church's continual prayer for Peter, we must assume.

A servant Rhoda, a detail that suggests wealth and a house large enough to have an upper room to accommodate a hundred or more, hears him at the gate and runs to tell the others, without unlocking the gate, however. They say, "You're out of your mind" and "It's his angel," as if they, too, are participants in a night vision. Peter is at last let in but finally has to go to "another place" for safety, and in the continuing nightmare, Herod "examines" the guards, most likely a euphemism for torture, and then executes every one of them. It's for this reason, in a sense, that Luke takes the time to supply minute details; all the witnesses to these details, and to the impossibility of Peter escaping by other than a supernatural act, are now dead, shut up for good. This is one miraculous event the Jerusalem populace isn't going to hear about.

But Peter is alive and probably later informs Luke, in the way in which he later dictated his gospel to John Mark, as a faithful witness. We know he wrote epistles. Why no gospel? It would appear that no apostle is to be seen as having particular ascendance; Peter did what he was called to do. None of the writers of scripture wrangled about who would write what. They worked in one sense as every writer does: helplessly—doing what they had to, but to a degree no writer nowadays can imagine; their helplessness was under the direct weight of God's Spirit.

If the Spirit still inspires prophetic or charismatic utterance, then it must direct the stunning utterances some writers attain trying to string together five words that make sense. This is the untenable position that some poets and hymn writers from the past, and the present, too, have assumed: that their words arrive through the Spirit. The dangers inherent in this should be obvious, without trying to imagine how a writer of that conviction would deal with an editor who said the whole thing had to be scrapped. If such works are of the Spirit, they should appear in scripture, as they appear in our hymn books—Deuterocanonical, I guess.

There is an interesting note before Peter leaves for that "other place," which is probably a house not as well known to the authorities as this house that seems a locus of the new covenant. Peter says, "Report these things to James and the brethren." So another James, besides the one who has died under Herod, exists in Jerusalem and seems a person of authority. Historical consensus is that this James is the younger brother of Christ (Mark 6.3) and is the author of the Epistle of James. As Acts continues to unfold, James seems to assume apostolic authority in Jerusalem, or certainly becomes a pillar of power in the church, but if he was directly called by Christ to apostolic office, no evidence for this exists.

Herod cannot locate Peter and travels to Caesarea, the beautiful port built by Herod the Great—the center of Roman government and the city in which this movement in Acts began, at the house of Cornelius, the Roman centurion. In a brief glance by Luke at local history (the history in scripture is accurate, and should be read so), we learn that Herod is of a mind to engage in war with the people of Tyre and Sidon, but that they have an advocate in Blastus, Herod's chamberlain—the implication being that Herod would like to make war on them but doesn't quite dare to without Rome's approval.

Gaius, an earlier Roman emperor, rewarded Herod's fidelity by giving him the tetrarchies of his relatives Philip and Lysanius, and the present emperor, Claudius, has added Judea to his rule, enlarging his realm to nearly the size of the one held by his grandfather, Herod the Great. This is why the people of Tyre and Sidon come to Blastus seeking peace; they're aware of Herod's ingratiation with Rome. Their country, Phoenicia, is dependent upon Samaria and Judea, Herod's domain, for its supply of food, Luke writes.

All of this surely flatters Herod's sense of power, and none of it is merely innocent local color or a physician's detail. It is meant to suggest Herod's mental state at the moment, after the deaths he has recently engineered, and also to illustrate the dependence of civil government upon the hand of God. Imagine unleashing Herod on somebody he hates, after his treatment of James and sixteen of his own guards. The earth, too, is the Lord's, and all that is in it; even the crops the Phoenicians need (a reversal of Israel's plight in the days of Joseph) depend upon the weather, His domain.

In Caesarea, "on an appointed day," Herod Agrippa dons his royal robes and mounts his rostrum, or throne, and begins delivering an address "to them," the representatives from Tyre and Sidon—but this is obviously a royal, public event, or else Tyre sent some wonderful flatterers, because Luke writes, "And the people kept crying out, 'The voice of a god and not of a man!'" Herod is at least a nominal Jew, and "because he did not give God the glory" but perhaps nodded, acknowledging that he was of His approximate stature, immediately an angel of the Lord struck him—the one that passed over Peter while he was in prison—"and he was eaten by worms and died."

Did he die immediately, his flesh a crawling mass of wormy gore, as we might imaginatively see it? The text only says that he is struck by an angel, at perhaps his finest moment, a further miraculous act of judgment. It may have been a wasting disease or a more immediate one—a closer examination would have brought an exact diagnosis: Luke knew which worms were what. But in the artful economy of Acts, where years elapse within a phrase, we're given a picture of the act and only a suggestion of the effect of its awful end.

All these angels. This is not fantasy; they are not fantastical, but further signs and wonders of an actuality: that God in Christ is acting out of the heavenly realm to confirm his direction over every act in Acts. In most all instances, it would not be farfetched to say that the appearances in Acts are direct interventions of the glorified Christ, who from a biblical perspective is the Angel of the Lord. It's this angel who appears to Abraham at the moment he intends to sacrifice Isaac and to Joshua after he crosses into Canaan, and who orders Joshua to remove his sandals because he is on holy ground—as Moses was instructed to do in the presence of the burning bush.

Peter, however, is told to pull his sandals on, because the arrival of the Messiah has made the earth His tabernacle. In another Old Covenant story, the wrestling match with Jacob, the angel is the *Angel of the Lord,* clearly a preincarnate appearance of Christ. In Cornelius' testimony about his vision, the man's *garments were shining.* This is the exact description of those who witnessed Christ's transfiguration with Moses and Elijah. It is this glory that Stephen sees in his glimpse of heaven, the same fieriness that blinds Saul when it faces him directly, without the mediation of a vision.

And so in most instances in Acts, and particularly when the angel is "The Angel of the Lord," it is a post-resurrection appearance of Christ. He sometimes also sends angelic ministers, and his Spirit appears at other times. In a true sense Jesus is, though a distinct person in the Trinity, the Holy Spirit—"the same in substance, equal in power and glory"—and it is the acts of Jesus you follow in Acts.

Why is it that we moderns, wrapped in our scientific veneer, believe in Carlos Castaneda's Don Juan and UFOs and reincarnated spirits that consult with musical-comedy actresses and employ them as amanuenses for their books, but balk at the mention of angels? We are better believers in speculative worlds of fantasy that do not exist.

ALL THE WORLD

and the Persecution of Paul

8

C O U N C I L S   A N D

B O U N D A R I E S

When the Pilgrims landed at Plymouth Rock, to quote William Bradford, "they fell upon their knees and blessed the God of heaven, who had brought them over the vast and furious ocean, and delivered them from the perils and miseries thereof, again to set their feet on the firm and stable earth, their proper element." The style of this passage, incidentally, with its repetition and parallelism, shows that its author knew the Bible; and it is a point worth making early in any treatment, however brief, of American literature and Christian doctrine that the Bible has been the greatest single influence on our literature.

Randall Stewart,
American Literature and Christian Doctrine

IN HIS ADDRESS at the Areopagus on Mars Hill, Paul tells the Athenian crowd that God made from one blood every nation on earth, and has determined their appointed times and the boundaries of their habitation. Luke has recorded how the Phoenicians were dependent on the agriculture of the domain of the now deceased Herod for their food. Such a dependency is a form of bondage, as the Israelites learned in Joseph's day, and I'm sure that most residents of the U.S. don't recognize their dependence on the farmers they sometimes malign.

Within the boundaries of the habitation where I presently live, this rectangular state located neither in the Arctic nor in the Midwest, the major ingredient of one-half of the bread consumed in the U.S. in one year is raised—hard red spring wheat. If that production weren't limited by the government, or bought up and stored by the government in reserves, or sold by the government to other nations at a price lower than the cost of the fuel and labor to produce it (more bondage), then the 15,000 or so farmers left in our state, exercising proper stewardship over the land, could bring in a harvest at least five times as great. Our state alone could provide bread for more than 600 million people for a full year.

The increase of crops, however, is dependent not only on stewardship and government, but on the weather, and for the last few years North Dakota has had hardly any snow or rain and is suffering from a drought as severe as any of the 1930s. When I was growing up in the state, about 90 percent of the residents were involved in farming. Since that time the population has hovered near 600,000, or about five people per square mile, but now it is beginning to decline, and the number of farmers still in business after the boom or bust attitude initiated by the government and bankers—*get big,* they counseled—and the foreclosures that as a result have followed so fast that nobody can keep up with even the local auctions, presently stands at about 3 percent.

To keep up on our situation, watch the bread rack at your store. And when you pick up your next loaf, remember that half of it came from here and that a community within the boundaries of this habitation is working to deliver your staff of life. Our nearest neighbors, the two most fiscally conservative, have managed to hang on, but if they're unable to get through this drought and their lights blink out to our north and south, we won't have any neighbors. It's not a mere matter of loneliness. When family-run farms fold, then outside interests, corporations and conglomerates, take over, and if they come to control the market, the price of your bread (ditto for spaghetti) could triple. Or worse.

So when farmers talk about the weather, so boringly as some say, they're actually considering the welfare of their occupation, which affects others, or are attempting to fathom the attitude God has taken toward them. Ag-college farmers scoff at this last attitude. They point to the cloud masses moving through the atmosphere that are tracked by satellites and simulated on TV (we got that in the Dakotas a while back), or the increasing greenhouse effect, or the hole in our stratospheric ozone. Through most of January, the month that tends to be the coldest here, it has been in the forties and fifties, even the sixties for a week, in this year of our Lord 1992. In these days people tend to point to the effects without stepping past the veneer of televised science to consider the source that moves clouds.

Wind? What's its source? A heating and cooling effect, and perhaps the stratospheric currents we're only beginning to learn about. And their source? The sun and perhaps evaporation, in the case of clouds. Evaporation? Water rising into the atmosphere. The source of water? The planet. Of heat? The sun. And what's their source? They appeared after a cosmic Big Bang, they say, a theory as durable as any, perhaps, and one whose basic premises adhere as well to the history of creation that scripture registers. No scientist recorded that. One of the most knowledgeable living scientists, Robert Jastrow, has stated that theology has as valid an explanation for the origin of the universe as science.[1] Public schools and even Christian schools will not tell you that the eras of the earth you must memorize as fact, as I did, are merely innovative guesses of people armed with data as complete as they could assemble at the time, as any honest scientist will confirm.

In the last decade and a half, the theory of the origin of the universe has changed several times in the scientific community itself, and it keeps changing, or evolving, as more data are assembled from within our stratosphere (and without) and computers attempt to crunch the data into something to suggest a pattern that will set newer boundaries. The probability of a cell that contains the DNA of life appearing, whether mud was struck by lighting or however you wish the first spark to ignite, and then evolving into a human being is about as great, as one number-cruncher has estimated, as the probability of a tornado assembling a 747 out of a junkyard.

One of the methods of estimating the age of the earth and the plant and animal life found on it or in it, carbon dating, is based on two suppositions: that the earth was about the age that scientists estimated it to be when carbon dating began (in the 1940s) and that there has never been in the entire history of the earth any radical change in the amount of sunlight reaching it, such as the radical change that everybody has experienced over the past five years.

The deterioration of the ozone layer, if that is what it is, may be the result of sin—all those stinky hair sprays from the fifties and sixties and seventies, which I thank God my wife never used. If that is what it is, its effects might be the beginning of a way to slowly move parts of the polar ice cap—other than by towing icebergs south, as some state governments have essayed—to the places afflicted by drought. This would be a farfetched and expensive process, but every person and every nation, too, must suffer the effects of sin and do their best to make restitution. There are few limits people won't go to when their lives and the lives of their children are at stake. For a loaf of bread. I pray that we will be able to continue to produce it. But this, again, is in God's hands and applies to this appointed time within every habitation where people presently dwell.

At this chapter's opening, in his paragraph on the Pilgrims, Randall Stewart is merely restating a commonplace that Christian writers and teachers of literature in our day are reluctant to claim.

C. S. Lewis never made a declaration quite so definitive about British literature, although he could have.[2] A contemporary of his, the eminent historian Sir Arthur Bryant wrote, "The most important element in our history has been the continuity of the Christian tradition."[3] In our culture it is not correct to mention a religion unless it's a dead one, or shamanistic, or declaimed by a bag person, now wealthy, whose battered Bloomie's bag is actually an oracle—or the one sanctioned by the powers that legislate universities: Humanism. Ours is the exact cultural agenda and atmosphere that Saul faces in Acts.

The rest of the book, or approximately its second half, covers the broader missionary acts of the church and the definition of "church" itself, as its structure begins to assemble while its geographic boundaries press farther outward, until eventually (but not in my version of Acts) they reach the shores of this continent, via the Pilgrims. It would not be inaccurate to say that the organization and shape of the church had to be established before it could spread abroad. This is certainly true of writing; the more shaped an oeuvre in idiosyncratic content and form (Dante, Kafka, Marquez), the more universal its appeal.

While Peter was opening the Covenant to every nation, Saul and Barnabas have been at Antioch, and it's best to take a backward loop to catch up with them. It has been written (11.19) that "those who were scattered because of the persecution that arose over Stephen traveled as far as Phoenicia, Cyprus, and Antioch, preaching the word to no one but Jews alone." Some of these, "men of Cyprus and Cyrene," reach Antioch, on the lower tip of present-day Turkey, just north of Syria, and begin speaking to Hellenists about the Messiah. Large numbers are converted in Antioch, and when the church in Jerusalem hears of it, they send Barnabas to investigate. He recognizes "the grace of God," rejoicing with the Antiocheans and encouraging them in the faith, and then goes off to Damascus to locate Saul, surely remembering Saul's fiery confrontations with the Hellenists in Jerusalem.

Barnabas and Saul return to Antioch and remain for a year (a small part of the fourteen when Saul is absent from Jerusalem) and meet "with the church" and teach "considerable numbers." Note the delegatory powers; Barnabas, sent by the church at Jerusalem to survey the scene, is so impressed that he fetches Saul to help teach; they add to the increase of the church without reporting back to Jerusalem. We learn at this point that it's in Antioch that the church was first called "Christian"— which was probably a derisive term, as Methodist and Calvinist and Fundamentalist were, originally, and in many instances continue to be.

Then we read, "And now in these days prophets came down from Jerusalem to Antioch." Travelers "came down" from Jerusalem in the parlance of the time, even when they were heading *up* north, as we would put it, because Jerusalem was on a mountain and was also the high holy city. These travelers are prophets. Do they arrive to check up on Barnabas? No, since the scriptures of the new covenant weren't yet written, these prophets, like the prophets of the old covenant, were portable sources of prophetic information (when they received it) for their terms on earth. One of these prophets, Agabus, who will continue to appear through Acts, seems a sort of mime; he never uses language in his early appearances, much less an exotic tongue, but appears to enact events that will take place. Now he "began to indicate by the Spirit that there was surely to be a great famine through all of the world." Was it the result of a drought like ours?

"And this took place in the days of Claudius," Luke reports, meaning the famine, another historical event. The gathering of common property in Jerusalem is set now in sharper light—it is city dwellers who suffer the most during a famine—and the next verse states: "Then the disciples, each according to his ability, determined to send relief to the brethren living in Judea." This they do, perhaps over the period of Herod's violence, because Saul and Barnabas are chosen to deliver the offering, and we pick these two up at the close of chapter 12, returning from their "ministry" to Jerusalem. So we can suspect that at least a decade has passed since the conversion of Saul.

The church at Antioch has its prophets, too, including "Manaen, who had been brought up with the tetrarch Herod," so it can't be said that prophets were exclusive messengers of a central church at Jerusalem. And note how closely Christianity has approached Herod's throne, since some translate Manaen's relationship as "Herod's foster brother." So perhaps Herod's ire toward James and Peter contains jealousy and fear that we can't trace. The group of teachers and prophets gathered at Antioch (13.1), a plurality of them, suggests that "the church at Antioch" may actually be a number of local churches; that is, the church for the Antioch Region. The probability of this is strengthened by the next act. As this church "ministered to the Lord and fasted," the Holy Spirit says, "Now set apart for Me Barnabas and Saul for the work to which I have called them."

Prayer and fasting indicate the serious intent of the church, and then its elders lay hands on Saul and Barnabas, as hands have been laid on "the Seven." Although Saul is an apostle and Barnabas one of the teachers or prophets in the Antiochean Church (13.1), they are "set apart" or sanctified by the laying on of hands for a specific work "to which *I* have called them." No detailed explanation is given of this work, but the Lord speaking through his Spirit has obviously informed the church that the two are to set off on a journey across the world to seek others of the way.

There is no mission board of origin in a higher church at Jerusalem, and it is the church at Antioch that calls and ordains them; both churches are under the headship of Christ. Saul and Barnabas will not visit missionary societies on their return trips, nor make tours to churches while on "furlough" with pleas for support. They will be self-supporting, a point Paul makes in his epistles (1 Cor. 9.1–15, 2 Thess. 3.8) and Luke in Acts (20.34, 28.30). This is the structure for missions taught by Acts. The local church should by means of prayer (and fasting wouldn't hurt) choose with care and ordain and send out missionaries from its own plurality of elders, and should expect those missionaries to support themselves on the field, while the church also tows the line in caring for its own.

A denomination or string of churches that meets with the missionary and his family only when they appear to solicit funding, and after that only every few years, should not undertake the responsibility of supporting a missionary. These churches don't have personal knowledge of the missionary or his family, don't know their spiritual state, and won't be able to oversee directly the missionary's doctrine or private life, so that any false teachings or depredations that occur in the field cannot, as they should, be halted that day.

Having said all this, it is discouraging to have to add that there is almost no church in the United States that adheres to any of these teachings disclosed in Acts.

Now the great sea voyages of the book begin, and as a commentator has said, "If a man's universe is the arena in which his mature energies are concentrated, the Aegean Sea was the center of Paul's world"[4]—a statement we might receive as a plausible truth if Saul's relationship to the world were merely Homeric. The writer does add "and the main centers of his activity were Corinth and Ephesus." But this doesn't set our vessel of the church off on the clear course Acts delineates, with Paul's ordination by the church centered in Antioch and his regular returns to it. It's another misinterpretation, this at the outer edge, of the meaning of the missionary work of the church.

Now I see I've started calling Saul Paul, but Acts will soon do that. And maybe you wonder what makes me say the Spirit has called him and Barnabas to undertake a missionary journey of sea-faring magnitude. They head straight for the coast, a short walk, for them, of a dozen miles or so, to Selucia, and board a sailing vessel for Cyprus. That quick. The student of Acts will recall that Barnabas is a Cypriot and that "men of Cyprus and Cyrene" were in the church at Antioch, so there are enough connections to suggest that Saul and Barnabas aren't sailing blind. They had contacts to pursue. "And when they reached Salamis," Luke writes, as if Salamis had been their goal all along, "they started preaching the word of God in the synagogues of the Jews."

The proclamation of that word is the power of God for salvation to all who believe, Paul writes to the Romans, to *the Jew first,* and also to the Greek. Now why would somebody who invented a religion palatable to Hellenists state this as the ground rule for delivering the gospel? Paul keeps to the blueprint set down by Jesus, who, when he first sent out his twelve apostles, instructed them to go not to the gentiles or Samaritans (Mat. 10.5–6), but to the lost sheep of Israel. I have heard it said that we are in a different dispensation, and in the sense that Christ has made the covenant new by filling out every shadowy type and ritual by the sacrifice of his own body, that is accurate, but in proclaiming the dispensation, as we may call it, initiated by Peter, Saul does not say, "First we must minister to the gentiles."

Nor does he. He goes first to the synagogues on this missionary journey commissioned by the Spirit. Until the destruction of Jerusalem and the Temple, Israel's sheep were the first to receive the call to return to the covenant; afterward, they were given an equal chance with the rest of the nations, until the day when they will all be called in and God's Israel made complete (Rom. 9–11). The application for our present day is one that many won't want to hear: missionaries and evangelists should be going, first, to the apostate church, as missionaries from black African churches are now arriving, properly, in the apostate U.S.

Two present details are relevant: John Mark is with Barnabas and Saul. He returned to Antioch with them after they delivered the famine funds collected for Jerusalem. If Mark is the "interpreter" of Peter, as the aged presbyter put it, he probably represented Peter's preaching as he heard it or as Mark practiced it himself. The Gospel of Mark is concerned primarily with the *acts* of Jesus, and to quote Machen, "Mark seems to be following with great exactness the scheme of early apostolic preaching as it is laid down in Acts 10.37–43."[5] The cited passage is an extract from Peter's sermon in the house of Cornelius, to the gentiles.

John Mark is now at Paul's side.

Then the synagogues, which in Greek means *assemblies:* with the Babylonian exile, the scattering of the central Jewish kingdom became widespread; there was never again a theocracy in Jerusalem, no new David. Though Ezra returned with exiles to rebuild the Temple and confirm the covenant, so that the throne of David would indeed be established forever, the intermarrying of the nation of Israel with other nations had begun; and though the walls of Jerusalem were rebuilt under Nehemiah and Jeremiah, the diaspora continued until it reached Italy.

Synagogues, local assemblies where the word of God was studied and prayers offered up, were built and became the locus of the far-flung Jewish communities. Their beginnings are suggested by Daniel, who defied Babylonian law by retiring to his house at a certain hour every afternoon to pray. Whatever the exact origin of synagogues (and it seems lost in history), their existence as places of assembly for God's people is mentioned throughout the gospels, and it is toward these synagogues that Saul now heads.

"And after they had gone through the whole island as far as Paphos"—to all its synagogues, I suspect; Paphos is on the southwestern coast of Cyprus, at the opposite end from Salamis—"they found a certain magician, a Jew and false prophet whose name was Bar-Jesus." Son of Jesus is the meaning, but the English barring of Jesus would also be apt. This false prophet is "with the proconsul, Sergius Paulus, a man of intelligence"—the administrator of Roman rule and a gentile, of course, who must have found Bar-Jesus helpful, or necessary, to have near. Sergius Paulus may have heard of the mission of Saul and Barnabas to the Jewish community through Bar-Jesus, for now he summons the disciples to him "to hear the word of God."

Elymas the magician, "for so his name is translated," Luke notes, in a sudden name-hopping, keeps contradicting them, "seeking to turn the proconsul away from the faith." Finally Saul ("who is also Paul"—again from Luke), filled with the Holy Spirit, stares him down and says, "O son of the devil, full of all deceit and craftiness, enemy of all righteousness, will you not stop perverting the right ways of the Lord?"

Not an irenic correction, as Jesus' to Peter on the same issue also was not: "Get behind me, Satan! You are an offense to me, for you do not savor the things of God but of men." You should recognize that Saul, through the Spirit, is able to see into people's intentions as Jesus was. Which is only the beginning, because with this first recorded apostolic sign from Saul, he steps into the realm of the miraculous and declares, "And now, behold, the hand of the Lord on you! And you will be blind, not seeing the sun for a while."

The identical affliction that Saul, now Paul, suffered himself! A mist and darkness fall on Elymas, and he, like Saul before, "went about seeking those who would lead him by the hand." The transformations and shifts of name are so swift they can slip past in a first reading, though we should register the proconsul *Paulus*, whose name some commentators suggest Paul took up—a minor note under the more momentous chord of spiritual change signified by a change in name: Abram to Abraham, Jacob to Israel, Simon to Peter. Does Paul pity in another the state he suffered as Saul? You can't find this in the text, except to realize that Elymas is in the darkness that brought Saul to light, and tradition has it that Elymas discovered in darkness, like Saul, infinite light—the bar removed from Jesus' entry.

The result is the same as always with any apostolic sign or wonder, even these darkest miracles of judgment: when the proconsul Sergius Paulus "saw what had been done, being astonished at the teaching of the Lord," he believed.

Paul and his companions, as Luke has it, put out to sea from Paphos to the port of Perga, in Asia Minor—the present country of Turkey—and John Mark, elusive enigma that he is, deserts them. This is how many commentators suggest the Greek here should be read ("leaving them he turned back"), and this is Paul's interpretation of the event (15.38). Paul and Barnabas travel a hundred and fifty miles overland to another Antioch, in Pisidia, near modern Aksehir. In the synagogue there on the Sabbath, the "officials," a plurality of elders it seems, ask Paul to give "a word of exhortation."

Luke cracks the door slightly on the doings inside a synagogue of his time, and the glimpse is the same as when Jesus reads from Isaiah in the synagogue in Nazareth (Luke 4.16–30)—a simple service, a "reading of the Law and the Prophets," and then an invitation to Paul: "If you have any exhortation for the people, say it." Paul's first recorded sermon is so significant it deserves scrutiny now, pared as close as I can pare it to the Greek, as it arrives in context. Rising and signalling with his hand, the timeless, international signal for requesting attention, Paul says:

> My brother Israelites and those fearing God, listen. The God of this people Israel chose our fathers and exalted the people when they lived as strangers in the land of Egypt, and He brought them out with a high arm. And for a time of about forty years he put up with them in the wilderness. And when he had destroyed seven nations in the land of Canaan, he divided their land to them by lot. And after that He gave

judges for about four hundred and fifty years, until Samuel the prophet. And afterward they asked for a king, and God gave them Saul the son of Kish, a man of the tribe of Benjamin, for forty years.

And when He had removed him, He raised up David to them to be their king; to whom He also gave testimony and said, "I have found David, of Jesse, a man after my own heart, who shall fulfill all my will." Of this man's seed God has raised to Israel, according to His promise, a Savior, Jesus—John having before proclaimed the baptism of repentance to all the people of Israel, before His coming.

And as John fulfilled his course, he said, Who do you think I am? I am not He. But behold, One comes after me, the sandals of whose feet I am not worthy to loose.

Men, brothers, sons of the race of Abraham, and whoever among you fears God, the word of this salvation is sent to you! For those living in Jerusalem, and their rulers, not knowing this One, or the voices of the prophets read to them every Sabbath, have fulfilled the Scriptures in judging Him. Finding not one cause for death, they begged Pilate to do away with Him. And when they had fulfilled all that was written concerning Him, taking Him down from the tree, they laid Him in a tomb.

But God raised Him from the dead, and He appeared for many days with those who came up with Him from Galilee to Jerusalem, who are his witnesses to the people. And we preach the gospel to you, the promise made to our fathers, which God has fulfilled to us, their children, in raising up Jesus; as also it is written in the second Psalm, "You are my Son, this day have I begotten you." And that He did raise Him from the dead, to return to corruption no more, He spoke in this way: "I will give you the holy promises of David." Therefore He also says in a psalm, "You shall not allow your holy one to see corruption."

For after he had served his own generation by the will of God, David fell asleep and was added to his fathers and saw corruption. But He whom God raised again saw no corruption. Therefore be it known to you, men and brothers, that through this One the forgiveness of sins is announced to you. And by Him all who believe are justified from all things, from which you could not be justified by the law of Moses. Therefore beware unless it comes upon you which is spoken of in the prophets: "Behold you despisers, and marvel, and perish; for I work a work in your days, a work which you shall in no way believe, though a man declares it to you."

The sermon is one the present-day church needs to hear: a history of its struggle to find a footing; a history of its wandering astray; a pronouncement of the hope available only in Christ, by way of insistence (as Peter also insists) on Jesus' bodily resurrection, in fulfillment of the prophecies of Scripture ("If Christ has not been raised," Paul writes elsewhere, "then our proclamation is worthless, and your faith is also worthless"), with an emphasis on Christ's lack of corruption, or freedom from uncleanness, as the perfect sacrifice. Christ then justifies believers in the sight of God as adherence to the law cannot, and those who remain lukewarm in their belief of all of this must be warned, in Paul's way, with a warning from scripture, here Habakkuk (1.5).

The effect? "The people begged that these words might be preached to them the next Sabbath." Jews and proselytes follow Paul and Barnabas, and are urged "to continue in the grace of God." On the next Sabbath nearly the entire city turns out, "and when the Jews saw the crowds," Luke writes, surely meaning the synagogue officials, or an establishment analogous to the Sanhedrin, "they were filled with jealousy, and contradicted what was spoken by Paul, blaspheming."

Paul and Barnabas say it was "necessary" to bring *them* the word of God first, but since they've repudiated it, judging themselves unworthy of eternal life, he and Barnabas are turning to the gentiles, and in support of this they quote from Isaiah 49.6. The gentiles rejoice, Luke writes, adding, "And as many as had been appointed to eternal life believed." God appoints or elects those he will call to belief (Eph. 1.4), which is relevant to those formerly outside the covenant; their will does not effect the call. The word now spreads through the boundaries of this part of the world.

But the existing church, angry as Hell, incites "devout women of prominence and the leading men of the city" to start up a persecution against Paul and Barnabas and drive them out of "their district"—perhaps the range of this synagogue's authority. The two are chased out of town.

At their next stop, Iconium, over a hundred miles east, they again speak first in the synagogue, so forcefully that a great number of both Jews and gentiles believe. But the Jews who disbelieve—and again this seems to mean established officials who stand to lose in the exchange—stir up the gentiles and embitter their minds against the brothers. Or, when you don't like what the Baptist preacher who is collecting all those converts is preaching, sit in the local coffee shop or bar and gossip among unbelievers about how his selfish stupidity is tearing the town apart. Which is what happens. As apostolic signs and wonders continue from Paul, and more adherents are added, the city divides down its center.

The gospel causes conflict and dissension; it always has and always will; Jesus warned it would divide even families, as it has. Now, with this city taking sides of belief and unbelief, an attempt is made by "both the Gentiles and the Jews *with their rulers*" (this supports my suppositions) to rough up Paul and Barnabas, and then stone them. The two hear of this and flee to Lystra and Derbe and the surrounding countryside, and then at Lystra run into problems of another kind. Paul is preaching when he notices a man who, as Luke says, was "lame from his mother's womb," with a disability identical to that of the man Peter and John met at the Temple. Paul says to this person in a loud voice, "Stand on your feet!"

The man leaps up, as the other did, and begins to walk, recipient of an apostolic sign. Healing as an apostolic sign contains these elements: a publicly known illness or incapacity, often in existence since birth; a reversal of the state in public, in the sight of many witnesses, in a total and immediate way, with proofs so conclusive that the presence of a miracle is universally acknowledged. Miracles attest to the power of Christ invested in his apostles and are a means of calling people to faith in Him. This first recorded healing by Paul doesn't by accident deal with the same disability Peter and John reversed, but in a gentile culture imbued with local legend, as Lystra was, of gods from the Greek pantheon visiting the area in the form of human beings, the crowd goes wild. The gods have come down to earth again!

They call Barnabas "Zeus," perhaps because of his bearing as a man of wealth (4.36), or his appearance or height in relationship to Paul, who is physically unimpressive, if we may take as description his statement in Second Corinthians 10.10. Paul they term "Hermes," or Mercury, the swift-footed messenger of the gods who carried the caduceus (or twined snakes) that is still the symbol of the medical profession. It was Paul who commanded the lame man to stand. A priest from the local temple brings oxen and garlands to the city gate to sacrifice to Paul and Barnabas, and in the crowd's reaction you will note that the religion of unbelief will do its renaming, too, to suit the purposes of the Church to its ends. It takes a great deal of untangling by Paul, who tears his robes in despair, finally, to restrain the mob.

"We're men of the same nature as you!" he cries, echoing Peter's words to Cornelius. We're here to preach the gospel of the God who created heaven and earth, he says, so you can turn from your empty idols—

But he doesn't get much farther, because at that moment Jews from Antioch and Iconium appear and win the frenzied crowd to their side. And then the sentence that the local officials have threatened to bring upon Paul takes place: the people start stoning him. As I sense the sickening thump and wallop of stones over Paul's body, I think of Stephen, as Paul must have, observing his slow death with the garments of the stoners at hand. Paul is stoned and dragged outside the city gates and left for dead—for the jackals and birds of prey, one of the most profane deaths of the covenant.

"For I will show him how he must suffer many things for my sake," Jesus said in their Damascus encounter.

There are always manipulators of power in a bureaucratic structure, even the church, though this shouldn't be. In my life I've watched the federal government deteriorate in almost every particular, because of the moral void left where before saints of excellence were called to serve, and the American government has existed for only two hundred years. University bureaucracies go to pieces every decade. In Paul's time, the church had existed since Abraham, for centuries, and it was God's church, not men's. So when I speak of the hierarchy within the existing church, or of synagogue officials, I'm referring to those individuals who have learned the skills of manipulation, as certain individuals always do, and exercise them out of envy or to shore up personal power, rather than exercising the mercy and justice of God. This same tendency is the shame of the modern Church.

One of the worst examples occurred when the higher critics, through their intellectual influence, altered the face of the church in Germany. The way to evil had been paved by the Prussian ideal of social education:

> One is amazed on studying the 1819 Code [of Germany] today to discover the extraordinary powers which the state assumed to coerce unwilling and negligent parents to have their children educated. . . Baptismal registers and the records of the civil authorities were laid open for inspection and the police were asked to give every assistance. . . . When this information had been obtained, it was used not merely to coerce unwilling parents to send their offspring to school, but also to ensure that the children arrived. . . . Thus, the state increased its power over the very lives of the people.[6]

Part of the process of this education was to instill in its students a sense of the necessity and "benevolence" of a central government. One of the adherents of the Prussian school, Robert Owen, a Scot, carried its ideals of "Social Democracy" to the United States and established in 1825 the utopian community of New Harmony.[7] Its longevity was usual for such utopias: two years. But in Germany, enforced by the government, that Prussian education continued, while on a higher level respected theologians at German seminaries began to say that their skills in literary research had led them to discover that the Bible was, basically, a flawed and polyglot production—the same teaching encountered by Kuyper in Holland. The Old Testament, especially, was untrustworthy, they said, but in spite of this one was to continue to believe with a kind of noble existential angst, of the sort they could muster, over this irreversible tragedy they had uncovered.

A new emphasis was put on Luther's view of justification by faith, which was seen as experiential and personal rather than as an exact imputation of Christ's flawless obedience to the law applied to every person unable to keep the law, and his death as the atoning sacrifice needed to clear each individual of his or her deserved death according to the tables of perfect justice given by Moses via God. Luther came to be seen as a "German nationalist rebelling against the Mediterranean world and against Renaissance humanism."[8] If you remove the law as the standard for measuring the effect of grace in a person's life, or as the measure of your acts, you remove the ethics from Christianity, and any possibility of an ethical culture.

Fichte, one of the higher critics, influenced Alfred Rosenberg, who became the official philosopher of the regime of Adolph Hitler,[9] and Friedrich Delitzsch, a writer of the commentary in every pastor's library (Keil and Delitzsch), further "influenced Rosenberg against Paul and the Old Testament."[10] The poet Peter Viereck carefully followed the spiritual battle in Germany as it rose through the twenties and thirties into the forties, and perhaps it's best to view it through his eyes, as he watches it take shape in 1941:

> The famous Catholic refutation of Rosenberg [circa 1935] proves convincingly that Christianity is inseparable from the Old Testament, that the connection is umbilical and introduced not merely by Paul but by Jesus Himself. Hitler has called the Old Testament "the Bible of Satan"! Rosenberg calls it "tales of pimps"! He blames it in part for today's "frightful Jewish overlordship" in Germany. All this horrifies both Protestants and Catholics of Germany, especially his demand that "the so-called Old Testament must be *abolished*" officially. Ever more Nazi educators of the young [in those schools already set up] follow his advice to replace instruction in the Old Testament by "nordic sagas from Wotan on."
>
> *Mein Kampf* and the Twenty-five Points of the official party platform demand "positive Christianity." Rosenberg defines positive Christianity as Germanic, negative Christianity as Etruscan-Syrian-Jewish-African. The latter is non-Aryan, the former carried on the spirit of nordic paganism. Rosenberg accuses the established churches, Protestant and Catholic, of always selling out Germany to the negative heritage. . . .
>
> How much Christianity remains in Rosenberg, the "true Christian," after he throws out its love, its universalism, the whole Old Testament, and all of the New Testament connected with Paul? . . . Our conclusion is that Hitler's and Rosenberg's positive Christianity means nordic paganism plus lip-service to a falsified Jesus.[11]

When Rosenberg's philosophy became the official doctrine of the Nazi regime, those who had been educated in the Social Democratic German schools, the "brownshirts" (this was their school uniform), began to idolize and enforce this teaching at every level, and we know the rest. But Nazism could not have advanced if Christianity had not been disassembled, if not deconstructed, at every German seminary by the higher critics. So when as human beings we believe that we know better than what Luke or Paul or Jesus taught—all of whom taught the Old Covenant—

the conclusions we reach can be perilous. The churches of our day would do well to take heed.

In Lystra and Iconium the pattern of the last portion of Acts is set in place: the proclamation of the gospel, the unreserved response of some, and then the restraining reaction of civil or church authorities, often directed against Paul—though at this point that seems ended. As the disciples stand around outside the city gates, however, Paul gets up and goes right back; he enters the city, whole. The next day he and Barnabas travel to Derbe, fifty miles away, and after preaching there and adding disciples, they return to Lystra and Iconium and Antioch in Pisidia, encouraging the churches. But there is this new note from Paul: "Through many tribulations we must enter the kingdom of God."

Paul's return to the churches where he has preached is an act ignored by most popular, modern evangelists, and even many missionaries. And something of perhaps even greater import occurs at this point; the institution of *local* church government. Elders are appointed in the new churches, establishing the authority of plural local rule. The term in Greek for elder is *presbyter,* which is synonymous with bishop in its usage, and though Paul and Peter are apostles, they also refer to themselves as elders of the church. We have seen Paul participate in the local (and perhaps regional) government of the church at Antioch. A single elder or bishop is not installed in any local church in any chapter of Acts, and a plurality of presbyters seems the consistent scriptural teaching, Old and New—from the time of the establishment of elders to serve with Moses, through the Levitical priesthood, to the plurality of officials in the local synagogues of the foreign lands Paul now tours.

After the churches brought into being by his preaching have been encouraged, and the biblical form of government has been installed in each, Paul and Barnabas again sail along the south coast of Turkey (Pamphylia and Cilicia) all the way back to the church at Antioch—"from which they had been commended to the grace of God for the work that they had accomplished." They gather the church together, as a missionary who has been sent out by a local church should do, and report what has happened, along with how God has opened His faith to the gentiles.

Paul and Barnabas spend "a long time" at the church in Antioch. We don't know exactly how long, nor the length of their journey, but taking into account the vicissitudes of travel then, and the chronology in the second chapter of Galatians, we must assume it's been fourteen years, at the minimum, since Paul's last visit to Jerusalem. Now he is about to take another trip to that holy city, for the apostolic event commonly known as the Jerusalem Council.

As with many matters of the church, then and now, the event rises out of dissension. Some disciples from Judea arrive at the church in Antioch, saying, "Unless you are circumcised according to the custom of Moses, you can't be saved." Paul and Barnabas debate with them, not on whether gentiles should enter the church, but over the proper form for receiving them. "Circumcision is nothing, and uncircumcision is nothing," Paul might say (1 Cor. 7.19), "but what matters is keeping the commandments of God."

"They," the plurality of elders at Antioch, appoint Paul and Barnabas and some of their own number to "go up to Jerusalem to the apostles and elders about this question." The matter apparently can't be settled locally and perhaps even regionally, so they will consult with the next authority, or appeal this to a higher court of the church.

This act has led, through the centuries, to the formation of an ecclesiastical hierarchy, as it might be seen, or to levels of government within the church, and to the calling of councils and assemblies and synods (over and above local church government) in all but the most independent branches of the church. As the delegation from Antioch passes through Phoenicia and Samaria, they announce the conversion of the gentiles, which brings "great joy to all the brothers." So there are churches with elders there.

In Jerusalem they are received by *the church,* and by *the apostles* and *elders*—again a layering of authority to be examined soon. At this first council of the newly forming church, after a bit of discussion, Peter stands and explains how God through "his mouth" has called in the gentiles, making "no distinction between us and them, purifying their hearts by faith. Now therefore why do you tempt God by putting a yoke on the neck of the disciples, a yoke that neither our fathers nor we were able to bear?"

Paul and Barnabas relate the "signs and wonders" God has performed among the gentiles, and then James, the brother of Christ, the one who seems to be acquiring authority in the Jerusalem church (because of his relationship or resemblance to Jesus?), stands and says, "Even as Simon has declared: how God at the first visited the gentiles to take out of them a people for his name, and the words of the prophets agree to this." He quotes Amos, who is echoing Isaiah, Jeremiah, and every prophet who foresaw this widening of the kingdom.

Then he suggests a mid-course: "That we write to them to abstain from things contaminated by idols, and fornication, and things strangled, and from blood." This finds approval with the assembly, and the quote from Amos reinforces the apostles' pattern, as it is established over and over in their sermons, for referring to relevant portions of the canon of the old covenant for spiritual and doctrinal matters in the emerging church. Barsabbas, called Judas (possibly the author of the book of Jude), and Silas are chosen to accompany Paul and Barnabas to deliver the first written communication, or epistle, of the Christian church—the entire text of which is reproduced by Luke—to the church at Antioch.

At Antioch, they gather "the multitude together," and read the letter to rejoicing at the "encouragement" or comfort it brings. So some in this church were obviously concerned about whether they should be circumcised or whether they were in the wrong. Then Silas and Barsabbas further encourage the Antiocheans with "a lengthy message." I hardly need to waste breath wondering how many modern churches would be encouraged by their method. I know of pastors who, if their sermons last thirty minutes, have been admonished by members for causing their roasts to cook dry. For our television-addicted generation, God is merely an amulet of convenience on a chain of complaints, and not to be attended to as regularly as the six o'clock news.

Silas remains at Antioch, and "some days afterward," Luke reports, in the intimate dramatic mode in which all of Acts is cast, Paul says to Barnabas—and here I see an aging, more unkempt Paul, short beside Barnabas, turning to his companion and smiling, perhaps putting a hand on his shoulder—Paul says to Barnabas, "Let's return and visit the brethren in every city where we proclaimed the word of the Lord, and see how they're doing."

It would be pleasant for Luke (and me) to report that their camaraderie continues, but this is the occasion of the most shocking disagreement in Acts, and it is included to edify our present-day church. Barnabas wants to take John Mark along, but Paul points out that though John Mark began the first journey with them (12.25), he "deserted them" in Pamphylia, and such "sharp disagreement" rises between Paul and Barnabas that Barnabas breaks off from Paul, takes John Mark, and sails for Cyprus, his homeland, without Paul's blessing.

"All happy families are alike but an unhappy family is unhappy after its own fashion." So Tolstoy opens *Anna Karenin*,[12] with a maxim that applies equally well to this family, the intimate body of believers, once we examine the source of most every disagreement in the church. Paul is saying that, from his point of view, John Mark, whose family was at least fairly well-to-do and who is, further, a cousin to the well-to-do Barnabas—another family matter!—has not been thoroughgoing enough in his service to God. Barnabas disagrees, and it is in exactly this fashion that the church, even when it is faithful, has disagreed over the ages: when one believer's sense of the extent of faithful service or interpretation of proper faithfulness is set against another's. The unhappiness then follows after the fashion and particulars of each sad case.

But in this one it would be imprudent not to pause and say, as I must, that Barnabas was wrong.

I know, I've heard arguments for his gift of consolation and making friends, and that he was the one who befriended Paul in his outcast state. But these ignore the apostolic office and the subtle hint supplied by Luke (15.39): when Paul asks Silas to travel with him, they "are commended by the brethren to the grace of God." These are nearly the same words of institution that graced Barnabas and Paul on their first journey. No such send-off is given to Barnabas and John Mark. None is. Both Barnabas and Paul were called for their first journey, it's true, by the Spirit and the laying on of hands, but Paul, an apostle chosen by Christ, would have authority of revelation that Barnabas didn't possess.

In a case in the church of two possible rights (rather than a right and a wrong), the lesser authority must bow to the higher, or to the general will of the church at large.

Since Luke has reported earlier that Barnabas was "a good man, full of the Holy Spirit and of faith" (11.24), I must assume that he was sincere, as I often am when I lose my temper or want my way. But he was wrong. The surest indication is that he is never again mentioned in Acts, by our gentle-natured Luke writing under the authority of the Holy Spirit, nor is he mentioned again by Paul, I believe, if we were able to sort his epistles with absolute chronology. Paul will grant Barnabas credit where credit is due when he writes to other churches of the history of the church, which indicates his own lack of animosity, and though he obviously becomes reconciled again to John Mark (1 Tim. 4.11), he does not after this "recommend" Barnabas to the church.

So Paul, with his new companion Silas, travels north and then east by land, through Cilicia and Syria, "strengthening the churches." They travel to Derbe and Lystra, the area of Paul's stoning, and a curious moment occurs in Lystra, when Paul meets Timothy, "the son of a Jewish woman who was a believer" (see 2 Tim. 1.5) but whose father is Greek. Paul wants Timothy to join him, and circumcises him, in spite of the Jerusalem document he's been reading in the churches, because the Jews in the area know Timothy's father was a gentile.

Has Paul lost his gracious mantle, or what? Doesn't this authorize contextualization? Contextualists, or those who advocate contextualization, want to adapt portions of doctrine or church practice to suit the practices of an existing culture. An indigenous tribe might wear voodoo masks, as an example, for the rite of initiating a young man into adulthood, so wouldn't it be okay to wear the same masks when a young person is baptized? Let me add that my method of taking scripture at its face value and attempting to find its meaning, in order to apply it to the present-day church, might be seen by some as primitive as an aborigine's (though there is a growing underground of my kind in the U.S., too), so will my doctrinal views be incorporated into the church?

I don't believe this is a question anyone wants to answer with the seriousness with which I pose it, and I mean it to illustrate an actual dilemma: a contemporary reluctance to examine scripture, but a bustling hurry to examine every artifact of the cultural context. Paul was an apostle who received the word directly from the Spirit, the Head of the Church, and in every instance I can find of his facing a problem caused by the cultural context—in synagogues, with the Hellenists, with homosexuals, or with the artisans of Ephesus—he hit it head on with the antithesis of scripture. He was as unrelenting in this as he was faithful.

So has he, in this encounter with Timothy, become a contextualist? He has returned, rather, to a sign of the old covenant, not the masks of Greek drama of the culture, and I have to presume he made the right decision; Paul knew the particulars of the case, as I do not. He obviously doesn't want to be stoned again, though there's no indication this bears on his decision (the opposite, considering Galatians 2.3–5), and perhaps this was one way to protect covenant members of the household, the Lois and Eunice he mentions so warmly in his second epistle to Timothy. The document he is delivering to the churches "in the cities" of the area does not state that no one can be circumcised, ever; all members of the old covenant, including Peter and James and John and Paul himself, are in fact circumcised. The document states that circumcision isn't necessary for membership in the church, and that there are other minimal guidelines, all of which fall under old covenant law, that are to be observed by those who wish to maintain responsible membership.

Since the neighborhood knows that Timothy's father is Greek, or a gentile, and Paul wants to take Timothy into this faith that he claims is the apotheosis of the old covenant, he has to weigh both sides. And in making the concession he makes, which he does purposely to keep from offending fellow Jews, as the text suggests, he can be seen as stating in the strongest possible terms, You are no more cut out of the covenant, as you seem to think from the way you've treated me, than Timothy is now permitted in. What we're disputing about is different signs to mark that covenant. God admits or bars no one by the *sign,* you know that. He established the covenant with our father Abraham before delivering him any sign. *The essential covenant remains the same.*

In affirmation of this, we immediately read that "the churches were being strengthened in the faith, and were increasing in numbers daily." Paul and his group travel on through the Phrygian and Galatian regions, a wide swing west of hundreds of miles, because they are forbidden by the Spirit to speak in Asia, and they obey. Then the "Spirit of Jesus," named here particularly, forbids them to enter Bythinia. Was the time not ripe, or the fields not white for harvest?—a phrase that means the beards on the wheat and the barley have dried to a pale amber that looks white under the sun, indicating that the grain is hard ripe, a time when farmers within the boundaries of our habitation start up their swathers or windrowers and combines.

Does Jesus appear directly to Paul? Is this one of his many post-incarnate manifestations? Which I should modify by saying, Is it one of his many post-incarnate appearances to one of his apostles? If *you* see him in the present, you should, like Martin Luther, pick up an inkwell or a computer and throw it at him and demand that he be gone, knowing that this is one of the appearances Satan is able to take (he can assume the appearance of *an angel of light*) to deceive. Jesus did return, or come again within the lives of those who heard him speak, when he caused the temple at Jerusalem to be desecrated ("the abomination of desolation") in A.D. 70 by Augustus, who sacrificed pigs there and then razed it to the ground.

So having received a message from the Lord himself, Paul and his group go from Mysia to Troas, on the coast south from Constantinople, and there Paul experiences what has come to be known as the "Macedonian Vision," a term I hear used to excuse all sorts of wayward behavior, which is possible if you assume that you, like Paul, are directly spoken to by the Spirit. In the night, "a man of Macedonia was standing and appealing to him," as Agabus appeals to Paul, but with speech, saying, "Come over to Macedonia and help us."

At this moment, just when we feel there can be no more surprises in this well-woven book, and certainly no technical ones, the next sentence goes, "And when he had seen the vision, immediately we sought to go into Macedonia, concluding that God had called us to preach the gospel to them." Swift as the light that can suffuse this room with desert heat, but wholly unobtrusively, in a mere shift of personal pronoun, Luke is present, standing among the rest, waiting to board the ship for Macedonia.

9

REALMS BROADER

AND DOMESTIC

THE APPEARANCE OF LUKE is similar to another moment in scripture, in the book of Ezra. Following a proclamation from King Artaxerxes to the Israelites in Babylon, freeing those who wish to return to Jerusalem to rebuild the Temple, the "I" appears. Ezra, their leader, is with them. In Acts that temple is still being built, in the form of the church, the "you" addressed at Corinth—"You are the temple of God"—and not individuals, as the passages in the third and sixth chapters of First Corinthians are usually taken to mean. The Spirit is with and within each believer, but the temple the Spirit is building is made up by the incorporation of the living stones (1 Peter 2.5) of all believers.

Ecclesia is the word for "church" in Greek, and means nearly the same as synagogue: an assembly of a public sort. In the new covenant, *ecclesia* refers in particular to a gathering of God's people, or a society of Christians. People in our culture have come to think of *church* as a building, or in some instances a particular denomination (which is closer), and though there are many ways in which the word is used in the new covenant, it is never used to refer to a physical building. Here are several important instances:

175

"Salute the brothers who are in Laodicea, and Nympha, and the church which is in her house"[1] (Col. 4.15). This is a society of Christians so small it can assemble in one house.

"Then news of these matters came to the ears of the church that was at Jerusalem." The reference is to the time when Barnabas was sent to Antioch, and here *ecclesia* means a society of Christians from the same city, which includes, as Acts has enumerated, several thousand.

"This is the one [Moses] who was in the church in the wilderness along with the angel who was speaking to him on Mount Sinai. . . ." We meet our angel again (see also the explicatory verse in 1 Cor. 10.4). The extract is from Stephen's testimony before the Sanhedrin (7.38), and *ecclesia* here denotes a society of believers so large it makes up an entire nation, numbering about two million at the time.

"And God has set some in the church, first, apostles; second, prophets; third, teachers; after that miracles; then gifts of healings, helps, governments, diversities of tongues." You find a built-in hierarchy of order in Paul's first letter to the Corinthians (12.28), and now *ecclesia* refers to the society of Christians presently on the earth. Thus the mention of apostles, prophets, and tongues.

"Husbands, love your wives as Christ loved the church, and gave himself for it." Here is the largest society of Christians yet, all those for whom Christ died—everyone presently living on earth and everyone in heaven, and all the elect yet to be born or called into the church.[2]

The last two examples, especially, refer to the temple being built by the Spirit through Paul's journeys, although he is always careful to set in order the local realms of government in that church. Paul has now been joined by Luke, who is clearly familiar with the sea and sea craft, and for a time the church is borne on water, as the ark of Noah was, and there is a sense of fresh air hitting the sails: "Then having set sail from Troas, we ran a straight

course to Samothrace, and the next day to Neapolis, and from
there to Philippi, which is the chief city in that part of Macedonia
and a Roman colony. We remained in this city for some days."

Nobody is there to meet them, though, and the man who beck-
oned doesn't appear. Paul doesn't seem discouraged that hundreds
of people aren't clamoring to hear him. Not even one. It looks
bad for church growth. On the Sabbath he and the rest go outside the city gates to a river, where they suspect (or have heard)
that Jewish believers gather to pray. From the hints and develop-
ments in this chapter (16), we come to understand there isn't a
synagogue in Philippi—for a specific historical reason: "It was a
capital offense for Greeks and Romans to celebrate the Sabbath, or
practice Jewish rites."[3] The adherence of Jewish believers to their
faith was so firm it threatened the authority of Rome; or the
Roman emperor specifically, whose office at this point in history
was seen as worthy of worship. Claudius was a god.

At the river Paul and Luke and the disciples encounter Lydia,
a seller of purple fabrics, a woman who is obviously engaged in the
commerce of the world, most likely a widow, and "a worshiper of
God." The "Lord opened her heart to respond" to Paul's message, which is the only way the gospel can be received, not by any
person's decision to receive it. Lydia and her household are baptized, the first recorded converts in Europe. In describing the baptism of Lydia, the construction of the sentence allows for a passage
of time, and suggests something further: "And when she and her
household had been baptized, she urged us saying, 'If you have
judged me to be faithful to the Lord, come into my house and
stay.'" The baptism seems to have been at or near her house, to include all its members, and not at the river.

There are few instances of such moving hospitality (perhaps
Abigail's to David is an equal), and Lydia has since exemplified for
Christians the attitude they are to embody.[4] Certainly hospitality
is a lost art. It is even accurate to say, considering this and other

passages (Rom. 12.13, 1 Tim. 3.1, 1 Peter 4.9), that the loss of the art signifies spiritual decline in the church. Christians tend to be like most other people: they entertain out of social exigency, or they admire their guests, or it's their turn, and not out of gratitude for the gift of Christ. This is the way in which hospitality should rise from a Christian, and there ought to be gratitude in the understanding that hospitality, too, is a gift of God, a spiritual gift, and a necessary expression of the renewal at the center of a Christian life. Our homes and the food on our tables, additional gifts, should be offered as openly as the gospel now being offered to the broader world.

If more churches taught this, we might see effects of the kind we see at Lydia's house. A group of believers begins to gather there, or a locus of worship is established, for we learn next that "as we went to prayer, we met a slave girl possessed with a spirit of divination who brought her masters a great deal of gain by fortune-telling." This girl follows Paul and Luke and the rest, crying, "These men are bond-servants of the Most High God and are proclaiming to you the way of salvation!"

She does this for days, until Paul, grieved, turns and says, "I command you in the name of Jesus Christ to come out of her!" His grief is based on the understanding that the spirit has become the young woman's personality and that the departure will not be peaceful, for spirits are known to "tear" their victims. At Paul's command, the spirit is gone.

It has correctly named, through the young woman, the Lord whom the disciples serve, as demons in the gospels say to Jesus, "You are Jesus, the Christ, Son of the Most High God." Even demons in their hierarchy acknowledge his Person. The men who have used the young woman's spiritual bondage (to be discussed in connection with Sceva's sons) realize that their source of income is gone. The gospel affects pocketbooks; like church members who are asked to tithe, or tithe and then some (Luke 6.38), they're angered. They drag Paul and Silas before the authorities, and say, "These men, being Jews, are troubling our city greatly, and are teaching customs that it is not lawful for us to accept or follow, being Romans."

Smart men; they point out that their adversaries are Jews. They know how to hit where it hurts with local rule. The magistrates rip off their clothes and order them to be flogged, perhaps with rods; Roman heralds or lictors carried fasces, bundles of rods with an axe in the center, that signified Roman rule, and these rods were unbundled and used to enforce Roman law. Paul and Silas are then thrown in jail, under the command of a man memorialized since as the Philippian Jailer. He takes them to the inner prison and locks their feet into stocks.

At midnight, as Paul and Silas pray and sing hymns of praise—the Psalms Paul has sung in worship since childhood—there is an earthquake. The man of the Macedonian vision has arrived, and all the doors of the prison slam open, and the shackles of Paul and Silas break. For emphasis I add the witness of two modern poets: *And each in the cell of himself is almost convinced of his freedom*[5] and *I hear / my ill-spirit sob in each blood cell, / as if a hand were at its throat . . . / I myself am hell; / nobody's here.*"[6]

The jailer wakes, and you can imagine his incredulity and shaggy disarray. Then I feel in my bones his next act. He draws his sword, impetuous as Peter, intending to kill himself—death is anyway his end if anybody escapes, as with the sixteen Herod executed. The jailer has the misplaced temerity to judge himself and carry out his sentence to execute, though this earthquake of course wasn't caused by him. He lives by some code of standards, clearly, and autonomously blames himself. Paul prevents him from carrying out this act, however, calling out to him that nobody has escaped, and the jailer, who by now must feel tossed in every direction after obviously observing and listening to Silas and Paul, comes over, "trembling," falls at their feet, and says, "Sirs, what must I do to be saved?"

Why do I identify with this jailer? I turn away and see a character from a novel of mine, wearing only a robe, step through a shadowy wall in galloping strides that have worn one heel raw, grab a fencing foil out of a resounding brass umbrella stand, hold its tip to his stomach, and fling himself on the floor on top of it.

"Believe in the Lord Jesus Christ, and you shall be saved, you and your household," Paul and Silas tell this man who has prostrated himself before them. Again, they emphasize the covenant, and I hear their words as though it's me at their feet. I've tried to approach this moment from so many angles I'm not sure I wish to again, but for those two above, and anyone who cares to listen, I say, "I was separated from my wife. I'd finished a book that took ten years, and in that sense things were resolved, but there was no resolution to other matters. At thirty-five I'd received the critical attention I'd hoped to have by the end of my life, and money, but what did I have? A disorganized, scattered life with no peace. By the time I was reconciled with my wife, I'd lost my father, who had meant a lot to me and had, in spite of prejudices he'd faced, held to the faith his father had. In the midst of this continuing lack of resolution, a moment of real *crisis* came, when I had to say, or I realized—however it happened, because it happens in wordlessness—I knew I would never live the same life."

Or I say, "I was catechized as a child and went to parochial school. I pretty much tried to live by that faith until I was about twenty. There was a period of falling away then, rebellion, agnosticism, and all the rest that many young people go through, until about the time of writing my first novel. I felt a resurgence of faith then, and a confirmation of it, in that our first child, a daughter, was born just after the book was finished. We had her baptized. There was a further falling away, and that pattern kept up through the writing of my next book, which is, I think, an overtly Christian novel. There were soaring periods of prayer during the work on it. I began to read the Bible then. Right after it was published, my father died, and the effects of his death, which are too complicated to go into, drove me to the approximate point my character is in when he throws himself on the fencing foil."

These moments when eternity collides with the body we carry through each day: "Things that I wrote about began to happen in my life as I'd write them, or would seem to, or I'd see shades of them in the newspapers. At other times it felt I was holding parts of the world in place, or affecting it in ways that weren't entirely healthy. Then, about four months after the book was out, my father died. All through it I'd been fighting belief, because I was dealing with generations whose lives were built around the Bible and Christ, and I'd come to the moment of saying, Yes, I believe, but then, as for me, well, let me do what I want. And proceeded to do it. My father had always been an example to me of what a Christian could be, and when he died it was not only as though my past had been severed, but there was no one I could talk to whose motives I could wholly trust about what had been happening *around* the writing of the book. . . . It was written specifically for him. Fortunately, he'd lived long enough to go through the galleys of it with me. We passed them back and forth, nearly wordlessly, with small questions to one another here and there, across the hallway of a retreat house where he was working as a janitor and had got me a room. I lost consciousness once, is the only way I can describe it, and the next thing I knew I had his slippers on and he was walking me up and down a long hallway."

"And they spoke the word of the Lord to him and to all who were in his household." That word was spoken to mine in my crisis. How does that word enable the jailer's household, and indeed the household of God, to be distinctive? We're to be a preserving salt to the world, yet remain set apart, or sanctified, by the renewal of the Spirit. We're to be ready to give a defense to anyone who asks for an account of the hope that is in us (1 Peter 3.15), with meekness and fear. The extracts above are taken from interviews, the first the most recent, from late 1991, and the final the most distant, from 1979.[7] They don't speak of the hope I hold, quite, and they aren't fiction. All are attempts to give an explanation to the question, *How is it that you believe?* I'm not sure a rational explanation can be given, but every Christian should try.

What is Christian literature, or fiction? Any novel produced by a person who claims to be Christian? A novel in which there is a conversion? Of course not. The conversion of the Philippian jailer is the only "crisis conversion" in Acts, and then there's the next morning. For the rest of his life the jailer will attempt to embody in everything he does the distinctiveness of his faith. Christians used to examine these distinctions, in order to find ways to apply them to every occupation, but now they're generally ignored. It would not be proper, most would agree, to be a Christian housebreaker. If you agree, you've entered the realm of ethics, and we'll have to decide where we're going to go to get our ethics.

If you say that it's merely common sense, then I would have to say that I've met people who believe it's common sense to be housebreakers, and worse, and they believe they're ethical. There is an ethical nature to every work of art. How then do we define those ethics? Christians largely do what the culture tells them to, or as the world defines the doing of it, whether it's painting a triptych or bending the IRS code, instead of pausing to ask what the Christian way in that instance ought to be, much less what the distinctives of their occupation should be as defined by scripture.

Late that night in Philippi, the jailer incorporates a new outlook on his daily tasks. He bathes the ragged backs of Paul and Silas (Christian art should bring *comfort*, even when it hurts, at the minimum), and then in a sense they do the same; they baptize him and his household. The jailer feeds them, an act related to Saul's taking his first food in Damascus. I once wondered whether it wasn't the Lord's Supper being celebrated on these occasions (see also 20.11), but in this instance I think not, because the elements of worship aren't present, as at other times.

You sense a holy aspect of gratitude, however, to each meal that is absent in our overstocked and brightly packaged era, and it's certain the jailer is extending the same hospitality that Lydia did. The scene is equally domestic. Even if this passage and others aren't explicit enough to identify them as communion per se, they are clearly times of communing, opportunities for the self-less expression of concern for others that all Christian art and acts should embody. The jailer, the text reads, is rejoicing greatly, and the next day he has cause to rejoice further. He won't have to continue to incarcerate the brothers who have brought his life to eternal rest. The city magistrates send their police with a message that the jailer delivers to Paul: "The judges have sent word to let you go. So come out now, and go in peace."

But Paul says, "They've beaten us in public, we who are Romans and uncondemned, and thrown us into prison, and now they're sending us away in secret? No, indeed! Let them come themselves and bring us out." What, is Paul ungrateful?

When the authorities hear Paul's demands, they arrive, fearful, and beg him and Silas to leave—the lesson being that civil authorities, too, are under God's jurisdiction (Rom. 13, 1 Peter 2.13), and exist to administer justice with righteousness: to reward good and to punish evil. The only way to measure righteousness is by the standard set in scripture, and rulers are to be held to their prescribed roles. In this instance the authorities tremble, as they should, for not adhering to established civil law. Paul's appeal to his citizenship (as Americans appeal to theirs overseas) is an appeal to the rights and privileges of the justice of the nation he serves.

I've heard people argue that Paul's protest is a form of worldly wisdom that will entrap him (see 1 Cor. 1.18–21), since his insistence on Roman citizenship carries him to Rome, where tradition, not scripture, has it that he was executed. This is a misconstruction of Paul. The wisdom of the world that denies the gospel is what Paul opposes—the realms of rationalism and education that are revered for their "scientific" value. Because God ordained governments inside the boundaries of habitations, Christians must appeal to those governments, and when a government or its officials turn unrighteous, vote them out, or through an upright minor official resist or rise against them, as the Russian populace has risen, as the colonists of America rose up.

Paul does not take the advice of these unjust judges and run off. Now that he's thrown enough of a scare into them to cause their chins to wobble, he goes to Lydia's. In this household of the local church, he meets with believers and encourages them before he departs. First things first. Then he and Silas, minus Luke—"we" has vanished—travel by land, for a distance of a hundred miles, to Thessalonica. They speak in a synagogue there for three Sabbaths, gathering believers, "along with a multitude of God-fearing Greeks and a number of the leading women." With this further reference to women, it seems clear that a new point is being made; the gospel cuts across not only every race and station in life, but gender.

Again the establishment becomes jealous, and gathers loiterers from the market place into a mob; they assault a domestic residence, the house of Jason, where Paul and Silas are believed to be hiding. When the two can't be found, the crowd drags Jason before the magistrates, shouting, "These men who are turning the world upside down have come here! And Jason has welcomed them, and they all act contrary to the decrees of Caesar, saying there is another king, Jesus."

This is exactly the point that the civil rule of any country, including the present U.S., can't bear to see—honor to an authority that transcends Caesar's central rule, by those who know they must serve God rather than men. The crowd is so incensed that after Jason has paid bail for his release, he and "the brethren" send

Paul and Silas away by night. If the civil authority is so unrighteous you see no possibility of justice ahead, and nobody is placed in danger by your action, you flee, as Paul has before.

He and Silas arrive in Berea, several dozen miles south, and go straight "into the synagogue of the Jews." If they were proclaiming a new religion, and I were a Jew observing their actions from the outside, I would by now be irritated. But they are proclaiming the fulfillment of the law and the prophets, as commanded by the Spirit, as the Bereans right away recognize. The men of the synagogue in Berea receive the word with eagerness, "examining the Scriptures daily, to see whether these things were so."

Now interesting things happen all at once. The more I read Acts, the more I'm amazed at the way people got around on foot, because the Thessalonicans have heard that Paul and Silas are in Berea, and a group of them arrives and starts stirring the people up. Then this: "Immediately the brethren sent Paul away, to go toward the sea, but both Silas and Timothy stayed on." So Timothy is still with Paul, but the question to ponder is whether Paul, an apostle, is obeying the consensus of local church government— "the brothers" who send him off. Paul always arouses the greatest ire, it appears, presumably from his ability to argue out of the law and the prophets, but here is an interesting example of the possible operation of one level of church government. Would the elders of a church in Cracow tell a pope it was best that he ship out? Would he? Would a Methodist bishop? The stated clerk or moderator of a Presbyterian General Assembly?

However it may be, Paul sails to Athens, accompanied by the group who got him to the coast, and then instructs them to send Silas and Timothy to him, and settles down in Athens to wait. Paul wait? I think of him as a lifelong resident of New York, America's holy city, who has come to an area like Detroit or New Orleans, and now stops in a grocery store (along with banks, our temples) and finds ahead of him in line a local resident who does not have her money ready as in New York, but after her groceries are rung up she sets her purse on the counter and opens it, takes out her billfold, pages through it for dollars, and when she's found the right amount of these and laid them down, she opens a change purse and starts digging in it for the correct silver, while Paul, having noticed the household gods on every shelf, is about to get down in a crouch and yell, "Let me through!"

The only one Paul waits on, to paraphrase him, is God. His spirit is so provoked by Athens, a "city full of idols," that after he speaks in the synagogue "with the Jews and the God-fearing Gentiles," he also speaks in the open market place, day after day. Stoic and Epicurean philosophers meet with him—a picture of the prevailing sources of wisdom of that period—and wonder, "What does this babbler say?" Some think he's speaking of foreign gods, because he proclaims Jesus and the resurrection. Babbler? Paul could tell them what Babel meant. He never shuns conflict, which the gospel is bound to bring, and now the philosophers take him to the Areopagus on Mars Hill not to face the Areopagite court, for a change, but to give him a chance to address a larger audience.

In a footnote to his century, Luke adds, "For all the Athenians and the strangers visiting used to spend their time in nothing else than telling or hearing something new." The footnote could apply to ours. The nearly insatiable need in humankind for the new, which once was satisfied by visiting and gossip, or the highfalutin gossip of Samuel Johnson and entourage in the chop shops and coffeehouses of England, down to the coffeehouses of the sixties in New York and Paris, is now universally fulfilled by television. An hour of refried news is enough to convince those in the numb state TV induces that they've heard something new. The philosophers in our sophisticated, electronic age, Luke, are Oprah and Donahue.

It is possible that the Areopagite council is gathered on its stone seats—see "ruins"—and to this audience of magistrates and intellectuals, Paul says, "Men of Athens, I see you are superstitious of the gods in everything." He mentions that he has seen a local altar inscribed TO AN UNKNOWN GOD, and says that the God they are worshiping in ignorance he is here to proclaim.

This God, Paul says, is the creator of all things, the Lord of heaven and earth, and does not dwell in temples made of hands; is the Spirit who gives life and breath to all things, the uniter of nations, the determiner of time and events and the boundaries of habitations for a purpose. We should seek God, he says: "Perhaps we might grope for Him and find Him, though he is not far from each one of us; for in Him we live and move and exist, as even some of your own poets have said, 'For we also are His offspring.' Being then the offspring of God, we ought not to think that the Divine Nature is like gold or silver or stone, an image formed by the art and thought of man. Therefore having overlooked the times of ignorance, God is now demanding that men everywhere repent, because he has appointed a day in which He is going to judge the world in righteousness by a Man whom He appointed, and has given proof to all of this by raising him from the dead."

When they hear of a resurrection, which in Greek means to stand up from the dead, some sneer but others say, "We shall hear you again concerning this." Paul tags them at least twice; that they have acknowledged the existence of God (Psalms 19, Rom. 1), and that His nature doesn't participate in the nature of objets d'art. This model sermon for missionaries and pastors who face people who have never heard of God, but do sense or acknowledge His presence, has its effect. Bystanders are converted, two of whom are named; Dionysus the Areopagite, or one who sits on the council of the Areopagus, and Damaris, a woman, yet another woman.

Paul now travels to Corinth, seventy miles down a narrow neck of land to the Peloponnesus peninsula, and meets Aquila and Priscilla, recent exiles from Italy due to the heat the emperor is feeling, apparently, from believers: "because Claudius had commanded all the Jews to leave Rome." Again, the intertwining of the faith that many attempt to divide is seen as one. Paul labors with this couple at the trade they hold in common, tent making, the means by which Paul—self-supporting missionary par excellence—pays his way. And of course Paul is teaching in the synagogue on every Sabbath, and when Silas and Timothy finally trace him down in Corinth, "Paul was pressed in the spirit and testified to the Jews that Jesus is the Christ."

Did the presence of young disciples press him to further diligence? When he is again opposed in the synagogue, he returns to a domestic setting and teaches in the house of Justus, adjoining the synagogue. Then Crispus, "the chief ruler of the synagogue, believed on the Lord with all his house." Once again we have the household rule of covenant, and when word of this gets round, "many of the Corinthians believed and were baptized."

Then the overseer of all acts enters in a night vision, and the Lord says to Paul, "Do not be afraid, but speak, and do not be silent. For I am with you, and no one will attack you in order to hurt you, for I have many people in this city." Luke then notes, more calendarlike now, that Paul remains in Corinth for eighteen months. But when Gallio is named deputy of Achaia, the Jewish leaders, apparently sensing an ally, bring Paul before Gallio's judgment seat, accusing him of persuading the people to worship God contrary to their law. Gallio won't hear the case, since it isn't a matter of wrongdoing or a crime, and Paul is set free.

He sails with Priscilla and Aquila to Syria, and in Cenchrea has his hair cut to keep a vow—perhaps to be in Jerusalem for Pentecost. We learn no more of it. The detail is included, I suspect, not to suggest he is keeping the old covenant vow of a Nazarite, but to impress on us that he was involved in serious business, and that the teachings of the old covenant carry weight. In Ephesus he "reasons with the Jews in the synagogue," and when they ask him to stay, he says, "I will return to you if God wills," acknowledging his servanthood, and departs from his tent-maker friends. He sails on across the Mediterranean to Caesarea, goes to Jerusalem, "to salute the church," and then back to the local church in Antioch, a breakneck pace, but home again at last.

And now you might blink a bit at the disappearance of Paul, who has dominated two-thirds of Acts, because as he travels through the upper country of Phrygia and Galatia "strengthening the disciples," the focus turns on Priscilla and Aquila, his Christian friends. In Ephesus, an eloquent Alexandrian Jew, Apollos, who is called "mighty in the Scriptures," appears and speaks and teaches accurately about Jesus, but seems aware only of the baptism of John the Baptist. Priscilla and Aquila take Apollos aside and teach him "more accurately," surely about the Holy Spirit.

Does Priscilla, or Prisca (as named in Romans 16.3), execute in this instance church authority? She does indeed join her husband in straightening out Apollos' doctrine, as it needs straightening in most of us, but there is no mention of her speaking or teaching on her own. Paul arrives back in Ephesus from his travels, and when he discovers disciples who have never heard of the Holy Spirit, he teaches them, baptizes them, and lays on hands, and they begin to speak in tongues and prophesy. There is this interesting note, "And there were in all about twelve men," or the same as Christ's apostles. By now you should know it is only an apostle who can confer the Spirit and the gift of tongues directly by the laying on of hands (no one else does this in Acts, that power Simon wanted to buy), but is Paul's teaching to be seen here as the only authoritative teaching?

What I'm edging toward, of course, is the issue of women in church office, and I would as soon edge past it.

It's night again, and as I climb the steps toward the room where my son is asleep, I hear a scratch race down the stairwell wall and my neck hair bristles. An arrangement of branches on the landing.

I don't fear a night vision but do sense the visionary nature of reality, existing coincident with the eternal spirit world, grow thin in the absence of light. In my son's room I pause to make sure he's asleep and then walk past his pine bunk bed and in the dark climb the wobbly ladder to the darkness of our tower. Cold black light glints off aluminum insulation we've fastened in place, and to the south, out a bow window that forms most of that wall, I watch our neighbor's yard light winking in the wind.

I'm barely able to make out the fields of the farm lying in that direction, under a light dusting of today's mica-thin snow, the first that's remained since late October. To the north, out a kind of porthole, beyond the chimney smoking from our woodstove (and the ghostly rims of my reading glasses that lately remain even when the glasses are removed), I can see faint yellow lights far off near the highway. This tower rose partly by whim. The close quarters of our elderly farmhouse had been added onto several times by Ivan and Enid or their parents, and we wanted to build a sun room on the south, in a gap where two previous additions hadn't been joined, but when I framed up to their roofs, one on each side, I discovered four separate pitches I would have to match, and decided why not go up another story, to enlarge our son's room, and once I was up that high, looking down on this countryside that draws the eye to every horizon, I thought, Why not one more?

I didn't count the cost or the time the tower would take when I began, and we've worked at it as we've been able to. The ground floor is finished, the second is getting done, but this level hasn't been sheetrocked and contains the chilly emptiness of anything new made by human hands. It isn't my workroom, as our rural mail carrier imagines; the view is too tempting, a distraction. My granary next to the barnyard is better, in the proper setting for a person of my ambition to consider his estate. This tower is for my wife.

For the past two years my son and I have been working to complete it for her. I can still picture his look when he was twelve and stood below holding a rope that was to keep me from falling as I balanced at the top of a ladder and lugged the large ladder rafters that form the overhang—nearly two hundred pounds apiece—up to a thirty-foot height one sparkling fall afternoon. From here I hope my wife will have a better sense of the house and the farm radiating from it resting under her control.

If she sees a piece of land from here that she likes, or sees one she likes driving down a road, and she has the means at hand, she ought to be able to buy it. I've largely turned our accounts and finances over to her; I've acknowledged both scripture and the gifts she's been given in this realm by my act (see Proverbs 31), although both of us understand that, as with Harry Truman, the buck stops with me.

And ratiocination seldom takes the day.

"Come, let us reason together," I hear people say, but when those words occur in Isaiah, God doesn't mean let me hear your ideas and I'll share mine and we'll see whose are the most valid. This is how many apply this passage from Isaiah, once it's pulled out of context, and those who seem prone to do that are often otherwise reasonable people who would be appalled to see a fundamentalist, say, do biblical wrenching of the kind. Educated people run on rationality until they encounter a situation beyond their control—an accident, a troubling situation with a daughter or son—and then give it up or change enough to realize that rationality isn't necessarily the engine running the universe.

Immediately following "Let us reason together" is this: "Though your sins be as scarlet, they shall be white as snow; though they be red like crimson, they shall be as wool."

What is being asked for (at the period of Uzziah through Hezekiah) is a reasonable confession from God's Israel of its sin, to be followed by repentance, so that their sins like scarlet will be white. Wiped out. The promise wasn't wholly fulfilled until Christ, and the "logic" of this is the issue Peter confronts in the house of Cornelius; forgiveness falls on *all* who believe. The book of Isaiah teaches exactly this, and this is the reasoning that covenant people must use, understanding that even a superhuman gift to reason, when it exalts itself against the knowledge of God, must be repented of, too.

So when somebody says "Let's reason together" in the sense of rationalism's superiority, it arouses suspicions in me. It always seems that the person suggesting it is searching for a reason to go his or her own way—perhaps because I also know that the great manipulator of contemporary American politics was more enamored of this verse than any other. "Come, let us reason together," Lyndon Baines Johnson used to say when he wanted others to knuckle under to his will.

The Church has reasoned with the world so much on so many topics, on the world's terms, that vast tracts of the church have come to accept the sociopolitical correctness of our culture, rather than the teachings of scripture. The issue of women in church office is such an issue, if not an issue of the past, decided ages ago, when women began to participate in Quaker sessions; or anyway decades ago, as women were ordained pastors in denominations across America; or for others when Mary Baker Eddy set up her church in Boston at the turn of the century. Indeed, a black woman was recently ordained a bishop in the Episcopal Church, though she remains unrecognized by the nominal head of that church, the Archbishop of Canterbury.

One of the oldest Christian institutions, however, and one of the largest, the Roman Catholic Church, has so far resisted ordaining women as pastor or elders or deacons, although Roman Catholicism has for centuries had orders of nuns ("Get thee to a nunnery," Hamlet says in 1594)—the establishment of which might be partially explained by 1 Timothy 5.9–10. The small denomination in which I presently hold membership, the Orthodox Presbyterian Church, recently completed a three-year study on the role of women in church office—a sixty-page document citing from scripture—and came to the conclusion that the offices of elder and deacon are not open to women, if Scripture is the only guide.

Sola Scriptura, the rallying call of civilization during the centuries of the church fathers, from Athanasius to Augustine, and the time of the Reformers—Hus, Luther, Calvin, Knox[8]—is no longer popular. The decision was not entirely happily received, nor did it find "approval with the whole congregation" (6.5). At least one local church has left the denomination due to this study.

It was a decision reached by a committee of men, of course, and the lone dissenter to the majority opinion, the president of a seminary on the West Coast, agreed on the office of elder, but felt that the diaconate, in light of a reference to Phoebe (Rom. 16.1), was available to women. Our assembly has asked local congregations to respond to the decision, and I hereby officially state that this is not an official response, although it may contain allusions to one somebody might someday attempt.

To deal with an accusation that rises both from the culture and within the church, it's necessary to say at first that Christianity has never been the faith of misogynists who cloister their misogyny under patriarchs. Schopenhauer was an unbeliever who sat under the higher critics Schleiermacher and Fichte in Berlin; Voltaire repudiated Christianity, as Rousseau and Goethe and Nietzsche— all notable misogynists, to my sense—repudiated it. Jesus commends the woman who pours expensive oil on his head as one who will go down in history wherever the gospel is heard. Paul commends dozens of women in a similar manner in his epistles to the church, and it is to Paul that most of those who study scripture turn (Gal. 3.28) when they speak about the ordination of women.

Women who are adherents of Christianity do not wear veils
that cover their faces and follow a dozen steps behind their husbands, or even in deferential rear-guard fashion, as in Japan, nor
have they ever in the history of Christianity. I believe a woman
should be treated as my equal as much as any man in the body of
the church. In Galatians 3.28, this exact attitude is embodied in
scripture itself, in salvific terms, from the perspective of acceptance
in the sight of God; that He, in offering salvation to every individual of every nation on the earth, makes no distinction between
Jew or Greek, slave or free, male or female.

I believe children should also be included here, in view of the
terms of the covenant (2.39), and Jesus' teaching about them.
But once you are called by the nondiscriminating Spirit to faith in
Him, you must observe the rest of the teachings of scripture, and
these speak of structures of protection both in the home (Eph.
5–6, Col. 3–4) and in the church (1 Cor. 11, 1 Tim. 3, Titus 1–2)
and in daily life—all of both covenants.

In a portion of one of my novels, which is cast in the form of
entries a woman makes in her diary, I was attempting an explicit
plea for the recognition of a woman as equal to a man, certainly in
the matter of salvation. She is called to faith into the church, but
she never assumes that the free expression of her feminine individuality would override her responsibilities to her children, nor
particularly suit her to assume the role of pastor or priest. And
once she has children, the tensions between her responsibilities
and her freedom are indeed the heart of her matter. It's a conflict
common to most parents with daughters and sons whose person-
alities are apparent from birth. In our responsibility to care for
them, we understand that their individuality can't be allowed free
reign, yet we are the only ones who, given the time, can truly
nurture to the full that individuality in each of them. Yet we want
our own future. The possibilities of working out these tensions,
which can involve remorse or worse for both husband and wife—

and will affect their offspring for the rest of their lives—is possible for the Christian within the structure provided by scripture.

I don't believe the solution for a woman is necessarily to take a job, which is the point at which most American males become feminists: when there is material advantage to being one. Many men have, in the crassest sense, cashed in on their wives. They have used the urge and tension in women as a means of doubling their income. My wife and I, who in the seventies were feminists, charter subscribers to *Ms.*, began to see that when we were equal but on opposite sides of an ultimate decision, we could only revolve in ratiocination or worse, since there was no standard except current practice (and whose practice did you then finally refer to?), until one or the other gave up or gave in.

This left us making fewer and fewer mutual decisions; we did things on our own. We have been married over twenty-five years and are still working out interfamilial and gender tensions, and I will admit that at times it isn't easy for either of us. But we have a structure to operate within, as each living human being uses the structure of language to make sense, instead of flailing in incoherence that adapts to any rules—otherwise known as meaninglessness. Before we were called by the Spirit of God to confess faith in Christ, as Lydia and Crispus were called—from different angles and perspectives at a time when we had separated and were about to be divorced—there was no hint of a structure. There was no standard of reconciliation; there was no hope.

In a passage quoted earlier from Ephesians, Paul through the Spirit instructs husbands to love their wives as Christ loved the church and gave his life for it. That's entire dedication and selflessness. And wives are instructed to submit to their husbands as to the Lord. Entire dedication and selflessness. Paul then compares marriage to the church, which he says is a mystery, and at least one element of explanation to the mystery is that Christ referred to himself as a bridegroom. He was preparing himself for the church, his bride. He gave himself over to her wholly, to the point of death, so that she would be built on his perfect foundation. In this way, husbands should give themselves over to their wives, but not so they as women are built up in the ways of the world. That is why wives are to submit to their husbands *as to the Lord* and not according to a manufactured agenda.

I have been made more aware of the distinctness of my sexual nature and identity, as I've been made more aware of my wife's, through this teaching, while we both have been more wholly united than before by the Spirit that builds up and teaches us in every realm, as it teaches the church. We are also united in the church, under its rule, and under its head. A portion of this unity is expressed in a passage from a story by Wendell Berry, "A Jonquil for Mary Penn," in which Mary, the central character of the story, begins by thinking of a neighbor's description of her husband, Elton:

> Walter Cotman always spoke of Mary as Elton's "better half." In spite of his sulks and silences, she would not go so far as "better." That she was his half she had no doubt at all. He needed her. At times she knew with a joyous ache that she completed him, just as she knew with the same joy that she needed him and he completed her. How beautiful a thing it was, she thought, to be a half, to be completed by such another half! When had there ever been such a yearning of halves toward each other, such a longing, even in quarrels, to be whole? And sometimes they would be whole. Their wholeness came upon them like a rush of light, around them and within them, so that she felt they must be shining in the dark.[9]

The light of the Spirit has made my wife and me shine as one in ways that were unknown to us before we entered the church as children and fell in faith at her feet, before Christ. My wife's gifts to the church are used for their own merit and are also used whenever mine are; my gifts are used through her as long as they are under the Lord and remain faithful to him. For this is a mystery, Paul says, that the head of woman is man, and the head of the church is Christ, and the head of Christ is God. This structure of coordinating order permeates the church and Christian life at every level.

I would not want one of my children to be ordained; and, yes, I'm aware that there have been child preachers. Miriam and Aaron did not want Moses, in his foreshadowing of Christ, to be the prophet of God to Israel. It probably never seemed fair to some men that the tribe of Levi alone was chosen to furnish priests for the tabernacle (what about us Gadites and Danites and Josephites and the rest?); and Korah and Dathan and Abiram, as Levitical priests chosen by God, did not want to submit to Moses and Aaron (Num. 16), and so were destroyed. It's a matter of biblical record that when Jesus chose the twelve apostles, and one of them the devil, signifying his choosing in all realms, he chose no woman. Elders, males, are ordained in the churches by Paul and Peter. This isn't cultural neglect, but a refining of order in the church established by Christ.

Paul remains in Ephesus for two years, teaching in the house of Tyrranus, a schoolmaster most of us suspect we've met, and a practice begins that has been cashed in upon by hundreds of charlatans since. Handkerchiefs and aprons are carried from Paul and used to heal and to drive out demons. Not that I believe Paul was a charlatan—I don't—or that evil spirits do not exist. They surely do. This is one of the instances in which an apostle performs wonders stranger even than Jesus performed, as He prophesied would happen.

Is there a problem in Paul's ministry, that he keeps attracting demons? Jesus attracted more; he was at the center of the final, ultimate battle to control the souls of men, and every satanic and demonic power available joined arms to destroy his ministry and person. The head of that power (reread *That Hideous Strength*) was undone by Christ's resurrection from the dead, but the beast has been cruelly flailing people in its death throes since, as Hitler's Nazi rule continued in cruelty two years after its actual death. And now in Paul's ministry to the gentile nations, these demons, bad losers all, want to do in him and his disciples, as they want to devour every living soul on earth.

In Shirley Nelson's careful examination of the Frank Sandford Shiloh cult, *Fair Clear and Terrible*,[10] she includes an account of a demon-possessed fellow that should set your hair on end. The society that will accept Castaneda's Don Juan, a recasting of the malevolent "legion," or shape-shifter, or an actress's New Age "deep throat," who speaks in the retrograde platitudes of Edgar Cayce's malign familiar, somehow finds it difficult to accept the presence of evil. This is an indication of how selective we are in our beliefs and how we continue to allow ourselves to be deceived by the master of that process, Satan.[11]

Enough recent books have appeared, *The Ultimate Evil, Children of the Lie, Unholy Spirits*, and more, to signal to us that something is amiss, in case we missed it in scripture, so it's no good feigning ignorance. And there are more than enough recent news accounts to document the worship of Satan, and its demand for human sacrifices (as the worship of Molech demanded human sacrifice), for anyone to pretend this is a subject for the Dark Ages. *It's worse now.* The present unprovoked violence, such as the shooting of children on a playground, or a crowd in a fast-food restaurant, or a family by a son, should move us to set aside for good the idea that people are getting better and better, as a banal platitude goes. Sin entered the world by Adam, and all the imaginings of our hearts since, scripture says, are evil continually. Even the righteous acts we prize the most have the appearance, in the eyes of God, of filthy rags (Isa. 64.6).

Evil doesn't always make the blatant appearance some of the examples above might suggest, as America's adopted Russian émigré and recent Nobel laureate Joseph Brodsky points out in "A Commencement Address": "Such is the structure of life that what we regard as Evil is capable of a fairly ubiquitous presence if only because it tends to appear in the guise of good. You never see it crossing your threshold announcing itself: 'Hi, I'm Evil!'

"A prudent thing to do, therefore, would be to subject your notions of good to the closest possible scrutiny, to go, so to speak, through your entire wardrobe checking which of your clothes may fit a stranger. That, of course, may turn into a full-time occupation, and well it should. You'll be surprised how many things you considered your own and good can easily fit, without much adjustment, your enemy. . . . To put it mildly, nothing can be turned and worn inside out with greater ease than one's notion of social justice, civic conscience, a better future, etc. One of the surest signs of danger here is the number of those who share your views, not so much because unanimity has the knack of degenerating into uniformity as because of the probability—implicit in great numbers—that noble sentiment is being faked."[12]

In these words addressed to graduates of Smith College in 1984, Brodsky not only refers to Jesus' view of dealing with evil (Mat. 5.29–42—is it only exiled Russian émigrés who as writers quote scripture?), but sees so far into the center of standardless American society that he anticipates the evil "unanimity" of ideological and political correctness whose intolerant fakery plagues every American university.

A central teaching of Christ is that you can't serve two masters. It's one or the other; or, as Bob Dylan puts it in his rousing song, "Ya gotta serve *some*body." Paul in his missionary journeys and his epistles teaches, as Christ did, that you are in bondage to Christ or Death, Christ or Mammon, Christ or demons. And so the possessed young woman refers to Paul and the disciples as bondservants of the most high God, through a demon truly knowledgeable on bondage—as Christians should confess to be servants and call on the renewing Spirit to displace the spirits they previously served.

In Ephesus, a sort of exorcism trade sets up, and the seven sons of the chief priest, Sceva, begin to command evil spirits to leave by "Jesus whom Paul preaches." Or they do this until one spirit says, "I recognize Jesus, and I know about Paul, but who are you?" Again there is a sense of an order of authority in the church, a spiritual kingdom, even among demons. The possessed man then attacks a pair of Sceva's sons and tears their clothes so badly they run off naked. The entire scene does not depict a neutral middle ground, any more than the rest of scripture does, but a battlefield in which good is pitted against evil.

This is why the author Stephen King is so popular among young people. Not that he isn't popular with the middle-aged and elderly, too, including Christians, but it's among youth that you find his most fervent adherents. Young people are not as tutored as their elders in the philosophy that insists human nature is improving every day, and from what they see even at school, they understand evil is abroad. King's work confirms this evil, as the novels of few contemporaries do. And though it would be improvident to say that King's view is clearly biblical, he does, like the good journeyman he is, keep reporting on the presence of evil in yet another aspect of American life with each new book, and young people sense that there is more truth to his view than to the platitudinous exclamations and fantasies of fiction called "Christian."

When news of the attack on Sceva's sons gets around, fear falls on the city, as it should on any setting where Satan has an upper hand, "and the name of the Lord was being magnified." This is the result of every apostolic sign; the Lord attests to his power through his apostles, and his word spreads and is magnified. The fear that falls on Ephesus is obviously the fear that leads to repentance, because a period of confession and turning from evil begins in the city, including the first recorded book burning. Magicians and sorcerers gather their incunabula and source materials on demonology and begin "burning them in sight of all; and they counted up the price of them and found it to be fifty thousand pieces of silver."

Say a million dollars' worth in present currency. Evil never comes cheap. That's largely its temptation: *this could cost me my life*. The book burning is done out of the sorcerers' free will, please note, in a repentant mode, as if to say, "This black magic I here abjure." It is not imposed on them by a censor; nor does a censorious group alter history by forbidding any further books to mention, say, that Paul came preaching and performing signs and wonders, or that the Pilgrims prayed at the first Thanksgiving. Here is an admission that the "arts" the sorcerers practice are the reverse of, or in opposition to, the gospel Paul has been teaching. "So the word of God was growing mightily and prevailing."

After a tour through Macedonia and Achaia, presumably to strengthen the churches (20.2), Paul again prepares to return to Jerusalem, and speaks prophetic words: "After I have been there, I must also see Rome." He has probably heard of this capital of the civilized world at every turn in his journeys, and probably has received detailed accounts from Priscilla and Aquila. Could it be worse than Athens? But at the moment a reaction rises from another special-interest group, as it were, other than the magicians.

Demetrius, a silversmith who fashions shrines to Diana, assembles the artisans and workmen of the city, and says, "Men, you know that our prosperity depends on our business." Amen! "And you see and hear that not only in Ephesus, but in almost all of Asia, this Paul has persuaded and turned away a considerable number of people, saying that gods made with hands are no gods at all." A good listener. The danger, he warns them, in this fervent speech of an inciter of crowds, is not only that their trade will fall into disrepute, but that the temple of Diana will be treated as null. They begin shouting with rage, "Great is Diana of the Ephesians!"

Soon the whole city is caught up in the confusion. The crowd drags two of Paul's disciples into the amphitheater, and when Paul wants to go into this assembly, which has the aura of a lynch mob, the disciples won't let him—again the implication of a local restraint on Paul. Finally a magistrate, a just one, the town clerk, persuades the crowd to disperse and pursue legal means if they have a complaint, or they'll be culpable, he says, for their uproar—in one of the first recorded labor riots, rising in this instance against the gospel.

Paul swings through Macedonia again, giving "in these districts" (another sense of levels within the church) hearty exhortations, and ends again in Greece. By a mere naming of a list of those with him, we receive a sense not only of the personal nature of Christianity but of the success of the gospel in Berea, Thessalonica, Derbe (where Paul was stoned), and Asia. "But these had gone on ahead," we read, "and were waiting for us at Troas." Luke again is present. The sail from Philippi takes "five days," and with the group that has gathered at Troas Paul and Luke remain seven more.

"And on the first day of the week, when we were gathered together to break bread," Luke writes, reaffirming for the new covenant church that the Sabbath is to be celebrated on the first day of the week, when Christ broke free of the bonds of death. Here the breaking of bread seems the sacrament of communion, or Lord's supper, because of what follows. We receive from Luke an exact description of a worship service of the fledgling church. Paul, who is anxious to leave the next day, and so appears to have remained for this Sunday service, preaches to those present, and his speech goes on past midnight. A long sermon. Then there is a physician's detail: "And there were many lights in the upper room where they were assembled."

A lot of people, a lot of torches burning; little oxygen. It's difficult enough to remain attentive to long sermons under the best conditions, but they seem to strike hardest at youth, as here. Eutychus, a young man who has apparently found a good vantage point above the crowd but is inhaling smoke and carbon dioxide, a boy who will be held forever dear by those who tend to nod off, is, as Paul keeps talking, "overcome by sleep" on the third-story window ledge where he's sitting. He falls over backward to the ground. When people get to him, he's dead. An early casualty of the gospel? Paul runs down the stairs and outside and falls on the boy as Elijah fell over the widow's son, also dead. Taking him in an embrace, Paul says, "Don't be alarmed, for his living soul is in him." After a breaking of bread that seems a regular meal, Paul continues to talk until daybreak, and the dead young man, to everyone's joy, walks away alive.

Paul wants to be in Jerusalem for Pentecost, and on the way there he calls the Ephesian elders, a plurality of them, to him in Miletus. No minister or pastor, not even one of the balky and headstrong priests in J. F. Powers's novels or short stories, is able to go it alone. No single individual can bear the oversight of an entire congregation alone, and none should be asked to undertake such a chore. It's never undertaken by anyone in the church of Acts.

Paul is waiting at Miletus, in a coastal harbor, on a beach with its ocean smell, and when the Ephesian elders gather, he says, "You yourselves know how I lived with you in all seasons, from the first day I came into Asia, serving the Lord with all humility of mind and tears, and enduring plots that fell my way through the Jews; and how I kept back nothing that was profitable, but have shown you and have taught you publicly, and from house to house, giving testimony both to the Jews, and also to the Greeks, of repentance toward God and faith through our Lord Jesus Christ.

"And now I go, as a captive to the Spirit, to Jerusalem, not knowing what will happen to me there, except that the Holy Spirit testifies in every city, saying that bonds and afflictions await me. But none of these things move me, nor do I count my life dear to myself, so long as I might finish my course with joy, and also the ministry which I received from the Lord Jesus Christ, to testify fully the gospel of the grace of God.

"And now I know that none of you, among whom I went proclaiming the kingdom of God, will see my face again. Therefore I testify to you on this day that I am innocent of the blood of all. For I did not hold back from declaring to you the whole counsel of God. Therefore take heed to yourselves, and to all the flock over which the Holy Spirit has made you overseers, to feed the church of God that He has purchased with His own blood. For I know that after I depart savage wolves will enter in among you, not sparing the flock. And from among your own selves men will arise, speaking perverse things, in order to draw disciples away after them.

"Therefore, watch; and remember that for the space of three years I never ceased to warn all of you night and day with tears. And now I commend you to God and to the word of His grace, which is able to build you up and give you an inheritance among all who are sanctified. I have coveted no man's gold, or silver, or clothing. You yourselves know that these hands have ministered to my needs, and to those who were with me. I have shown you all things, that by working in this way we ought to help the weak, and to remember the words of the Lord Jesus, how He himself said, *It is more blessed to give than to receive.*"

Paul falls to his knees and prays with them, in this parting that expresses as strongly as any passage in scripture the bond of love between believers. Does he cry, God be with you! He might, but the text doesn't say that. What it does explicitly say is more significant: everybody on the beach is weeping. Christianity is a personal religion, a religion of close relationships that deals with people one on one, ministering to them and encouraging them to grow with each other in the faith, and now these heartbroken elders embrace Paul and kiss his neck, grieved most deeply by his prophetic words: None of you will see my face again.

10

THE EARTH ITSELF

IN THE CHURCH I presently attend, four elders read Hebrew and Greek. Two are particularly adept at koine Greek, and another took his degree, cum laude, in Attic Greek and philosophy. They all will have a chance to study these reflections for accuracy. There are five other elders, at least one of whom has a grasp of biblical theology as profound as any I've encountered. Most of the elders attended college at least for a time, and they hold five advanced degrees among them, but the theologian, gray-haired, never finished high school. He reads and studies daily, while running a farm and ranch operation; he teaches adult Sunday School and, on occasion, preaches. During the week other elders hold Bible studies, with prayer afterward for local and broader realms.

There are fifty-three members on the roll of the church, which is an exact number. There is not a loose person, and no one is unaccounted for. The elders practice oversight and discipline, and visit each member at least once a year. They hold catechism and church history classes for children at three different levels, and in one of these, at the present, the study of the Westminster Confession and Catechism by G. I. Williamson, mentioned earlier, is used. Once when I was in New York City, a young East Indian woman came up after a worship service in Brooklyn and said that she had read Williamson's study on the Confession of Faith on the subway, on her ride to work at an investment firm and back, and that the meaning of the teachings of the church started overtaking her faster than the subway stops.

There was a shine of solidity to her face as she said this, and I felt I understood her gratitude. When I began to pick up the strings of my spiritual life after the clop of that guillotine that came down in college, I turned to the Bible, but the actual turning was more indirect than that might sound. I was in my late twenties and wanted to check a phrase, "the wages of sin is death," to use in a novel. Then for another novel I was working on at the same time, the one that took a decade, I needed to find where in the Bible it said that wives must submit to their husbands, remembering that sermon I had heard at four or five. My wife, to whom I did not intend to read the verse, came from a background that included reading the Bible, and she showed me how to use a concordance.

She has ministered to me for more than twenty-five years, but her knowing hand here proved to be not only time-saving but providential, in the course our lives were to take. Because as I continued to work on this novel that traced the course of several generations of a family from the upper Great Plains, I had to refer to scripture. The family was made up on both sides of recent immigrants, and the values that they and their predecessors, the Church Fathers and Pilgrims and Puritans, adhered to (and sometimes didn't) were based on the Bible, so it seemed only fair to them, and to my readers, to discover what the Bible said.

When the house where an unclean spirit dwells is swept bare, Jesus says, referring to a person's spiritual state (Luke 11.24–26), then that house is susceptible to the entry of a variety of worse spirits—a more vivid way of saying that the world as it was formed abhors a vacuum. That house swept clean but rapidly filling with piling characters and creatures was exactly my state over that decade. I read the Bible and recognized its wisdom but was not able to order it, along with edges of my own mind, into a coherence I could live with. Or didn't know what to do with it when I could. Passages and verses seemed to contradict others, yet the pull of its truth on my conscience afflicted me so much I was divided and maddened, drawn and quartered in my intellect.

I reached the moment of no exit I've tried at different times to describe, and it was then that a pastor who was familiar with the work of G. I. Williamson began talking to me and my wife in our home. This pastor served in the Orthodox Presbyterian Church, a denomination that withdrew from the mainstream of presbyterian churches in the 1930s.

One of the leaders of that withdrawal, John Gresham Machen,[1] whose introduction to the New Testament has been one of my most consistent helps, was a Professor of New Testament at Princeton Theological Seminary; indeed he was teaching at Princeton when he wrote the study I've drawn from for mine. Earlier in his life, he had tasted some of the teachings of the highest biblical criticism at its source, in Germany, at the universities of Marburg and Göttingen, and then later had grown wary when he saw those teachings begin to appear in the Presbyterian Church in America.

Machen left the glory of that ivied bastion, Princeton, to help found Westminster Seminary in Philadelphia, drawing to it the Dutch scholar Cornelius Van Til and the Scot John Murray, among others—a well-represented worldwide community—and Machen was instrumental in establishing what is now known as the Orthodox Presbyterian Church. He was an exuberant scholar, one of the few biblical scholars able to refer with equal ease to the classics or Shakespeare (indeed, he once expected to be a classicist), and he would travel anywhere to explain the rationale of what only years before he would have judged as sinful schism: the formation of a new church.

He didn't live to see the fruits of his service, perhaps at least partly because it didn't occur to this elegant and patrician Baltimore native that he would ever have to face a North Dakota winter. In December of 1936, at a time when he was unwell from overwork, he traveled to a small rural congregation in Leith, North Dakota. Leith is now nearly a ghost town; boarded-up buildings grayed by weather line the single block of its main street, and even the post office has closed down. But in 1935 there was in Leith what Machen perceived to be a faithful congregation, and he came by train from Philadelphia to speak to the church at the request of its pastor. Everybody remarked about his ill health and coughing, which seemed to worsen, and eventually he had to be taken to a hospital in Bismarck. He died there on January 1, 1937. His last words, dictated for a telegram to his colleague John Murray, were "I'm so glad for the active obedience of Christ. No hope without it."

I'm sure there were those in the mainline presbyterian churches who suspected Machen had received his comeuppance. There was surely joy in many hearts that he was dead; in his fifty-five years he produced a dozen books, including a Greek *Grammar* still in use in seminaries, and he was one of the most erudite defenders of the faith of Christ in the first half of this century, equaled in intellect by only one other, C. S. Lewis, but a better theologian, since Machen heard the Bible read in his household from the time of his birth. If he had suspected that he should be struck down for schismatic acts, he probably would have prayed, Lord, strike me down. It was only after years of struggle that he left the church of his first love, and once he was dead, there was never quite the same dynamism in the struggle against its latitudinarian trends.

His death was due to a severe case of pneumonia, according to the medical records, and the pulpit he spoke from at Leith during his last week of life stands at the head of the church where my family and I worship each Sunday. A child of some members of the Leith congregation, present in the church building the night Machen spoke (the covenant was honored at Leith), apparently caught the same strain of pneumonia from Machen; two weeks later this child died in the Bismarck hospital where Machen had died. The parents of the child, now in their eighties, are still living. They are members of the church I attend. The present pastor of the church is G. I. Williamson. He was called from New Zealand to serve it at a time when I was teaching at a university in New York state.

It wasn't until a further teaching assignment took me to London that I was able to spend much time with him. We at last got together for two days in June, when he was on his way to an ecumenical conference in Zimbabwe and had a layover at Heathrow. We took the tube together to Westminster Abbey, and after some urging on my part (wearing a King's College sweater that was a gift from my students and speaking in the East Side accent then in the vogue, all vowels), I persuaded a keeper of the keys that he was in the presence of an august scholar, and we walked together, Williamson and I for the first time, into the spacious barrenness of a room at the front of the cathedral that the vicar explained was now not in use: the Jerusalem Chamber. Henry VIII could have entered and sat before the primitive fireplace and reclined with the softening ease of those who stare at the ocean as if listening to internal music.

The church over the entire world is made up of living tissue like this. It persists in spite of every division, including the separation of physical death.

Which is a roundabout way of saying that the pastor who began to talk to me and my wife was an effective teacher—we joined the church he pastored—and that this wee denomination rightly has a reputation for stalwart teachers. It wasn't until this pastor pointed out to me, in Williamson's clear language, the Five Points, as they're known, that the seeming contradictory nature of the

Bible, which had had the effect of drawing me off in several directions at the same time, began to settle into sense. These points gave me, more than anything, a center of focus, and then the scriptures of both covenants started to cohere, and suddenly an internal rearrangement took place as all of the passages of the scripture that I held in my mind and any I chanced to look at when I opened a Bible started tumbling into place at the feet of the one who is the source of all language, Christ.

These five points are also known as Calvin's Five Points (an acronym for them is TULIP), although Calvin himself never formulated them. They were drawn up by a church council, the Synod of Dordt, to refute as heresy the five points of the Dutch theologian Arminius. "Calvin" is such a dirty word in the modern evangelical world I find myself straining against a reluctance to mention him at all, though I should know better. From the reaction I've seen in Christians merely to his name—similar to the reaction of university professors to scripture—you'd think he was responsible for the ills of the church. It's largely due to Calvin and his ordering of Scripture into what is known as systematic theology, in *The Institutes of the Christian Religion*, that protestant churches exist as they do. So if it's your view that they shouldn't exist, then probably he is a dirty word. But if you belong to a protestant denomination, you should examine your conscience.

Calvin has received press as bad as the press accorded to Solzhenitsyn, and that press is identical to the press the academy and evangelicaldom in general has given the Puritans. For good reason, perhaps. The Puritans were Calvinists. So were the Pilgrims. To offer a glimpse of the other side, you should know that during the time of Charles I, the monarch beheaded by order of Parliament, there were women in England who called themselves prophetesses. They didn't always have good things to say about Charles during his reign and were abused, imprisoned, or executed by him. One of those who was imprisoned, the prophetess Lady Eleanor Davies, loved anagrams and thought that O. Cromwell suggested "Howl Rome" (Charles I's wife was a Roman Catholic and his reign was supported by the Church in Rome), and in an account related in *The Weaker Vessel* by Lady Antonia Fraser, this prophetess visits Cromwell himself, the Ur-Puritan of all time:

> When the Army was at its headquarters at St Albans in 1648, Lady Eleanor presented to him a book of her prophecies first printed (with dire results) in 1633. She superscribed the book *The Armies Commission*, adding the verse: 'Behold he cometh with ten thousand of his Saints to execute judgment on all.' . . . Smiling at the superscription, and putting on his 'specticles' [*sic*], Cromwell gently observed: 'But we are not all saints.'[2]

Cromwell reenacts the apostolic attitude; though he is to be sovereign ruler of the realm of England, the Lord Protector, he openly receives a woman who is viewed as controversial as an equal in belief. On a matter of biblical teaching, including a truth about the troops under his command, he is gently corrective on scriptural grounds.

The Puritans have at last found a congenial historian in Leland Ryken (who has also written on the literature of the Bible), in the recent *Worldly Saints*.[3] America's Puritan and Pilgrim heritage, two strains of Calvinist protestantism—one offering retreat from, the other confrontation with the world—is a subject that touches on this country's and its churches' survival, yet is of such complexity (a complexity beyond the scope of these reflections) that it's best to point you to a recent book, *Anti-Calvinists: The Rise of English Arminianism*,[4] by Dr. Nicholas Tyacke, a British scholar. Tyacke has studied letters, books, and records of the leaders of the Church of England from 1590 to 1640, and has found that the "Arminians" in seventeenth-century England, who viewed the monarch as the head of the Church of England (and later called themselves Anglicans), became a Crown party inside the Church and acted as an ecclesiastical arm of the state. This is the ecclesiocracy that everybody in America fears, when they think they fear a *theocracy*. A theocracy must have its ruler directly appointed by God, as the apostles were appointed by Jesus: a David or a Solomon.

Calvinists disputed the authority of the Crown over the Church, and theirs, which was the majority view (see the first Lambeth Articles written at Cambridge in 1595), held sway from the end of the Spanish Armada until the reign of Charles I: "That Calvinism was the *de facto* religion of the Church of England under Queen Elizabeth and King James may surprise those brought up to regard Calvinists and Puritans as one and the same. Such an identification, however, witnesses to the posthumous success of the Arminians in blackening the reputations of their Calvinist opponents; until the 1620s Puritan, as a technical term, was usually employed to describe those members of the English Church who wanted further Protestant reforms in liturgy and organization."[5]

The primary blackening was by Richard Montague, chaplain to James I, who in *A New Gagg for an Old Goose* claimed that all Calvinists were Puritans, and described "Puritanism and Popery as Scylla and Charybdis, and said that the Church of England stood in the gap between. . . ."[6] The Calvinists in the Commons of the house of Parliament, a majority of that body, reacted in anger, and Montague was denounced. But when Charles I took the throne, Montague rose in importance in the court and wrote another book, *Apello Caesarem*, in which he called Calvin, who helped form and run the peaceable government of Geneva, an extremist (a false idea held to this day), and said that the State should rule through "experts." One of these was Archbishop Laud, an Anglican; Laud, while claiming no essential changes in the church would be made, began to institute elaborate rituals nonexistent in the Church of England before his time, rewrote the Book of

Common Prayer, abolished preaching, and began to burn at the stake "dissenters," who of course were "Puritans."

These were the issues that brought the majority, now treated as a fringe group, to the point we all can trace, because of the upheaval: revolution—not simply rebellion or civil war, but revolution, years before the French Revolution, and one that engendered the American Revolution, after a boatload of the "Puritans" sailed the sea and formed the Massachusetts Bay Colony. The Pilgrims, true dissenters and separatists, arrived on the same shores only years before at Plimouth Plantation, and first attempted to establish a utopian community. Between their actual Scylla and Charybdis this country will eventually rise or fall.

And so we sail, and "running a straight course we came to Cos, and on the next day to Rhodes, and from there to Patara. And finding a ship sailing over to Phoenicia, getting all aboard, we set sail. And sighting Cyprus, and leaving it on the left, we sailed into Syria, and came down to Tyre, for the ship was to unload its cargo there."

Disciples at Tyre warn Paul not to go to Jerusalem, but after he and his group have stayed a week, they head for the ship. There is a scene like a reprise of Paul's farewell to the Ephesian elders, but more domestic. Here whole families, with all their children present, walk with Paul and his group from the city to the beach, and then everybody kneels in the sand and prays with him.

The next ship takes the group to Caesarea, where we meet up again with one of the Seven, Philip, who years ago taught the Ethiopian eunuch out of Isaiah, and so by the Spirit's direction established the branching of the church over the entire earth. Philip is now called "the evangelist," which not only lends a certain propriety to the use of that term in the church, but suggests two other possibilities: that a deacon may rise in office, or that the ordination of The Seven was not to the office of deacon to begin with.[7]

We also learn that Philip has four daughters, virgins, who are "prophetesses," a reminder that this is still an era when, though apostles are present, the words of the New Covenant are not inscripturated and available to all. No prophecies from the young women appear in the text (they would have been of temporal matters, most likely, suited to the time), but it's relevant to note, in the order we find everywhere in the church, that they are of the family of Philip, who was directly ordained by the apostles, and that their title, if not office, persisted into Cromwell's time. And to note, too, that when prophecy for the church itself arrives, although the young women are resident, it does not arrive from them.

Agabus, that silent scriptural embodiment who seems Paul's nemesis, appears. He goes straight to Paul and unwinds Paul's belt, wound about his outer garb like a girdle, and binds Paul's hands and feet, and then, as if to guarantee that the mime of his prophecy is not misunderstood, Agabus for the first time in the text of Acts speaks: "The Holy Spirit says these things: So shall the Jews at Jerusalem bind the man whose belt this is, and deliver him into the hands of the Gentiles."

The cryptic turn of the prophecy, with its suggestion of Christ's betrayal, surely affects Paul. Again he is warned about Jerusalem, this time by a prophet of the church, in a prophecy that runs this way: The established church in Jerusalem, of which you were once the most zealous devotee, will not only not listen to the gospel from you but will bind your hands and feet as you used to bring members of the Way, bound, to them. Then they will deliver you to the gentiles, members of those diverse nations you've been visiting in your missionary journeys, and they will—

But the prophecy ends, and the only course is to follow Paul as he pursues his goal, Jerusalem. Once there, he meets with James and "all the elders." The church in Jerusalem listens to his report, particularly about the wonders God has wrought in foreign nations. The assembly then praises God, and Paul is told: "You see, brother, how many thousands of Jews there are who believe"—in reference to Jerusalem, undoubtedly—"and they are all zealous of the law. And they have been informed that you teach all the Jews among the other nations to forsake Moses, saying they ought not to circumcise children, nor to walk according to the customs."

This explanation gets to the heart of the problem. Not to circumcise children would be to say there is no covenant, which no right-thinking Jew could abide. Paul never has said any such thing, but rather baptizes to place the seal of the new covenant on believers. There are, however, also customs and traditions that the hierarchy, who administrates these, wants to keep preserved. Some of the customs may have been prescribed by the old covenant, but probably just as many were not; the Greek is *ethos* and means "rite" as often as it means a ritual prescribed. This was the point on which Jesus excoriated the Pharisees—for adhering to the rites and customs of tradition, and ignoring the weightier matters of the law (Mat. 23.23, Mark 7.7–9).

So what will Paul do, they wonder. They assure him a multitude is going to be gathering, because the news is out that he's here. Then James and the elders suggest what some see as a form of subterfuge. They ask Paul to participate in a ritual purification, along with four others who have taken a vow, so the Jewish hierarchy can't accuse him of disdaining Mosaic law. Paul has never shunned or denied the weight or authority of the law, though he always insists it is ineffectual in saving anyone from sin, and in consenting to undergo the ritual—he does consent—he is bowing to the wisdom of the local church. That wisdom isn't meant to appease, but to teach Jerusalemites, through Paul, that there is no discontinuity between the ethics of the law and the gospel the church now declares.

Paul goes with the others and is purified the next day, and then enters the temple, to signify the accomplishment of the days of the purification, until the time when an offering will be made. This offering is one of many the guardians of the temple wish to preserve. But when the days of purification are nearly up, Jews from Asia see Paul in the temple and cry, "Men of Israel, help! This is the man who teaches everyone everywhere against the people and the law and this place!" Meaning the temple. They claim Paul has brought in Greeks and polluted the holy place.

Paul hasn't, but earlier he was seen in Jerusalem in the company of an Ephesian, Trophimus, probably a convert from that city of sorcerers. Such a multitude has gathered, the seizure of Paul seems planned—"all the city was moved, and the people ran together." The tumult spreads as Paul is dragged from the temple and its doors slammed shut. This clangorous detail resounds through the rest of Acts: the established church has shut Paul out, and the only direction he can travel now is away from it. As he will, appearing before those rulers and kings prophesied to him years ago in Damascus. The doors closed against him will also bring down the judgment Jesus said would take place in the lifetime of his listeners; the destruction of the temple in A.D. 70.

As the mob prepares to kill Paul, the news gets to the Jerusalem chiliarch, or Roman commander of a thousand troops, and he rushes into the city with guards and centurions. The crowd stops beating Paul when the cohort arrives, but the chiliarch has Paul bound with chains and asks who he is and what he's done. There's such an uproar, the chiliarch can't make sense of it, and he commands his soldiers to carry Paul to the fortress. And they literally have to carry him, bound, up a set of stairs toward their barracks, because of the violence of the crowd, shouting now, "Do away with him!"

At the door to the fortress, Paul says to the commander, Claudius Lysias, "Is it lawful for me to ask you something?" And Claudius Lysias, in surprise, says, "Do you speak Greek? Then you are not the Egyptian who before these days caused a riot and led four thousand men of the assassins into the wilderness?" This is probably one of the rising rebellious groups that will soon bring Rome down in war upon Judea, and there is more than a hint here, too, of the perception outsiders had of Moses during the Exodus.

Paul says, "I am a Jew of Tarsus in Cilicia, a citizen of no mean city. And I beg you, let me speak to the people."

The commander honors his request, perhaps because of the status of Tarsus as a Roman protectorate. After Paul motions with his hands to quiet the crowd, he shifts to "the Hebrew dialect," that quick, another tongue, and tells the Jerusalemites how he persecuted Christians to death. Then he recounts his experience on the road to Damascus. The crowd is silent, listening with interest—and it is a wonderful story in itself—but then Paul mentions a further event, during a visit to Jerusalem, when the Lord appeared to him and said, " 'Hurry and go quickly out of Jerusalem, for they will not receive your testimony about me.' And I said, 'Lord, they know that I imprisoned and beat in every synagogue those who believed on You. And when the blood of your martyr Stephen was poured out, I also was standing there, consenting to his death, and holding the garments of those who killed him. And he said to me, 'Go, for I will send you far away among all the nations.' "

Here the people in the crowd pull off their cloaks and throw dust in the air, crying, "Away with such a fellow from the earth, for it's not fit that he should live!"

Lysias orders Paul to be examined, by scourging, or the whip, apparently a common form of "examination," thinking this will get Paul to confess why he has aroused the people. But as Paul is tied in place with thongs, he says to a centurion, "Is it lawful for you to scourge a man who is a Roman and uncondemned?" The soldier runs to Lysias to ask what to do, permitting us to examine the question of civil disobedience, which has affected the church since, is affecting it now, and threatens to affect in ways it never has, as the protest against abortion continues to escalate.

If the Jerusalem Sanhedrin, which was the government and hierarchy of the old covenant Church, can also be viewed as a civil authority, as it seems it partly was, then the apostles went contrary to that authority when they preached the gospel (chapters 4 and 5). But the command to preach arrived from the Spirit, from Christ, who, to those who accept him as Messiah, is the Lord of the Church. The apostles, and especially Paul, do get into trouble and do cause civil strife, but always through the declaration of the gospel, not a sit-down demonstration, and the trouble nearly always originates within an established religion—whether it's the idol fabricators in Ephesus, the Sanhedrin, or local synagogue officials.

The concept of passive resistance, which isn't found in the gospels but is a precept of Mahatma Gandhi, based on the teaching of that eminent nineteeth-century novelist Count Leo Tolstoy, has often been adopted by the church. To derive passive resistance from Jesus' teaching that if an enemy slaps you on one cheek you should turn the other, you have to transpose personal insult into the arena of public protest. Most passive resisters haven't been slapped to begin with, and I've never seen anyone make a similar transposition for the following teaching from the same part of Matthew 5, that if a man sues you in court and takes away your coat, you should give him your cloak—a demand by Christians that everyone who loses a legal suit be compelled to give up double what was asked for in the suit. Jesus is speaking in hyperbole, for emphasis, in this passage, and when he is slapped himself (John 18.23), he rebukes the person.

The writer with perhaps the greatest sensitivity to language, Joseph Brodsky, recognizes in the essay mentioned the hyperbolic quality of Matthew 5.39–42: "The meaning of these lines [*lines* denotes poetry] is anything but passive, for it suggests that evil can be made absurd through excess; it suggests rendering evil absurd through dwarfing its demands with the volume of your compliance, which devalues the harm. This sort of thing puts a victim into a very active position, into the position of a mental aggressor."[8]

The practice of passive resistance has become a cultural trend; the act of rescuing from death the progeny of women who have decided to have them aborted, an act of conscience. An excess? Rather than rule on the merits of either (except to say that those who oppose abortion are discriminated against as few protestors are), I believe the acts of the apostles teach another way. When a local branch of government is not legislating as scripture calls it to (Rom. 13, 1 Peter 3), one must appeal for relief from that government to a higher civil authority—as Paul does to the Roman government under which Judea was a protectorate. I realize how hopeless this can seem, when our present-day government appears corrupt at its roots, but persistence to excess (Luke 18) can wear away even august pillars and walls of marble.

I was once taken to court. An armed sheriff appeared at our door to hand me a summons. It was the year of our move to North Dakota, and we had found, after the liberties of the East, that it was contrary to state law to send our children to any school but a public school, period. There were some parochial schools, similar to the one I attended when I was a child, still in operation, but they were allowed to exist only under a kind of grandfather clause, as long as they taught the same curriculum as the public schools and allowed their teachers, who had to be certified by the State, to be overseen by the State Department of Public Instruction.

My immediate family had moved from North Dakota when I was eight, and I had returned for visits over the years, never suspecting I would settle here, but now that I had, in a kind of culmination of the spiritual odyssey my wife and I were on, I was, as a thirty-six-year-old and a Christian, appalled to find myself facing this law. And in my native state! By now I knew there is no neutral ground for education, certainly not in a system that forbade both the old covenant and the new (the Ten Commandments removed from all classrooms; the Bible never to be commented upon, if it was read—until a teacher recently had to remove from his classroom a Bible merely on a shelf), while it funded the banalities of New Age and the Eastern religion of Transcendental Meditation.

We started to teach our children at home. Illegal. I drove the dozen miles into town to "reason" with our local state's attorney, and he said, "I could fine you two hundred dollars a day! I'll throw you in jail!" I was still not entirely well, from that thorn in my flesh (psoriasis and hypoglycemia, ailments that originate in the liver—weakened, no doubt, by years of hedonistic abuse, plus other complications, so you won't keep guessing), and this was a dozen years ago, when the Christian community was not prepared to support our stand. I was not capable of the rigors of active resistance on my own; I caved in. We sent our daughter to the parochial school, a two-hour bus ride every day (the same ride as to the public school), and began to work with other parents to establish a Christian academy.

Our daughter had an excellent English teacher, a nun of the old school, and we were grateful for that. We talked to the local parish priest who was, it turned out, really only the figurehead of the parochial school; it was run by the superintendent of the public school, he admitted. He agreed that we should start a Christian academy, and was encouraging us to do that when he said, "Just a minute," and went inside his house. He came back to the porch where we were sitting and held out a booklet. "I can tell you know this is what you're up against," he said, and handed it to me. I'd heard about it but had never seen a copy: *The Humanist Manifesto.*[9]

The glossy exterior of our present-day world, whose homogenized finish is perfected by TV, has numbed most Christians to the truth that a spiritual battle is under way. The academy we founded with other parents was illegal, and that's when the sheriff appeared. The fathers of the children were taken to court, and lost, and were fined, over the protests of a state's attorney, ten dollars apiece. A height in cynicism, I thought at the time, and refused to pay it. The fine was illegal. We appealed to the district court and lost, then appealed to the state supreme court and lost, and for a while our appeal scratched at the doors of the U.S. Supreme Court, but was never heard.

A new Superintendent of Public Instruction was elected by a ground swell of Christian voters, and he said he interpreted the law to permit him to declare a qualified school approved. He would so declare ours, he said, and he did, and it was. But the drive to it was over twenty miles, two ways, and by this time my wife and I were convinced that the proper forum in which to teach our children (Deut. 6.4–7, Eph. 6.4, Col. 2.8) was at home, at least until they were mature enough to bear the ragging and cultural pressures that most Christian adults seem unable to bear. The next time the sheriff appeared, we started packing. We fled to New York state, and, unqualified to teach my own children in my home state, I taught graduate students at the largest university in the world, the SUNY system.

An impression was made by those committed parents, however, through their use of courts of appeal, by making public the inequities of the legal code, and by speaking and working with righteous legislators, and today it is legal in North Dakota, within limits, to educate one's own child in freedom from the state. The effort didn't solve the problem of public education, or education in general, but was a way of seeking justice that eventually worked, as it did for the widow against the unjust judge (Luke 18)—as Paul, a Roman citizen, now appeals for his civil rights under Roman rule; and Paul, as an apostle, represents the *Church*.

But should he turn to civil authority? In 1 Corinthians 6, Paul rebukes members of the church in Corinth for taking one another to civil magistrates over matters they should settle themselves. For Christians the first recourse must be the courts of the church, but in our modern churches so little oversight and discipline exists that just the mention of a church court, which for centuries embodied biblical justice, provokes suspicious bafflement. This court doesn't exist if your church is so local and independent you have no session or consistory of elders, and no court of appeal after that.

A board of deacons or trustees won't do. Trustees may manage property well, and deacons who dispense mercy and aid and goodwill to the church and community are needed (1 Tim. 3.8–13), but Paul never institutes trustees or deacons in any church. He instead ordains elders to an office of service and spiritual responsibility by "the laying on of hands of the presbytery." These elders are responsible for the members' living souls. In his farewell to the Ephesian elders, when Paul mentions that he is free from the blood of all, he's echoing Ezekiel (33–34), who says to the watchmen of Israel to warn the flock of dangers and to feed them, and if they are faithful to do this, they will not be responsible for the blood of anyone, even if the flock fails to take heed. But if the overseers refuse to warn the flock, and a life is taken, a soul lost, the blood is on their hands.

The court of the church, composed of elders, is the court Paul enters over and over in Acts, by going first to local synagogues. When he got in trouble at the temple, a high court, he was obeying the council of the apostles and elders in Jerusalem, a court that presently is politically powerless. If a church has abandoned equity and justice and the magistracy hasn't, yes, a church or even a church member may appeal, as the court of last resort, to a civil magistrate.

The commander Lysias arrives in a rush after he has received the message from the centurion, and says to Paul, "Tell me, are you a Roman?"

"Yes," Paul answers.

"I acquired this citizenship with a large sum of money," Lysias, most likely once a slave, tells Paul.

Paul says, "I was born free," and in the considerable dimension of meaning his statement contains, Paul is saying he is a natural-born Roman citizen, an inheritor of the rights of that citizenship. But also that he was born into the covenant established with Abraham, which was defined in every detail by Mosaic law, and as an inheritor of that covenant, which has reached its fulfill-ment in Christ, he has been infinitely and eternally freed. He has, indeed, been born once again into life within that covenant.

Lysias is now afraid for having shackled Paul; and in the morning he looses him and takes him before the Sanhedrin, trying to discover from them what they have against Paul.

Paul looks over the council with Stephen's earnestness, and says, "Men, brothers, I have lived in all good conscience before God until this day."

The high priest, still Ananias, has a man standing next to Paul slap his mouth. Does he turn his cheek?

"God is going to strike you, you whitewashed wall!" Paul cries. This is nearly exactly Jesus' rebuke to the scribes and Pharisees (Mat. 23.27). Then Paul goes straight to Jesus' point. "For do you sit to judge me according to the law, and against the law command me to be struck?" He is calling the high priest, the minister of God, to conduct a proper trial, as Jesus does in John 18. Paul has not been found guilty of anything, and the courts of the church, under God's law, can't invent their own modes of operation.

Bystanders rebuke Paul for reviling the high priest, and Paul says, in a sudden retraction, "I was not aware, brothers, that he was high priest. For it is written, *You shall not speak evil of a ruler of your people.*" Paul honors the priest's authority, too. I don't believe that Paul's statement is ironic, as I once did; he is too diligent about the law and, after irony, wouldn't command the consideration he does in his next appeal.

Noticing that the council is divided between Sadducees and Pharisees, he cries out, "Brothers, I am a Pharisee! I am on trial for the hope and resurrection of the dead!"

A new brouhaha begins, this one religious, as Pharisees rise in Paul's defense, and such dissension develops that Lysias is

226 A C T S

afraid Paul will "be torn to pieces." He returns him to the fortress. A lesson about ecumenicity, or faiths joining together, can be learned from this; if the bodies wishing to form a union are as diverse in their beliefs as the Sadducees and Pharisees, there is no true union, and disagreement only grows until the church is paralyzed.

Now, more than forty men, Luke writes, swear not to eat or drink until they've killed this troublemaker. That their vow includes a fast suggests its origins, and then they appear before the chief priests and elders and say, "We have bound ourselves together under a great curse that we will eat nothing until we have killed Paul." They ask the Sanhedrin to send for Paul through Claudius Lysias, as if to question him further, and they will be lying in wait to seize him.

It's not too farfetched to say that this desire to assassinate, at least a person's character, can also rise from movements that purport to be ecumenical, since it happens often. Those who wish to hold to biblical standards, as Paul does, are viewed as impediments to union, and are branded as reactionaries, or worse. When Machen demurred from the Auburn *Affirmation,* which stated that the central teachings of Scripture affirmed by the apostles—such as the resurrection of Christ from the dead—did not need to be attested to by potential pastors in order for them to be ordained, his character was pilloried. He was called, by the least offensive, a fundamentalist. And he finally came around to saying, in his affable way, that if it were a choice between lesser evils, being called a liberal or being called a fundamentalist, he would settle for fundamentalist.

With news of the plot to assassinate Paul, the primacy of the covenant in the church again asserts itself. A child, the son of Paul's sister, overhears the plotters talk, and works up the courage to enter the fortress and tell Paul, his uncle. Paul has a centurion guide the boy to Claudius Lysias who, in a touching gesture, takes the boy by the hand and leads him aside so they can speak privately. A godly magistrate. The boy repeats the story, getting every detail right, as Christian storytellers should, in their direction of souls toward life or death. The boy is a faithful witness. But should he be believed? Claudius Lysias is sensitive to several sides: that a band of men led by an Egyptian, called the assassins, is roaming the wilderness; that the crowd in Jerusalem, and even the Sanhedrin (which at the minimum is the local church authority), has not honored Paul's civil rights, as he, a Roman commander, must.

He is a faithful commander and a prudent man; he knows his duty to his emperor in a way many Christians do not know theirs to the Lord of the church. He assembles two hundred soldiers, two hundred spear bearers, and seventy horsemen—aware of the magnitude of the threat to Paul's life. It is his duty to preserve that life until Paul stands trial, and now, not even waiting until the next day, under the cover of night, he has his troops march, with Paul on horseback, down the mountainous countryside to Antipatris, a distance of thirty miles, a rugged overnight march. Lysias has sent along a letter, explaining details of Paul's case to the governor, and on the coastal plain the foot soldiers turn back and the cohort on horseback (able to outrun the robbers that were commonplace) continues to Caesarea, about thirty more miles, to the court of Felix, the Roman governor.

Though a boy has been used in the providence of God to preserve the life of an apostle of the church, I would still not want to ordain him, or any of my children, to serve in the church. It's more than a matter of what I want or don't want, on this and other issues (1 Tim. 3.6, Titus 1.5–9), but of what I encounter in scripture. Felix says he will hear Paul's case when his accusers arrive, and gives orders for him to be kept in Herod's Praetorium, which is the Roman governor's official residence.

In five days Ananias arrives with elders and a Roman attorney, Tertullus, and this attorney, after an oratorical preface meant to ingratiate him and his cause to Felix, claims that Paul has stirred up dissension among the Jews and desecrated the temple. Paul denies this and adds an unvarnished confession that arrives from the Spirit, I can say, not only because he's an apostle but because Jesus predicted this exact moment (Mat. 10.18–20) and said "the Spirit of the Father" would speak through Paul. "But this I confess to you," Paul says, "that according to the Way which they call a sect, I do worship the God of our fathers, believing all things that are written in the Law and in the Prophets. And I have a hope in God, which these men cherish themselves, that there shall be a resurrection of the dead, both of the just and the unjust. In view of this, I exercise myself always to have a blameless conscience before God and men."

Felix, "having a more exact knowledge of the Way, put them off," the text reads; he says, "When Lysias the chiliarch comes down, I will examine the things about you." He gives a centurion orders to keep Paul in custody, yet allow him freedom, and to permit his friends to minister to him.

In a few days Felix returns with Drusilla, "his wife who was a Jewess," a partial explanation of his knowledge of the way, and summons Paul to "speak about faith in Jesus Christ." As Paul reasons about righteousness, self-control, and the judgment to come, Felix gets so upset he locks him up again. Felix keeps summoning Paul to speak with him, hoping Paul will give him "silver," so he can free him, but Paul doesn't, since this isn't righteous either. The charade goes on for two years, a period over which Paul produces some of his greatest theological masterpieces, many of the Pauline epistles. Felix seems to welcome his successor, Porcius Festus, and to stay on the good side of the people he's been governing, he leaves Paul in chains.

Festus travels to Jerusalem and is met by members of the Sanhedrin, who beg him to have Paul brought to Jerusalem (after first setting an ambush for Paul along the way), but Festus says that those among them who have authority may come down with him to Caesarea: "If there is anything amiss in this man, let them accuse him."

They arrive and present a number of charges but are unable to prove any of them, and again Paul maintains his innocence.

Then he appeals to the Emperor, Caesar.

Festus confers with the Sanhedrin, and at last turns to Paul and says, "To Caesar you shall go."

Herod Agrippa II (a new Herod after the other's bout with the worms) and his wife Bernice, however, stop in for a visit, and a sense of how governors and kings act behind closed doors is conveyed. After the visitors have been present for several days, Festus says, "A certain man has been left in bonds by Felix, about whom, when I was in Jerusalem, the chief priests and elders brought charges, wishing me to condemn him. To them I said, It is not the custom of the Romans to deliver any man to death until the one being accused has his accusers there, face to face. So when they had come, without any delay I sat on the judgment seat and commanded the man to be brought, and when the accusers stood up against him, they didn't bring charges of any such crime as I expected, but had some points of disagreement with him about their own superstitions, and about a certain dead man, Jesus, whom Paul asserted was alive." Festus mentions that Paul has appealed to "Augustus."

"I would like to hear the man myself," Agrippa declares.

Festus says, "Tomorrow you shall hear him."

And so the next day Paul, by now accustomed to court procedure, is called into the hearing room in the midst of the pomp set out for King Herod—a reminder of the trial of Christ. In the working of providence, Christ was tried by a Roman civil authority, Pontius Pilate, and declared innocent—"I find no wrong in this man"—so that his innocence and atoning death for the sin of others would fulfill His Father's demand for absolute justice, the just dying for the unjust.

Festus, using courtier's speech, justifies his summoning of Paul before Agrippa by saying that this examination is to give him something to write to Caesar: "For it seems to me unreasonable to send a prisoner, and not to name the charges against him." Agrippa tells Paul he may speak for himself, and Paul says he is fortunate to be able to make his defense before the King, "because you are an expert in all customs and questions among the Jews." One can imagine Agrippa nodding at the reference to the Jewish ancestry of his family.

Paul mentions his strict Pharisee upbringing, and says, "And now I am standing trial for the hope of the promise made by God to our fathers, to which our twelve tribes hope to attain, serving God fervently day and night. For the sake of this hope, O King, I am accused by the Jews." Paul must glance at Festus, because his following "you" refers to "you people" in general: "Why is it thought a thing incredible to you if God raises the dead?"

"I truly thought in myself that I ought to do many things against the name of Jesus of Nazareth," he adds, then speaks of his zeal in persecuting "the saints," as he now calls them, "not only locking them up in prisons" and casting his vote for the death penalty, but trying "to force them to blaspheme; and being furiously enraged at them, I kept pursuing them even to foreign cities." Then Paul begins the story of his moment on the road to Damascus, and as he relates this second variation of the experience from his viewpoint, Theophilus surely remembers, as I do, the three recountings of the conjoining vision of Cornelius and Peter, and follows Paul's words more closely, noting new emphases, or the expansion of relevant details for this new audience, although the central story remains the same.

Then Theophilus realizes that through these examples Luke is instructing him in the witness of the gospels, their structure and relationship to one another—especially the first three, known as the synoptics. Theophilus is aware that some of the details seem to differ, and has wondered how to "harmonize" these different accounts. Now, through Luke's use of three versions from Paul of his Damascus experience, Theophilus understands the form and method behind the gospels. They weren't meant to harmonize, in an important essential; they are individual compositions. Or when they cover the same event, with a dissonant harmony, one witness merely elaborated with further details. The blind Bartimaeus is not confused with other blind men in Matthew and Luke. They are other blind men—Jesus met up with dozens, or hundreds, over his time on earth—and now as Paul gives witness to a different perspective on his own story (as that story is revealed in deeper detail to him, too), details in the gospels that before confused Theophilus clarify and shine with a new solidity, as if jewelry is assembling itself before his eyes.

Each gospel arrives through a different doorway, he thinks, looking up from Luke's account. Mark's came straight from Peter, as Luke has said. The need of each person in the church at a specific time in history, like me at this moment, was in the mind of the Spirit. So the gospels were written at the Spirit's prompting by those who saw the endlessness of Jesus' acts from different angles. The coherence of their truth is overseen by the Spirit, so the Spirit never attempts to cause dissimilar incidents to jibe when they never did in the first place. Now Paul is giving his version of the moment I saw him undergo from the outside, in that blinding light, and though I see the details build, I still know it's the same story (as at the look of cold black light at my windows *I* interpose myself to add that I've attempted to illustrate the same phenomenon, in a limited way, by reprinting extracts from interviews over the years, of the turn my own life took at one exact moment). The retellings of Paul reinforce one another and take me to a deeper dimension with each telling, and he seems to mean to drive that home, when he says that in everything he has ever said he has said "*nothing but what the Prophets and Moses said was going to take place*—that Christ should suffer; that by His resurrection from the dead, He would be the first to proclaim light to the people"—including Agrippa—"and to all the nations."

"Paul!" Festus cries. "You're out of your mind! Your great learning is driving you mad!"

How I love Luke for not suppressing this for fear it's what many might think! Then Paul turns to Agrippa and says, "King Agrippa, do you believe the Prophets? I know that you do."

Agrippa says, "Do you persuade me to be a Christian in so little time?"

"I would to God that, whether in a little or a long time, not only you, but also all who hear me this day, might become such as I am, except for these chains."

Except for these chains. This is the excess of empathy for others that does evil in. At this the king rises up, and the governor rises, and Bernice, and the courtiers with them; and once everybody is behind closed doors again, Festus and Agrippa consult and agree that Paul has done "nothing worthy of death or imprisonment." One can then imagine Agrippa lying back on a couch and sighing, and then staring off as he says, "This man might have been set free if he hadn't appealed to Caesar."

Paul has testified that he was born free, though, and as he begins a months-long sea journey toward Rome, still in chains, along with prisoners under the guard of a Roman centurion and other soldiers, his words surface with further meaning. Luke is with him again, so the commodious freedom of the sea is felt, capped by their open fellowship upon it, and Luke tells us that Paul is allowed to greet other friends at Sidon. Then the sailing suddenly isn't easy. The sea grows so rough that Paul warns the centurion they shouldn't leave a port in Crete; it's October, the winter storms are beginning, and Paul has sailed these seas so often he senses danger. But the centurion listens to the helmsman and captain, professionals, and the ship sets off.

Right away a stormy wind called Euroclydon bears down on them, and on the second day they lighten the ship. On the next they throw over all its tackle, and for days they're driven helplessly by this wind that is so severe it blots out the stars and the sun. Within his freedom it is Paul who, though aware of the dangers they face, encourages the crew to be of good cheer, for there will be no loss of life, he says—only of the ship. On this storm-lashed and drenched deck, with no rudder or sails, where waves come buckling over everybody hanging on for life, it is otherworldly cheer that Paul offers. "For tonight an angel of God stood beside me," he says, "whose I am and who I serve, saying, Fear not, Paul! You must stand before Caesar. And behold, God has given you all those who sail with you." The Angel of Acts.

If the sailors are cheered, their cheer is sooner or later dashed, because for fourteen days the belabored craft is engulfed by the same storm. Then members of the crew begin sounding land, a danger at their rate of travel, and throw over sea anchors from the stern to slow the driven craft, and other sailors, pretending they're going to cast out additional anchors from the bow, start lowering a lifeboat to escape. Paul cries to the centurion, "Unless they remain in the ship, you can't be saved!" The soldiers cut the ropes and the boat falls into the consuming sea. Now day is dawning and Paul urges everybody to eat, since nobody has even eaten in several days, and says, "For this is for your deliverance. For not a hair shall fall from the head of anyone."

Then Paul takes bread, giving thanks to God before the crew, and begins to eat, and this encourages them so much they also take food, and then toss away the remaining wheat to lighten the ship, its kernels showering over wind-torn waves with a sound like ripping silk, and we learn after this last serving of the staff of life that there are two hundred and seventy-six people on board, more than on the *Mayflower*. At last land is sighted and an attempt is made to let the ship run its own free course toward shore, but it is swept away in the midst of two converging seas and the worst occurs—it runs aground and the violent waves start breaking it up. The acts that everybody then become engaged in, on this ship that in miniature pictures the world, are the same ones that are everywhere ordained by God and that we are daily caught up in as we attempt to persevere in faith.

In sustaining Paul in the freedom he has confessed, so that he will arrive at Caesar's feet as he has been promised, God not only preserves the life of Paul and the lives of the rest of His elect (including Luke, who will record this) for the purposes He has ordained for them, He also preserves with them every life across the earth itself, because of the church at its center that He preserves. So when the soldiers in their fear want to kill the prisoners, to make sure they don't escape, the cumulative prophecies of Paul have their effect on the centurion. He forbids them to do their will but rather perform the will of the Father, on earth as it is in heaven, as Paul has explained that will, and all hands abandon ship as best they can.

Two hundred and seventy-six end up on the shore alive.

This is Malta, the sailors say, and when a viper appears from the kindling used for a fire on the island, and fastens itself to Paul's wrist, and the natives who look savage but are kind (Luke writes) wait for him to die, Paul rises free even of this, unharmed. He is to reach Rome, he's been told by his Messiah, and when he has traveled overland and nears the city, and crowds travel out to greet him, Paul thanks God and takes courage, though he stands in chains. The desire of his heart has been granted, he has arrived in Rome, freed into the life his mentor Gamaliel taught him their Messiah would bring, not by His reign over an earthly kingdom like David's or Solomon's, or the one Augustus now governs, but by a release from the bondage of death into the state in which Jesus is the first fruits: eternal life.

Whatever any church or council or civil authority has done to Paul, or tried to do, he has attained the authoritative peace that passes understanding, resting through faith within the life purchased by Christ for him. Paul is permitted to rent a room in Rome, and although the local Jewish authorities visit him, and some believe and some do not, there isn't a suggestion of even the slightest disturbance; and though a centurion still stands guard over Paul, and Paul for the next two years resides under the shadow of Caesar, we learn at the close of Acts, which remains as open-ended as any *New Yorker* story centuries before that magazine was founded, and which I will let run on its own to its natural end, that Paul "was welcoming all who came to him, preaching the kingdom of God, and teaching concerning the Lord Jesus Christ with all openness, unhindered."

So my joys and revels in these acts of the apostles are now ended. All of these, the major actors, as I foretold and reiterated at each step, were acting under the Spirit of Christ himself. And though some of the cities and locations revisited have melted since into air, into thin air—cloud-capped Jerusalem, the gorgeous synagogues, the solemn Temple itself—yet the eternally substantial pageant of the church itself has never faded, but grown more glorious inside the boundaries of every habitation with the passing of each century, and more enduring in my heart, as in yours, I pray, through the affirming power of the Spirit in these words given through God's gentle servant, Luke.

Who is dust, as I am, less than such stuff as dreams are made on; and even dreams are given us in sleep.

For indeed the acts of the apostles have by now reached the uttermost parts of the earth, their teachings taking hold over every area of the globe itself, including this secluded inland portion where I presently dwell. Last year our pastor undertook a study of Acts, and all that you have encountered here are questions I continue to consider as my family and I assemble to worship on the Sabbath with fifty others, many of them farmers, in the southwestern corner of this state distinguished by its mesas and buttes, in this congregation that has absorbed into itself the church from Leith and a neighboring church from Lark.

The building in which we worship is plain and unadorned, with a raised platform within an alcove where the pulpit stands, and to the left of the alcove is a door (EXIT, the sign above it says, to confound Sartre) leading to a room where children's classes are held. On sunny winter or spring or summer mornings, or those days of supernatural clarity that signify the fall, when the door is inadvertently left open, I'm able to see out a rear window to the ascending plain in its conjunction with the sky, blue against green or gold or white, depending upon the season, and my inner considerations seem less important than this picture of heaven over earth—a demarcation of the narrow interim in which we carry out our present-day acts.

NOTES

TO THE READER

1. J. Gresham Machen, *The New Testament: An Introduction to its Literature and History* (Edinburgh: Banner of Truth Trust, 1976), p. 9.
2. George H. Morrison, *Christ in Shakespeare: Ten Addresses on Moral and Spiritual Elements in Some of the Greater Plays* (London: James Clarke, 1928), p. 20.

CHAPTER 1: BEGINNINGS

1. See William Kirk Kilpatrick, *Psychological Seduction: The Failure of Modern Psychology* (Nashville: Thomas Nelson, 1983), or Garth Wood, *The Myth of Neurosis: Overcoming the Illness Excuse* (New York: Harper & Row, [1986] 1987). Both are good primers on the topic and Wood's notes to his second appendix offer a beginning bibliography—though I'm surprised neither mentions Janet Malcolm's *The Impossible Profession* (New York: Knopf, 1981), an extraordinary book.
2. Peter Makuck, *The Sunken Lightship* (Brockport, NY: BOA Editions, 1990), p. 75.
3. John Muir, *The Story of My Boyhood and Youth* (Madison: Univ. of Wisconsin Press, [1912] 1972), p. 27.
4. Noel Weeks, *The Sufficiency of Scripture* (Edinburgh: Banner of Truth Trust, 1988), p. 238.
5. F. F. Bruce, *Commentary on the Book of the Acts* (Grand Rapids: Eerdmans, 1954), p. 16. See Bruce's entire introduction.

6. Edward Carpenter, ed., *A House of Kings: The Official History of Westminster Abbey* (London: Westminster Abbey Bookshop, 1972), p. 170.

7. Carpenter, *House of Kings,* pp. 170, 302.

8. G. I. Williamson, *The Westminster Shorter Catechism: A Study Guide for Classes,* vols. 1 and 2 (Philadelphia: Presbyterian and Reformed, 1970); *The Westminster Confession of Faith, for Study Classes* (Philadelphia: Presbyterian and Reformed, 1964).

9. Robert P. Martin, *Accuracy of Translation and the New International Version* (Edinburgh: Banner of Truth Trust, 1989), pp. 41–74.

CHAPTER 2: THE DESCENT OF THE SPIRIT

1. Paul J. Achtemeier, ed., *Harper's Bible Dictionary* (San Francisco: Harper & Row, 1985); T. A. Bryant et al., *Today's Dictionary of the Bible* (Minneapolis: Bethany House, 1982); William Smith, *Smith's Bible Dictionary* (Old Tappan, NJ: Fleming H. Revell, 1967). These authorities agree on a distance of two thousand paces, derived from Exodous 16.29b: "Remain every man in his place; let no man go out of his place on the seventh day," or Sabbath: "In after times the precept in Ex.xvi. was undoubtedly viewed as a permanent law. But as some departure from a man's own place was unavoidable, it was thought necessary to determine the allowable amount, which was fixed at 2000 paces, or about six furlongs, from the wall of the city. The permitted distance seems to have been grounded on the space to be kept between the Ark [of the Covenant] and the people (Josh.iii.4) in the wilderness, which tradition said was that between the Ark and the tents. We find the same distance given as the circumference outside the walls of the Levitical cities to be counted as their suburbs." Smith, *Bible Dictionary,* p. 588; see also *Harper's Bible Dictionary,* p. 889. I cite here the dictionaries I will use to define terms throughout Acts.

2. Machen, *New Testament,* pp. 15, 16.

3. Machen must be credited for my close paraphrase: *New Testament,* p. 13.

4. Roland Flint, *And Morning* (Washington, D.C., and San Francisco: Dryad Press, 1975), from "Follow," p. 11.

5. *Harper's Bible Dictionary,* p. 769.

6. John Calvin, *New Testament Commentaries,* 12 vols., trans. John W. Fraser and W. J. G. McDonald (Grand Rapids: Eerdmans, 1965), vol. 6, p. 49.

7. See Meredith Kline's *Treaty of the Great King* (Grand Rapids: Eerdmans, 1963), not so felicitously written, or the more recent elaboration on Kline's thesis in Ray R. Sutton, *That You May Prosper* (Fort Worth: Dominion Press, l987), which is more readable but not, all in all, a book I unreservedly recommend.

8. Geoffrey W. Bromiley, *Children of Promise: The Case for Baptizing Infants* (Grand Rapids: Eerdmans, 1979), p. 99. This is an excellent little book on the subject, as is *The Meaning and Mode of Baptism* (Phillipsburg, NJ: Presbyterian and Reformed, 1975) by Jay Adams.

9. John Wilkinson, *Jerusalem as Jesus Knew It: Achaeology as Evidence* (London: Thames and Hudson, 1978), pp. 67, 97, 106–107.

10. Bromiley, *Children of Promise*, p. 107.

CHAPTER 3: MIRACULOUS EVENTS

1. This segment of the Kuyper story can be found in chapter 3 ("Books and a Book") of *Abraham Kuyper*, by Frank Vanden Berg (St. Catherine's, Ontario: Paideia Press, 1978), pp. 22–30.

2. C. S. Lewis, *Miracles: A Preliminary Study* (New York: Macmillan, [1947] 1976), p. 10.

3. W. K. Hobart, *The Medical Language of St. Luke* (Dublin, 1884), p. 34, as cited in Lloyd J. Ogilvie, *The Communicator's Commentary: Acts* (Waco, TX: Word Books, 1983), p. 80. Ogilvie's approximate rendering of the Greek follows.

4. Robert M. Grant, *Augustus to Constantine: The Rise and Triumph of Christianity in the Roman World* (New York: Harper & Row, [1970] 1990), p. 40.

5. Machen, *New Testament*, p. 33.

6. Machen, *New Testament*, p. 34.

CHAPTER 4: COMMUNION AND COMMUNITY

1. *Selected Essays of T. S. Eliot* (New York: Harcourt, Brace, [1960] 1964), pp. 351–352.

2. Machen, *New Testament*, p. 65.

3. Erik H. Erikson, *Ghandi's Truth* (New York: Norton, 1969), p. 180. In the seventies I used to imagine that only if Dr. Erikson worked with me personally would my community of internal problems receive proper communion.

4. *That Hideous Strength* (New York: Macmillan, 1946), p. 283.

5. *Selected Essays,* pp. 351–352.

6. I draw from an analysis by R. J. Rushdoony, an Armenian, not an Arminian, in his essay "Communion and Community," in *Law and Society* (Vallecito, CA: Ross House Books, 1982), pp. 132–137. I've heard Rushdoony dismissed by Christians, but often, as it turns out, by those who haven't read him; we have our hypocrites, too. He is a stimulating commentator whose scholarship is sound, whose bibliographies are monumental, and whose sources are unassailable; I've never discovered another Christian scholar quite as well read, and I don't know of one who has attempted to answer with similar erudition the question beneath all of Rushdoony's work: If not by God's standard, by whose?

7. From the last half of Matthew 25.

8. Randall Stewart, *American Literature and Christian Doctrine* (Baton Rouge: Louisiana State Univ., 1958), p. 64.

9. *Collected Poems 1909–1935* (New York: Harcourt, Brace, 1952), p. 105.

CHAPTER 5: THE WORD IN THE WORLD

1. Matthew 19.4–5. Jesus is referring to Genesis 1.27 and Genesis 2.23–24, and notice how he refers to these passages in Genesis, in the straightforward, unequivocal way he always refers to Scripture, as his sole authority.

2. See Roland H. Bainton, *The Reformation of the Sixteenth Century* (Boston: Beacon Press, [1952] 1961), excellent in nearly its entirety.

3. Jeremy Jackson, *No Other Foundation: The Church Through Twenty Centuries* (Westchester, IL: Cornerstone Books, 1980), ch. 7. A durable broad history by a British professor.

4. B. K. Kuiper, *The Church in History* (Grand Rapids: Eerdmans/ Christian Schools International, [1951] 1984), p. 167. Irenic and clearly written, this is one of the best primers on church history.

5. *The Encyclopedia Britannica: Fourteenth Edition* (London: The Encyclopedia Britannica Co., 1929), vol. 23, p. 823. For those who don't know, all editions of the Britannica after this date grow increasingly inaccurate on history and theology, either purposely or through the general disinformation that yearly becomes more stunning.

6. For a look at one questionable area of the fading practice of psychoanalysis, see Erik Erikson's analysis of Martin Luther, like Freud's

attempt at Michaelangelo, via tales and texts, in *Young Man Luther* (New York: W. W. Norton, [1958] 1962).

7. Anabaptist means "rebaptizer" and refers to the sect's practice of immersing adherents baptized by any other mode, besides rebaptizing any infants baptized by other churches, once adult.

8. John Murray, *Collected Writings*, 4 vols. (Edinburgh: Banner of Truth Trust, 1977), vol. 2, p. 335.

9. *Selected Essays* (New York: Harcourt, Brace , 1964), p. 330.

10. The author, Episcopalian by denomination, produces a controversial book (or two or three) a year, and with this one has hit about the right tone and page count, fifty (though the book was once an appendix to a 1,200 page commentary); even the polemics are amusing: "Higher criticism is today a backwater discipline that serves the needs of humanism by keeping linguistically skilled but stylistically handicapped scholars fully employed." Gary North, *The Hoax of Higher Criticism* (Tyler, TX: Institute for Christian Studies, 1989), pp. 39–40 (above, p. 47). Emphases in original.

11. Vanden Berg, *Kuyper*, p. 28.

12. North, *Hoax*, pp. 38–39.

13. John Updike, *Self-Consciousness* (New York: Knopf, 1989), p. 103.

14. Updike, *Self-Consciousness*, pp. 230–231.

CHAPTER 6: SAUL

1. For an example of such a house, see James B. Pritchard, ed., *The Harper Atlas of the Bible* (London: Times Books, 1987), p. 169.

CHAPTER 7: GENTILES AT THE GATE

1. A necessity for the church; compare 1 Cor. 14.40.

2. Francis A. Schaeffer, *The Complete Works of Francis A. Schaeffer*, 5 vols. (Westchester, IL: Crossway Books, 1982), vol. 2, p. 252. Emphases in original.

3. Not quite. My youngest daughter, now ten, recently left one too near and I read enough to feel fully confirmed in everything I say.

4. C. S. Lewis, *An Experiment in Criticism* (Cambridge: Cambridge Univ. Press, [1961] 1992), p. 56.

5. T. S. Eliot, *From Poe to Valery* (New York: Harcourt, Brace, 1948), pp. 18–19.

6. Lewis, *An Experiment*, p. 63.

7. Lewis, *An Experiment,* p. 69.

8. Disch, "Big Ideas and Dead-End Thrills," *The Atlantic,* vol. 269, no. 2 (February 1992), p. 94.

9. Disch, "Big Ideas," p. 87.

10. Disch, "Big Ideas," p. 94.

11. *Harper's Bible Dictionary,* p. 385.

12. A. Cleveland Cope et al., eds., *The Apostolic Fathers,* 34 vols. (Grand Rapids: Eerdmans, 1987), vol. 1, p. 151.

13. Machen, *New Testament,* p. 200.

CHAPTER 8: COUNCILS AND BOUNDARIES

1. "A Scientist Caught Between Two Faiths," *Christianity Today,* August 6, 1982, pp. 14–15. See especially Jastrow's statement (p. 15) that "these are the truths that are not accessible by scientific inquiry."

2. Lewis is dogmatic to the opposite degree: "The New Testament has nothing at all to tell us of literature." From "Christianity and Literature," in *Religion and Modern Literature,* ed. B. G. Tennyson and E. E. Ericson (Grand Rapids: Eerdmans, 1975), p. 48.

3. *A History of Britain and the British People,* 2 vols. (London: Grafton Books, 1986), vol. 1, *Set in a Silver Sea,* p. 26.

4. Pritchard, *Harper Atlas,* p. 172.

5. J. Gresham Machen, *New Testament,* p. 204.

6. Hugh Pollard, *Pioneers of Popular Education, 1760–1850* (Cambridge: Harvard Univ. Press, 1957), as cited by Samuel Blumenfeld, *Is Public Education Necessary?* (Boise, ID: Paradigm, [1981] 1985), pp. 36–37.

7. Blumenfeld, *Public Education,* p. 72.

8. Peter Viereck, *Meta-Politics: The Roots of the Nazi Mind* (New York: Knopf, [1941] 1951), p. 283 in the Capricorn edition updated by Viereck in 1951. This blockbuster used to be required reading at universities.

9. Viereck, *Meta-Politics,* p. 8.

10. Viereck, *Meta-Politics,* p. 286.

11. Viereck, *Meta-Politics,* pp. 286–87.

12. The proper translation of Anna's name; *Karenina* is a carryover from the Constance Garnett translation (near the turn of the century), and if you decide to read this magnificent novel, get the version by Rosemary Edmonds, available in a Penguin Classic paperback (New York: Penguin Viking, [1954] 1964).

CHAPTER 9: REALMS BROADER AND DOMESTIC

1. We meet a textual variant: many manuscripts read "Nymphas," which is masculine and renders the object, house, "his house," though some render it "their" house, as if Nympha (or Nymphas) were a family name.

2. This discussion of the Church is adapted from Thomas Witherow, *The Apostolic Church: Which Is It?* (Glasgow: The Publications Committee of the Free Presbyterian Church of Scotland, [1856] 1967), pp. 21–22.

3. Calvin, *New Testament Commentaries,* vol. 7. p. 72.

4. Karen B. Mains, *Open Heart, Open Home* (Elgin, IL: David C. Cook, 1976), a book also available in a Signet paperback (New York: New American Library, 1980) that I found in a second printing in a local library.

5. W. H. Auden, "In Memory of W. B.Yeats," widely anthologized, as in *The Viking Book of Poetry of the English-Speaking World* (New York: Viking, [1941] 1958), vol. 2, p. 1229.

6. Robert Lowell, "Skunk Hour," also widely anthologized, from *Life Studies* (New York: Vintage, [1956] 1959), p. 83.

7. To take these excerpts in order: the first is from an interview that appeared in *Renascence* (Vol. XLIV, no. 1, Fall, 1991), pp. 17–30, conducted by Dr. Ed Block, Jr.; the next is from *Radix* (Vol. 15, no. 1, July/August, 1983), pp. 15–17, done by the editor Sharon Gallagher through the mails, and later updated and revised for *The Bias Report* (Vol. 1, no. 5, May, 1989), pp. 2–5, and it's this version that I refer to; the last is from *Christianity and Literature* (Vol. XXIX, no. 1, Fall, 1979), pp. 11–18, conducted by Drs. Clarence Walhout, John H. Timmerman, and Edward Ericson, and privately printed in 1979 by William Kasdorf, Madison. None are acetate to page; since the reader wasn't an auditor, taking in my expressions and gestures, or semiotics, I fiddle with my sentences as spoken in an attempt to help supply them, bare on a page, with the sense I intended them to have when I spoke them.

8. For thumbnail sketches of these and other figures in the history of the Church, from Peter to Teresa of Avila to Francis Schaeffer, see *Great Leaders of the Christian Church,* ed. John D. Woodbridge (Chicago: Moody Press, 1988).

9. Wendell Berry, *Fidelity: Five Stories* (New York and San Francisco: Pantheon, 1992), p. 79.

10. Nelson, *Fair Clear and Terrible* (New York: British-American, 1989) p. 118.

11. Reader forewarned: a terrifying book on evil, for which you need firm spiritual footing plus a strong stomach, is Gary North's *Unholy Spirits* (Fort Worth: Dominion Press, 1986), a brilliant, scholarly study of satanic powers that is the best available; one indication of its being on the mark is that computers kept blowing as it was written and produced.

12. Joseph Brodsky, *Less Than One: Selected Essays* (New York: Farrar, Straus & Giroux, 1986), pp. 384–385.

CHAPTER 10: THE EARTH ITSELF

1. The following details on Machen's life are drawn from *J. Gresham Machen: A Biographical Memoir* (Grand Rapids: Eerdmans, [1954] 1955), by Ned B. Stonehouse, and from the accounts of others, still living, who knew Machen personally.

2. Antonia Fraser, *The Weaker Vessel* (New York: Knopf, 1984), citing Theodore Spenser, "The History of an Unfortunate Lady," *Harvard Studies and Notes in Philology and Literature* 20 (1938), p. 250. Lady Fraser's book far transcends easy polemics.

3. Academie Books (Grand Rapids: Zondervan, [1986] 1990).

4. Oxford Historical Monographs (Oxford: Clarendon Press, 1990). The following comments on Tyacke's book and British history are drawn from Otto Scott, "The Living Past," *Chalcedon Report*, no. 317 (Dec. 1991), pp. 3–4.

5. Tyacke, *Anti-Calvinists*, pp. 7–8.

6. *International Calvinism, 1541–1715,* ed. Menna Prestwich (Oxford: Clarendon Press, 1985), p. 222.

7. I won't beg the issue and am content to live with the offices the church has historically settled upon, but I suggest that someone more theologically and exegetically sound than I explore this area.

8. Brodsky, *Less Than One*, p. 389.

9. *Humanist Manifestos I and II* (Buffalo: Prometheus Books, 1973). After attempting for years to walk the waterfall of this ideology (for that is what it is, as much as Christianity) in the American university system, I resigned my professorship and along with others founded Bethel Institute for the Arts and Sciences (BIAS, Box 242, Carson, ND, 58529).